GROWTH, CYCLES, AND DISTRIBUTION

A KALECKIAN APPROACH

Hiroaki SASAKI

Kyoto University Press

TRANS PACIFIC PRESS

First published in 2014 jointly by:

Kyoto University Press
69 Yoshida Konoe-cho
Sakyo-ku, Kyoto 606-8315, Japan
Telephone: +81-75-761-6182
Fax: +81-75-761-6190
Email: sales@kyoto-up.or.jp
Web: http://www.kyoto-up.or.jp

Trans Pacific Press
PO Box 164, Balwyn North, Melbourne
Victoria 3104, Australia
Telephone: +61-3-9859-1112
Fax: +61-3-8911-7989
Email: tpp.mail@gmail.com
Web: http://www.transpacificpress.com

Copyright © Kyoto University Press and Trans Pacific Press 2014.

Edited by Karl Smith

Printed in Nagano by Asia Printing Office Corporation

Distributors

Australia and New Zealand
James Bennett Pty Ltd
Locked Bag 537
Frenchs Forest NSW 2086
Australia
Telephone: +61-(0)2-8988-5000
Fax: +61-(0)2-8988-5031
Email: info@bennett.com.au
Web: www.bennett.com.au

USA and Canada
International Specialized Book Services (ISBS)
920 NE 58th Avenue, Suite 300
Portland, Oregon 97213-3786
USA
Telephone: (800) 944-6190
Fax: (503) 280-8832
Email: orders@isbs.com
Web: http://www.isbs.com

Asia and the Pacific (except Japan)
Kinokuniya Company Ltd.

Head office:
38-1 Sakuragaoka 5-chome
Setagaya-ku, Tokyo 156-8691
Japan
Telephone: +81-3-3439-0161
Fax: +81-3-3439-0839
Email: bkimp@kinokuniya.co.jp
Web: www.kinokuniya.co.jp

Asia-Pacific office:
Kinokuniya Book Stores of Singapore Pte., Ltd.
391B Orchard Road #13-06/07/08
Ngee Ann City Tower B
Singapore 238874
Telephone: +65-6276-5558
Fax: +65-6276-5570
Email: SSO@kinokuniya.co.jp

ISBN 978-4-87698-394-0 (Japan)
ISBN 978-1-920901-12-7 (International)

List of Figures

4

List of Tables

Contents

Acknowledgements

I would like to thank my collaborators Shinya Fujita, Kazumitsu Sako, Jun Matsuyama, and Ryunosuke Sonoda. I would also like to thank Peter Skott, Eckhard Hein, Naoki Yoshihara, Takashi Ohno, Takeshi Nakatani, Takeshi Ikeda, Hideo Sato, Kenji Mori, Toichiro Asada, Takashi Yagi, Hiroyuki Yoshida, Kazuhiro Kurose, Hiroyuki Uni, Hiroshi Nishi, and Taro Abe for their useful suggestions and helpful comments. The publication of this book was supported by a President's Discretionary Budget of Kyoto University for Young Scholar's Research Results.

Preface

This book collects my contributions to the so-called Kaleckian model. The Kaleckian model is a kind of post-Keynesian growth model which, based on a principle of effective demand, investigates how changes in income distribution affect macroeconomic variables such as economic growth, output, and employment.

There are many books dealing with the Kaleckian model. The main contribution of this book is that it deals with not only the short-run Kaleckian model but also with the medium-run and long-run Kaleckian models. The definition and explanation of short-run, medium-run, and long-run are given in Chapter 1. In short, these are classified according to which variable becomes the adjustment variable in the corresponding run. Whereas a variable is assumed to be an exogenous variable in the short run, it might be assumed to be an endogenous variable in the medium and long runs. Since few existing studies deal with the medium- and long-run Kaleckian models, this book makes an important contribution to this field. This book is composed of Preliminaries (Chapter 1) and three parts. Each part is composed of two chapters. In the following, I explain the construction of this book in detail.

In Preliminaries (Chapter 1), I explain the Kaleckian model. Then, I distinguish short, medium, and long runs. Finally, I present the basic structure of the short-run Kaleckian model in detail and show the properties and results obtained from the model.

In Part 1, composed of Chapters 2 and 3, I develop the medium-run Kaleckian model. The medium-run Kaleckian model explicitly considers the accumulation of capital stock, which is assumed to be constant in the short-run Kaleckian model. In the short-run Kaleckian model, the capacity utilization rate and the profit share are endogenous variables. In contrast, in the medium-run Kaleckian model, in addition to these two variables, the employment rate becomes a new endogenous variable. When capital stock is not accumulated, we can identify the employment rate with the capacity utilization rate. However, when capital is accumulated, we must distinguish these two variables.

Chapter 2 is based on the paper entitled "Endogenous Technological Change, Income Distribution, and Unemployment with Inter Class Conflict," published in *Structural Change and Economic Dynamics*, while Chapter 3 is based on the paper entitled "Cyclical Growth in a Goodwin-Kalecki-Marx Model," published in *Journal of Economics*. The difference between these two chapters is that the model of Chapter 3 considers the reserve army effect whereas the model of Chapter 2 does not. The reserve army effect is an effect such that an increase in the employment rate exerts an increasing pressure on wages.

In Part 2, composed of Chapters 4 and 5, I develop the long-run Kaleckian model. In the medium-run Kaleckian model, the capacity utilization rate, the profit share, and the employment rate are endogenous variables. In the long-run Kaleckian model, in addition to these three variables, the normal capacity utilization rate and the expected rate of growth become new endogenous variables. The normal capacity utilization rate can be alternatively called the planned capacity utilization rate, which is a long-run target level of production of firms and a variable that represents the expectation of firms. Hence, in the long-run Kaleckian model, the two variables concerning long-run expectation become endogenous variables.

Chapter 4 is based on the paper entitled "Conflict, Growth, Distribution, and Employment: A Long-Run Kaleckian Model," published in *International Review of Applied Economics*, while Chapter 5 is based on the paper entitled "Is the Long-run Equilibrium Wage-Led or Profit-Led? A Kaleckian Approach," published in *Structural Change and Economic Dynamics*. The difference between these two chapters lies in the difference between the specifications of the firms' investment functions. In Chapter 4, I use an investment function in which investment depends positively on the difference between the actual capacity utilization rate and the normal capacity utilization rate. In Chapter 5, in contrast, I use two types of the investment function: one is an investment function in which investment depends positively on both the difference between the actual capacity utilization rate and the normal capacity utilization rate, and the profit rate; the other is an investment function in which investment depends positively on both the difference between the actual capacity utilization rate and the normal capacity utilization rate, and the profit share. In these chapters, I investigate whether or not the results of short- and medium-run models are obtained from the long-run model.

In Part 3, composed of Chapters 6 and 7, I return from the medium- and long-run model to the short-run model, and present extended short-run Kaleckian models, which will be extended to medium- and long-run models in the future.

In Chapter 6, I present a short-run Kaleckian model that considers regular and non-regular employment. This chapter is based on the paper entitled "The Macroeconomic Effects of the Wage Gap between Regular and Non-Regular Employment and of Minimum Wages," published in *Structural Change and Economic Dynamics*. In existing Kaleckian models, labor is assumed to be homogenous. In contrast, in this chapter, I assume that there are two types of labor and that wages are different between these labors. Using this model, I investigate how the wage gap between regular and non-regular employment affects the macroeconomy.

In Chapter 7, I present an open-economy Kaleckian model. This chapter is based on the paper entitled "International Competition and Distributive Class Conflict in an Open Economy Kaleckian Model," published in *Metroeconomica*. It investigates how international price competition affects the behaviors of domestic firms and domestic labor unions and in turn, how these changes affect the macroeconomy. The results of this chapter show that results obtained from the open economy model are not necessarily equal to those obtained from closed economy models.

Chapter *1*

Preliminaries

1.1 The Kaleckian model

This section explains a short-, medium-, and long-run analysis by using the Kaleckian model.[1] In short, these runs are classified according to which variable is regarded as endogenous.

Before explaining the analysis, we briefly summarize the Kaleckian model. The Kaleckian model is a kind of post-Keynesian growth model. According to Lavoie (1992, p. 297), the Kaleckian model has three constituents: a mark-up pricing rule in oligopolistic goods markets; constant marginal cost before full capacity; capacity utilization below unity. We can add a fourth constituent, a firms' investment function independent of savings.

According to Lavoie (1992, 2006), Del Monte (1975) is the first Kaleckian model. In the English literature, Rowthorn (1981) is the first Kaleckian model. Since the publication of Rowthorn (1981), papers dealing with Kaleckian models have proliferated. International refereed journals dealing with Kaleckian models include *Cambridge Journal of Economics*, *Metroeconomica*, *Journal of Post Keynesian Economics*, *International Review of Applied Economics*, *Review of Political Economy*, *Review of Radical and Political Economics*, *Review of Keynesian Economics*, *European Journal of Economics and Economic Policies: Intervention*, and *Bulletin of Political Economy*. *Structural Change and Economic Dynamics*, *Journal of Economic Behavior & Organization*, and *Journal of Economics* have also published papers dealing with Kaleckian models.

In the following, we will explain the outline of the short-, medium-, and long-run Kaleckian models. For simplicity, we omit open-economy aspects and financial aspects.[2] We must note that the definitions of short-run, medium-run, and long-run in

---

1) See Kalecki (1971) for his economic theory.

2) For open-economy Kaleckian models, see Blecker (1989, 1998), Bhaduri and Marglin (1990), Cassetti (2002), Cordero (2002, 2008), and Missaglia (2007). For Kaleckian models considering financial aspects, see Lavoie (1995a), Hein (2006, 2007), Charles (2008a, 2008b, 2008c), Lima and Meirelles (2007), Michl

this book are definitions that I think to be reasonable, although they might differ from
the definitions of other researchers.

1.1.1   Short-run model

Short-run model version 1

In the short-run model version 1, the price of goods and capital stock are assumed to
be constant. The discrepancy between demand and supply is adjusted through adjustment of the capacity utilization rate, that is, the quantity of output. Given that capital
stock is constant, the adjustment of output is equivalent to the adjustment of employment. Therefore, the short-run model version 1 is a model of employment adjustment.
Rowthorn (1981), cited above, is also a model of employment adjustment. In some
models, the capital accumulation rate is adjusted rather than the capacity utilization
rate (e.g., Cassetti, 2003), but these models are also models of employment adjustment
in nature. That is, the adjustment of the capital accumulation rate when capital stock
is constant is equivalent to the adjustment of the quantity of investment, and in turn,
the adjustment of the quantity of investment is equivalent to the adjustment of output.

Short-run model version 2

In the short-run model version 1, the price of goods is fixed. In contrast, in the short-
run model version 2, the price of goods is allowed to change. A typical example is
Cassetti (2003), in which both the capital accumulation rate and the profit share are
adjusted. In the Cassetti model, the adjustment equation of the price of goods set by
firms and the adjustment equation of the nominal wage set by labor unions are introduced, and consequently, income distribution (the wage/profit share) is endogenously
determined.

1.1.2   Medium-run model

In the short-run model, capital stock is assumed to be constant. If we want to investigate a longer time span, it is natural that we consider the accumulation of capital
stock. In this book, we define the medium run as a time period in which capital stock
is accumulated. In the short-run model, only the demand creation effect of investment
is considered and capital accumulation is not explicitly considered. We define a model
that considers capital accumulation as the medium-run model.

In the mainstream neo-classical growth model, an economy starting with small
capital stock approaches a steady state; in accordance with transitional dynamics, per
capita capital stock continues to increase and reaches some constant value in the end.
In the short-run Kaleckian model, such capital accumulation is not considered. Accordingly, it is problematic to compare the results obtained from the short-run Kaleck-

(2008), and Setterfield (2009).

ian model with those obtained from the neo-classical growth model. We cannot compare apples and oranges. For comparison, we must consider capital accumulation.

However, only a few Kaleckian models explicitly consider capital accumulation. To my knowledge, the only models are Dutt (1992), Lima (2004), Ohno (2009), and Sasaki (2010, 2011, 2013).

The reason for this is that if we want to explicitly consider capital accumulation in the Kaleckian model, as stated below, the employment rate (or the capital-labor supply ratio) must be an endogenous variable. The short-run models consider labor supply to be unlimited and the firms to employ as many workers as they desire at the given wages. However, it is reasonable to assume that labor supply is constrained in the long run. In this case, the equalization of labor demand growth and labor supply growth is an accidental occurrence. Thus, if labor supply growth steadily exceeds labor demand growth, then the employment rate will be zero; however, this is unrealistic. Therefore, to determine the long-run employment rate, we need a model in which the economically meaningful employment rate is endogenously determined. For this purpose, however, we must add one variable to the model, which necessarily adds a number of differential equations and complicates the analysis. For this reason, only a few Kaleckian models explicitly consider capital accumulation.

1.1.3   Long-run model

We have considered capital accumulation in the medium-run model. Are there any variables that are adjusted in the long run? We can endogenize some parameters that are constants in the short-run and medium-run analysis, which are considered as variables in the long-run Kaleckian model.

This is done to meet the criticisms of neo-Ricardians and Marxians, who claim that the Kaleckian model is a short-run or medium-run model but not a long-run model. In the Kaleckian model, the equilibrium capacity utilization rate diverges from the normal capacity utilization rate.[3] Critics assert that this divergence does not last and should vanish in the long run; accordingly, the Kaleckian model lacks logical consistency. For Marxians and Sraffians, the long-run equilibrium is a state where all variables are fully adjusted (Auerbach and Skott, 1988; Duménil and Lévy, 1999; and Park, 1997).

In contrast, some Kaleckians (Lavoie, 1995b, 2002, 2003; Dutt, 1997; Cassetti, 2006) introduce the adjustment process of the normal capacity utilization rate in the long run. They show that even in the long-run equilibrium where the actual capacity utilization rate and the normal capacity utilization rate are equalized, 'the para-

---

3) In fact, the difference in nuance between "the desired capacity utilization rate" and "the normal capacity utilization rate" is reflected in the difference in the positions of users of these terms. Critics of Kaleckian models use the term "the desired capacity utilization rate" whereas Kaleckians use the term "the normal capacity utilization rate." The term "desired" means that the desired capacity utilization rate is obtained by some optimization whereas the term "normal" means that the normal capacity utilization rate is set to a level that is obtained with experience.

dox thrift' and 'the paradox of cost' hold, which are important characteristics of the Kaleckian model. Here, the paradox of thrift means that an increase in capitalists' propensity to save lowers the rate of capital accumulation. The paradox of cost means that an increase in the real wage leads to an increase in the realized profit rate.

1.2   Short-run model

1.2.1   Adjustment of capacity utilization: Version 1

The short-run model is described by the following six equations:

$$Y = \min\{aE, uK\}, \tag{1.1}$$

$$r = mu, \tag{1.2}$$

$$p = (1 + \mu)\frac{w}{a}, \quad 0 < \mu < 1, \tag{1.3}$$

$$g_s = sr, \quad 0 < s < 1, \tag{1.4}$$

$$g_d = \gamma + \varepsilon(u - u_n), \quad \gamma > 0, \ 0 < \varepsilon < 1, \ \gamma - \varepsilon u_n > 0, \tag{1.5}$$

$$\dot{u} = \alpha(g_d - g_s), \quad \alpha > 0. \tag{1.6}$$

Equation (1.1) denotes the fixed-coefficients production function, where u denotes output; E, employment; K, capital stock; $a = Y/E$, labor productivity; and $u = Y/K$, the output-capital ratio. In the following analysis, we assume that the capital-potential output ratio is unity. From this, we can regard the output-capital ratio $u = Y/K$ as the capacity utilization rate.[4]

Equation (1.2) is the definition of the profit rate. Since we define $u = Y/K$ as the capacity utilization rate, the profit rate is equal to the product of the profit share m and the capacity utilization rate. Here, the profit share is the ratio of total profits to nominal national income.

Equation (1.3) denotes the mark-up pricing equation of firms, where p denotes the price of goods; w, nominal wage; and μ, the mark-up rate. Since nominal wage, the mark-up rate, and labor productivity is given exogenously, equation (1.3) means that the price of goods becomes constant. Using equation (1.3), we find that the relation $m = \mu/(1 + \mu)$ holds between the profit share and the mark-up rate. Since μ is assumed to be constant, the profit share becomes constant.

The left-hand side of equation (1.4), that is g_s, denotes savings standardized by capital stock. If we assume that workers spend all wage income on consumption while capitalists save a constant fraction s of profit, we obtain equation (1.4).

---

4) The capacity utilization rate u is defined as $u = Y/Y^*$, where Y denotes the actual output and Y^* denotes the potential output. The capacity utilization rate is decomposed into $u = (Y/K)(K/Y^*)$, where K/Y^* denotes the capital/potential output ratio and captures the production technology. If we assume that K/Y^* is constant, then u and Y/K change in the same direction. From this, we can regard the output/capital ratio as the capacity utilization rate. In this chapter, for simplicity, we assume that $K/Y^* = 1$. Therefore, we obtain $u = Y/K$.

The left-hand side of equation (1.5), that is g_d, denotes real investment of firms standardized by capital stock. Here, based on Amadeo (1986) and Lavoie (2006), we employ the Kalecki-type investment function: firms' planned investment depends positively on the capacity utilization rate.[5] The parameter γ denotes the capital accumulation rate independent of the level of capacity utilization, which can be interpreted as capturing the firms' expected growth rate. The parameter ε denotes the responsiveness of investment to the capacity utilization rate.

Equation (1.6) denotes the adjustment equation of the capacity utilization rate, where $\dot{u} = du/dt$. The capacity utilization rate increases when excess demand prevails in the goods market whereas decreases when excess supply prevails. The parameter α denotes the speed of adjustment of the goods market.

Note that in the short-run model, K, p, and m are all constant.

The short-run equilibrium is a situation where $\dot{u} = 0$, and hence, saving and investment are equalized. Substituting equation (1.2) into equation (1.4) and letting the resulting expression be equal to equation (1.5), we obtain the short-run equilibrium capacity utilization rate. Using the equilibrium value, we obtain the short-run equilibrium rate of capital accumulation.

$$u^* = \frac{\gamma - \varepsilon u_n}{sm - \varepsilon}, \qquad (1.7)$$

$$g^* = \frac{s(\gamma - \varepsilon u_n)m}{sm - \varepsilon}, \qquad (1.8)$$

where an asterisk "$*$" denotes the equilibrium value of a variable. Note that the profit share m is an exogenous variable. The short-run equilibrium values must be positive. From this, we need $sm - \varepsilon > 0$.[6] This implies that the sensitivity of saving with respect to the capacity utilization rate is larger than that of investment with respect to the capacity utilization rate. In what follows, we assume this condition.

To conduct comparative static analysis, we need the stability of the short-run equilibrium. The stability condition is given by

$$\left.\frac{\partial \dot{u}}{\partial u}\right|_{u=u^*} = -\alpha(sm - \varepsilon) < 0. \qquad (1.9)$$

Therefore, the short-run equilibrium is stable.

The effects of increases in the saving rate and the profit share on the short-run equilibrium are shown in Table 1.1. An increase in the saving rate lowers both the capacity utilization rate and that of capital accumulation. This is known as the para-

---

5) In another Kalecki-type investment function, the profit rate, in addition to the capacity utilization rate, becomes a variable in the investment function. Here, for simplicity, we employ only the capacity utilization rate as an explanatory variable of the investment function. In contrast, Marglin and Bhaduri (1990) assert that both the capacity utilization rate and the profit share should become explanatory variables of the investment function. In this case, various regimes are produced depending on conditions.

6) Since the capacity utilization rate has to be less than unity, we also need another restriction $\gamma - \varepsilon u_n < sm - \varepsilon$.

dox of thrift. An increase in the profit share lowers the capacity utilization rate. This implies that the short-run equilibrium exhibits a wage-led demand regime.[7] An increase in the profit share lowers the rate of capital accumulation. This implies that the short-run equilibrium exhibits a wage-led growth regime. These results are typical to Kaleckian models.

Table 1.1: Results of comparative static analysis in the short-run model version 1

	s	m
u^*	$-$	$-$
g^*	$-$	$-$

1.2.2   Determination of income distribution: Version 2

In the short-run model version 1, the profit share is constant. The profit share is obtained by subtracting the wage share from unity. In addition, the wage share is obtained by dividing the real wage by labor productivity. Accordingly, constant profit share means that both real wage and labor productivity are constant. Now, in this subsection, we assume that real wage endogenously changes but labor productivity is constant.

There are many ways to endogenously determine real wages. For example, we can introduce a real-wage Phillips curve into the Kaleckian models. In this subsection, we use the theory of conflicting-claims inflation developed initially by Rowthorn (1977). Cassetti (2003) is a representative study that introduces the theory of conflicting-claims inflation into a Kaleckian model. Since real wage is obtained by dividing nominal wage by the price of goods, we turn to specifying changes in price and nominal wage.

First, suppose that the firms set their price p to close the gap between their target profit share and the actual profit share. Second, suppose that the growth rate of the money wage w that the workers manage to negotiate depends on the discrepancy between their target profit share and the actual profit share. These ideas are specified as follows:[8]

$$\frac{\dot{p}}{p} = \theta(m_f - m), \quad 0 < \theta < 1, \, 0 < m_f < 1, \tag{1.10}$$

---

7) For classification of regimes in Kaleckian models, see Blecker (2002).

8) If we introduce equation (1.10), equation (1.3) becomes redundant when solving the model. Then, some might wonder if the mark-up pricing rule, one of the characteristics, is lost. If we want to retain the mark-up pricing rule, we can use a dynamic mark-up pricing rule given by $\dot{p} = \beta[(1 + \mu)(w/a) - p]$ (e.g., Raghavendra, 2006). In this case, we obtain $\dot{p}/p = \beta[(1 + \mu)(1 - m) - 1]$, which has a similar meaning to equation (1.10). That is, equation (1.10) essentially captures mark-up pricing.

$$\frac{\dot{w}}{w} = (1 - \theta)(m - m_w), \quad 0 < m_w < 1, \tag{1.11}$$

where m_f denotes the firms' target profit share; m_w, the workers' target profit share; and θ, a parameter that captures the bargaining power of firms.

The profit share is defined as $m = 1 - (wE/pY)$, which we differentiate with respect to time:

$$\frac{\dot{m}}{1 - m} = \frac{\dot{p}}{p} - \frac{\dot{w}}{w} + \frac{\dot{a}}{a}. \tag{1.12}$$

Substituting equations (1.10) and (1.11) into equation (1.12), we obtain the dynamical equation of the profit share.

$$\dot{m} = -(1 - m)(m - A - g_a), \quad A \equiv \theta m_f + (1 - \theta)m_w < 1, \tag{1.13}$$

where $g_a = \dot{a}/a$ denotes the growth rate of labor productivity and A denotes the weighted average of the firms' target profit share and the workers' target profit share.

Equations (1.6) and (1.13) comprise the short-run model. Note that $g_a = 0$ because labor productivity is constant. The short-run equilibrium is a situation where $\dot{u} = \dot{m} = 0$. In this simple model, equation (1.13) does not depend on u, and hence, we can easily solve the model for the short-run equilibrium value of the profit share.

$$m^* = A. \tag{1.14}$$

Substituting equation (1.14) into equations (1.7) and (1.8), we can obtain the short-run equilibrium values of the capacity utilization rate and capital accumulation rate when the profit share is endogenously determined.

In this case too, the short-run equilibrium is stable. Linearizing the system of differential equations that comprises of u and m and examining the property of the corresponding Jacobian matrix, we find that the trace and the determinant of the Jacobian matrix are negative and positive, respectively.[9]

Table 1.2 shows the results of comparative static analysis in the short-run model version 2. In this derivation, we assume that $m_f > m_w$. The firms attempt to set their targets as high as possible whereas the workers attempt to set their targets as low as possible. Therefore, the assumption that $m_f > m_w$ is reasonable.

The results of the capacity utilization rate and the capital accumulation rate are the same as those of Table 1.1. Since the profit share is endogenously determined in version 2, we cannot define a regime by using the relationship between m and u or m and g as in Table 1.1. Nevertheless, since an increase in m_f or m_w increases m^*, we define a regime by using the relationship between m_f (m_w) and u^*, or the relationship between m_f (m_w) and g^*. Since an increase in m_f or m_w lowers both the capacity utilization rate and the rate of capital accumulation, the short-run equilibrium exhibits

---

9) The characteristic equation corresponding to the Jacobian matrix leads to a quadratic equation whose discriminant is positive, and accordingly, the short-run equilibrium becomes a stable node.

both a wage-led demand regime and a wage-led growth demand regime.

Table 1.2: Results of comparative static analysis in the short-run model version 2

	s	θ, m_f, m_w
u^*	$-$	$-$
g^*	$-$	$-$
m^*	0	$+$

Part 1: Medium-run Kaleckian Models

Endogenous Technologocal Change, Income Distribution, and Unemployment with Inter-Class Conflict

2.1 Introduction

This chapter presents a Kaleckian model of growth that incorporates endogenous technological change and investigates the rate of economic growth, income distribution, and the employment rate.[1] Although a large number of attempts to endogenize technical progress have been made in mainstream growth theory, relatively less attention has been paid in the post-Keynesian tradition. In mainstream growth models, much emphasis is placed on technical progress as an engine of growth because supply-side factors determine economic growth. In contrast, because demand-side factors decide economic growth in post-Keynesian growth models, supply-side factors have not been considered so much. This is not to say that there have been no attempts to endogenize technical progress in the Kaleckian model. You (1994) introduces into a Kaleckian model technical progress in such a way that the growth rate of the capital-labor ratio depends on the rate of capital accumulation. In Cassetti (2003), induced technical progress known as the Kaldor-Verdoorn law (Verdoorn, 1949; Kaldor, 1966) is incorporated into a Kaleckian growth model. Stockhammer and Onaran (2004) also use the Kaldor-Verdoorn law to build a model based on Marglin and Bhaduri's (1990) work. They empirically test the model for the US, UK, and France by means of a structural VAR analysis. Lima (2004) develops a Kaleckian model in which endogenous technological innovation plays a significant role. In Lima's model, the rate of labor-saving technological innovation depends non-linearly on the wage share, which can generate limit cycles with regard to the wage share and the capital-effective labor ratio.

To endogenize technological change, this chapter adopts a technique such that the growth rate of labor productivity depends positively on the employment rate. This formulation is proposed by Dutt (2006) and Bhaduri (2006).[2] According to Dutt (2006),

---

1) See Kalecki (1954, 1971) for his economic theory. For the fundamental Kaleckian model, see Rowthorn (1981), Lavoie (1992 and 2006), and Taylor (2004).

2) Bhaduri (2006) proposes two specifications. One is employed in this chapter; the other is that the growth rate of labor productivity is adjusted through the gap between the growth rates of real wage and

this view of technological change differs from the mainstream endogenous growth theory in that it draws attention to the demand side of the economy: technological change occurs in response to labor shortages caused by the growth of employment rather than supply side which focuses on the research and development process. Bhaduri (2006) states that this captures a view that technological change is driven by inter-class conflict over income distribution between workers and capitalists. Bhaduri's (2006) model is not a Kaleckian one because income distribution is not determined by mark-up pricing. However, it bears similarity to the Kaleckian model in that effective demand plays a crucial role in determining output. In contrast, Dutt's (2006) model can be said to be Kaleckian, but it does not deal with such issues as income distribution and inflation because its purpose is to present a simple growth model that integrates the roles of aggregate demand and aggregate supply.

Our specification of endogenous technological change has the following theoretical implications. Conventional Kaleckian growth models assume that labor supply is unlimited and that firms employ as many workers as they desire at given wages. If, however, the labor supply grows at an exogenously given rate, there is no guarantee that the endogenously determined growth employment rate is equal to the growth rate of labor supply. Thus, if the growth of labor supply exceeds that of labor demand in the steady state, then the rate of unemployment will keep on rising, but this is unrealistic.[3] In contrast, the steady state unemployment rate in our model remains constant because the two growth rates coincide in the long run. Therefore, our model overcomes the weakness of existing Kaleckian models.

This chapter, however, is not the first attempt to consider the determination of the employment rate explicitly in the Kaleckian model. Stockhammer (2004) presents an augmented Kaleckian model that incorporates equations that determine employment and income distribution, and investigates the NAIRU (non-accelerating inflation rate of unemployment).[4] However, our model differs considerably from Stockhammer's model in the determination of employment and income distribution. Stockhammer (2004) uses an employment determination equation such that a change in the unemployment rate is given by the difference between the growth rate of exogenous labor supply and the rate of capital accumulation, and an income distribution determination equation such that the profit share depends on the unemployment rate. In contrast, we use an employment determination equation such that the growth rate of labor productivity depends positively on the employment rate, and an income distribution equation that results from the theory of conflicting-claims inflation. Furthermore, our model is different from Stockhammer's model in the variables used in the investment function and whether technological progress is exogenous or endogenous. With these differences, we obtain different results from those obtained by Stockhammer. In Stockhammer's model, the capital accumulation rate (and accordingly, the capacity utilization

---

labor productivity.

3) Cassetti (2002) also sees it as a problem that the long-run employment rate in the conventional Kaleckian model is not constant.

4) For the NAIRU, see also Stockhammer (2008).

rate) and the profit share are adjusted in the short run, while the unemployment rate is adjusted in the long run. However, employment (and accordingly, unemployment) necessarily changes with changes in the capacity utilization rate. Hence, it is reasonable to assume that these three variables—the capacity utilization rate, the profit share, and the employment rate—are adjusted at the same time. Therefore, we simultaneously analyze the adjustment process of these three variables.

The basic framework of our model is based on a series of Mario Cassetti's studies (Cassetti, 2002, 2003, 2006). In standard Kaleckian models, the level of money wage and mark-up are fixed and given exogenously, and accordingly, the price level is constant. Cassetti (2002, 2003, 2006) combines a Kaleckian growth model and the theory of conflicting-claims inflation, in which the rate of inflation is determined by negotiations between workers and capitalists (Rowthorn, 1977).[5] Kaleckian models that incorporate the theory of conflicting-claims inflation consider the effect of class conflict between workers and capitalist on income distribution, but do not consider its effect on employment. It is interesting to investigate how changes in the bargaining power of both classes affect employment.

The remainder of this chapter is organized as follows. Section 2 presents the basic framework of our model. Section 3 analyzes the existence and the stability of the long-run equilibrium. Section 4 presents numerical examples to show that the long-run equilibrium actually exists under plausible parameter settings and that each variable in the model converges to its long-run equilibrium value from an arbitrary initial value. Section 5 offers results of comparative statics analysis in the long-run equilibrium. Section 6 concludes the chapter.

2.2   Basic framework of the model

2.2.1   Adjustment in the capital accumulation rate

Consider an economy in which there are two social classes, workers and capitalists. Suppose that workers consume all their wages and capitalists save a constant fraction s of their profits. Let r and K be the rate of profit and the capital stock, respectively. Then, the real saving is given by $S = srK$, and consequently, the ratio of the real saving to capital stock, $g_s = S/K$, leads to

$$g_s = sr, \quad 0 < s \leq 1. \tag{2.1}$$

This corresponds to Harrod's actual growth rate. We ignore capital depreciation for simplicity.

Suppose that firms operate with the following fixed coefficient production func-

---

5) Lima (2004), mentioned above, is also an attempt to integrate the theory of conflicting-claims inflation with a Kaleckian growth model.

tion:

$$Y = \min\{aE, (u/k)K\}, \tag{2.2}$$

where Y denotes real output; E, employment; and $a = Y/E$, the level of labor productivity.[6] The capacity utilization rate is defined as $u = Y/Y^*$, where Y^* denotes the potential output. Let us define the ratio of the capital stock to the potential output as $k = K/Y^*$ and suppose that k is constant, that is, both K and Y^* grow at the same rate.[7] To simplify the analysis, we assume $k = 1$. Then, we obtain $u = Y/K$. Note that the relationship between the profit rate, the profit share (m), and the capacity utilization rate is given by $r = mu$ and the relationship between the capacity utilization rate, the rate of capital accumulation, and the profit share is given by $u = g/(sm)$.

Following the argument of Marglin and Bhaduri (1990), we specify the ratio of the real investment to capital stock, $g_d = I/K$, as follows:

$$g_d = Am^\phi u^\gamma, \quad A > 0, \ 0 < \phi < 1, \ 0 < \gamma < 1, \tag{2.3}$$

where A denotes a constant; ϕ, the elasticity of the investment rate with respect to the profit share; and γ, the elasticity of the investment rate with respect to the capacity utilization rate. Equation (2.3) means that the desired investment rate of firms is an increasing function in both the profit share and the capacity utilization rate. Accordingly, g_d in equation (2.3) corresponds to Harrod's warranted growth rate (Robinson, 1962). In conventional Kaleckian models, the investment function is assumed to depend positively on the rate of profit and the capacity utilization rate. Marglin and Bhaduri (1990), in contrast, argue that the profit share rather than the rate of profit should be a variable in the investment function. Their reasoning is as follows. The rate of profit is equal to the product of the profit share and the capacity utilization rate, that is, $r = mu$. Thus, it is plausible that a combination of high capacity utilization and a low profit share and a combination of low capacity utilization and a high profit share will produce different levels of investment even when the rate of profit is held constant at a given level.[8] Our specification of the investment function is based on Blecker (2002).[9] Since the investment function is not a linear but a Cobb-Douglas form, as will be shown later, different regimes can be produced according to the sizes of ϕ and γ.

---

6) Given the Leontief production function, a profit maximizing firm will choose employment and capacity utilization in such a way that $aE = (u/k)K$, from which it follows that $a = Y/E$.

7) Foley and Michl (1999) emphasize that, in capitalist economies, a combination of growing labor productivity and declining capital productivity (i.e., a rise in k in our model) is the typical pattern of technological change. They accordingly term the pattern Marx-biased technical change. When an economy experiences Marx-biased technical change, the rate of profit will decline as long as the profit share remains constant. In our model, such a biased technical change is not taken into consideration.

8) For details of argument, see Bhaduri and Marglin (1990).

9) If $\phi > 1$ in this specification, we have a profit-led demand regime in which an increase in the profit share leads to a rise in the capacity utilization rate. However, as Blecker (2002) points out, this is an extreme case. Hence, we assume $0 < \phi < 1$ in the following analysis.

An equation of motion for the capacity utilization rate can be formulated by

$$\dot{u} = \alpha(g_d - g_s), \quad \alpha > 0, \tag{2.4}$$

where α denotes the speed of adjustment. Equation (2.4) represents quantity adjustment by the capacity utilization rate in the goods market: excess demand ($g_d > g_s$) leads to a rise in the capacity utilization rate whereas excess supply ($g_d < g_s$) leads to a decline in the capacity utilization rate.[10]

Substituting equations (2.1) and (2.3) in equation (2.4), we finally obtain the dynamics of u as follows:

$$\dot{u} = \alpha(Am^\phi u^\gamma - smu). \tag{2.5}$$

2.2.2 Adjustment in the profit share

In the Kaleckian tradition, firms operate with excess capacity in oligopolistic goods markets and set their prices p with a mark-up μ on unit labor costs:

$$p = (1 + \mu)\frac{w}{a}, \tag{2.6}$$

where w is the money wage rate. It should be noted that $m = \mu/(1+\mu)$, that is, there is a one-to-one relationship between the mark-up and the profit share,[11] and accordingly, m and μ change in the same direction. Therefore, we can rewrite equation (2.6) as follows:

$$p = \left(\frac{1}{1 - m}\right)\frac{w}{a}. \tag{2.7}$$

Differentiating both sides of equation (2.7) with respect to time yields:

$$\frac{\dot{m}}{1 - m} = \frac{\dot{p}}{p} - \frac{\dot{w}}{w} + \frac{\dot{a}}{a}. \tag{2.8}$$

To know the dynamics of m, we have to specify the rates of change of p, w, and a.

We specify the dynamics of the money wage and price by using the theory of conflicting-claims inflation. First, suppose that the growth rate of the money wage that workers manage to negotiate depends on the discrepancy between their target real

---

10) When I is not equal to S, there is an unplanned inventory. For example, when the planned investment exceeds the planned saving, there is excess demand in the goods market. For the time being, this excess demand is compensated by the release of inventory, but when the inventory decreases, firms in the oligopolistic goods market try to increase production while maintaining prices, and as a result, the capacity utilization rate increases. Equation (2.4) describes this process.
11) The relationship between m and μ is given as follows:

$$m = 1 - \frac{wE}{pY} = 1 - \frac{w}{pa} = 1 - \frac{1}{1 + \mu} = \frac{\mu}{1 + \mu}.$$

wage rate and the actual real wage rate. Given labor productivity, to determine the real wage means to determine the wage share. Therefore, setting the target real wage rate is equivalent to setting the target profit share. Second, suppose that firms set their price to close the gap between their target mark-up and the actual mark-up. The target mark-up corresponds to the target profit share because, as stated above, the mark-up bears a one-to-one relation to the profit share. From these, the dynamics of the money wage and price can be described, respectively, as follows:

$$\frac{\dot{w}}{w} = \theta_w(m - m_w), \quad \theta_w > 0, \ 0 < m_w < 1, \tag{2.9}$$

$$\frac{\dot{p}}{p} = \theta_f(m_f - m), \quad \theta_f > 0, \ 0 < m_f < 1, \tag{2.10}$$

where θ_w and θ_f denote the speed of adjustment; m_w, the target profit share set by workers; and m_f, the profit share set by firms.

We can interpret θ_w and θ_f as the bargaining power of workers and that of firms, respectively.[12] We suppose $\theta_f + \theta_w = 1$ and define $\theta_f \equiv \theta$ because bargaining power is a relative concept. Then, we obtain $\theta_w = 1 - \theta$, where $0 < \theta < 1$.[13] We can take an increase in the unionization rate as a factor for raising the bargaining power of workers (i.e., a decrease in θ), and an increase in the market power of oligopolistic firms as a factor for raising the bargaining power of firms (i.e., an increase in θ).

Notice the difference between θ, and m_f and m_w. The parameter θ represents the relative bargaining power of firms (workers) and reflects the power to realize their demands. In contrast, m_f and m_w reflect their demands in the bargaining. To what extent their demands can be realized depends on θ.

Substituting equations (2.9) and (2.10) in equation (2.8), we obtain an equation of motion for the profit share:

$$\dot{m} = -(1 - m)[m - \theta m_f - (1 - \theta)m_w - g_a], \tag{2.11}$$

where $g_a = \dot{a}/a$ is the growth rate of labor productivity.

2.2.3   Adjustment in the growth rate of labor productivity

We now turn to the specification of endogenous technological change. Following Bhaduri (2006) and Dutt (2006), we describe the growth rate of labor productivity as follows:

$$g_a = \lambda e^{\beta}, \quad \lambda > 0, \ \beta > 0, \tag{2.12}$$

---

12) This interpretation is also adopted in Lavoie (1992, p. 393), Cassetti (2002, p. 192, and 2003, p. 453).

13) The constraint $0 < \theta_w, \theta_f < 1$ is also adopted by Dutt and Amadeo (1993), who, however, do not assume $\theta_f + \theta_w = 1$. Even if we impose only $0 < \theta_w, \theta_f < 1$, and not impose $\theta_f + \theta_w = 1$, we obtain similar results.

where e denotes the employment rate, which is defined as $e = E/N$ with N being the exogenous labor supply; λ, a constant; and β, the elasticity of the growth rate of labor productivity with respect to the employment rate.

Equation (2.12) shows that the growth rate of labor productivity is an increasing function of the employment rate. In general, the natural rate of growth is defined as a sum of the growth rate of labor productivity and that of labor supply. Although the growth rate of labor supply in our model is exogenously given, the growth rate of labor productivity is endogenously determined. Under our specification, therefore, the natural rate of growth increases while business is good (i.e., while the employment rate is high) and it decreases while business is bad (i.e., while the employment rate is low). The assumption that the natural rate of growth is endogenously determined is consistent with empirical studies by León-Ledesma and Thirlwall (2002), Libânio (2009), and Vogel (2009).

Using equation (2.12), we can show that in the long-run equilibrium, the growth rate of output per capita (Y/N) coincides with that of labor productivity (Y/E). In this respect, Sedgley and Elmslie (2004) empirically show the cointegration between the log of output per capita and the log of labor productivity.[14] Their evidence suggests that these two variables move together in the long run.

From equation (2.12), the rate of change of g_a is given by

$$\frac{\dot{g}_a}{g_a} = \beta \frac{\dot{e}}{e}. \tag{2.13}$$

From equation (2.2), employment is given by $E = uK/a$, and the employment rate is given by $e = uK/(aN)$, and accordingly, the rate of change of the employment rate leads to

$$\frac{\dot{e}}{e} = \frac{\dot{u}}{u} + g_d - g_a - n, \tag{2.14}$$

where n denotes the exogenously given growth rate of N.

Substituting equations (2.3) and (2.5) in equation (2.14), and substituting the resultant expression in equation (2.13), we obtain the dynamics of g_a:[15]

$$\dot{g}_a = \beta g_a [\alpha(Am^\phi u^{\gamma-1} - sm) + Am^\phi u^\gamma - g_a - n]. \tag{2.15}$$

From equations (2.13) and (2.15), we find that the elasticity β also means the speed of adjustment of g_a, and accordingly, the speed of adjustment of the labor market.

---

14) Their original purpose is to empirically test which model is more valid, the classical conventional wage share model proposed by Foley and Michl (1999) or the classical full employment model proposed by Pasinetti (1974). The growth rate of output per capita and that of labor productivity do not coincide in the classical conventional wage share model, whereas the two growth rates coincide in the classical full employment model. For this reason, we can know which model is more valid by examining the long-run relationship between the two variables.

15) We can use an equation of motion for e instead of equation (2.15) because e is related to g_a through equation (2.12). Naturally, we have the same results.

2.3   Existence and stability of the long-run equilibrium

From equations (2.5), (2.11), and (2.15), our model leads to the following system of differential equations:

$$\dot{u} = \alpha(Am^\phi u^\gamma - smu), \tag{2.16}$$

$$\dot{m} = -(1 - m)[m - \theta m_f - (1 - \theta)m_w - g_a], \tag{2.17}$$

$$\dot{g}_a = \beta g_a[\alpha(Am^\phi u^{\gamma-1} - sm) + Am^\phi u^\gamma - g_a - n]. \tag{2.18}$$

2.3.1   Existence of the long-run equilibrium

Long-run equilibrium is a situation in which $\dot{u} = \dot{m} = \dot{g}_a = 0$, from which we have the following three equations in order:

$$Am^\phi u^\gamma = smu, \tag{2.19}$$

$$m = \theta m_f + (1 - \theta)m_w + g_a, \tag{2.20}$$

$$Am^\phi u^\gamma = g_a + n. \tag{2.21}$$

From equation (2.19), we have

$$u = A^{\frac{1}{1-\gamma}} s^{-\frac{1}{1-\gamma}} m^{\frac{\phi-1}{1-\gamma}}. \tag{2.22}$$

Substituting $g_a = smu - n$ from equations (2.19) and (2.21) in equation (2.20), and substituting equation (2.22) in the resultant expression, we obtain

$$A^{\frac{1}{1-\gamma}} s^{-\frac{\gamma}{1-\gamma}} m^{\frac{\phi-\gamma}{1-\gamma}} - m + \theta m_f + (1 - \theta)m_w - n = 0. \tag{2.23}$$

This equation determines m^* (hereafter, equilibrium values are denoted with "$*$"). Using m^*, we can find u^* and g_a^*.

Let us explain the determination of m^*. We rewrite equation (2.23) as follows:

$$A^{\frac{1}{1-\gamma}} s^{-\frac{\gamma}{1-\gamma}} m^{\frac{\phi-\gamma}{1-\gamma}} + B = m + n, \tag{2.24}$$

where $B \equiv \theta m_f + (1 - \theta)m_w$. Each side of equation (2.24) is a function of m, and then, we can write each side as follows:

$$\text{LHS} \equiv F_m(m) = A^{\frac{1}{1-\gamma}} s^{-\frac{\gamma}{1-\gamma}} m^{\frac{\phi-\gamma}{1-\gamma}} + B, \tag{2.25}$$

$$\text{RHS} \equiv G_m(m) = m + n. \tag{2.26}$$

The intersection of these graphs determines m^*. $F_m(m)$ can be upward sloping or downward sloping depending on the sizes of ϕ and γ. $G_m(m)$ is a straight line such that the slope and the intercept are unity and n, respectively. From this, we obtain Figures 2.1 and 2.2. Both figures are drawn with the condition that $0 < m^* < 1$.

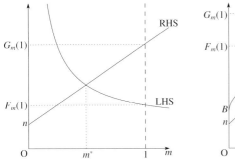
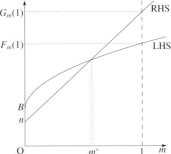

Figure 2.1: Determination of m^* ($\phi < \gamma$)   Figure 2.2: Determination of m^* ($\phi > \gamma$)

To obtain these figures, we need the constraints $B > n$ and $G_m(1) > F_m(1)$. Similarly, we can find the constraints under which economically meaningful values for u^* and g_a^* are obtained.[16] These constrains are summarized as follows:

$$m^* \in (0, 1) \Longrightarrow C1 : B - n > 0 \text{ and } C2 : 1 + n - B - A^{\frac{1}{1-\gamma}} s^{-\frac{\gamma}{1-\gamma}} > 0,$$

$$u^* \in (0, 1) \Longrightarrow C3 : s(1 - s)^{\phi - 1} - A(B - n)^{\phi - 1} > 0,$$

$$g_a^* > 0 \Longrightarrow C4 : A^{\frac{1}{1-\gamma}} s^{-\frac{\gamma}{1-\gamma}} B^{\frac{\phi-\gamma}{1-\gamma}} - n > 0.$$

The intersection of the conditions C1 through C4 is the necessary and sufficient condition for the long-run equilibrium values to be economically meaningful. Although it is difficult to obtain the intersection, numerical examples of parameters used in simulation below satisfy these conditions.

2.3.2   Local stability of the long-run equilibrium

To analyze the local stability of the long-run equilibrium, we linearize the system of differential equations (2.5), (2.17), and (2.18) around the equilibrium.

$$\begin{pmatrix} \dot{u} \\ \dot{m} \\ \dot{g}_a \end{pmatrix} = \begin{pmatrix} J_{11} & J_{12} & 0 \\ 0 & J_{22} & J_{23} \\ J_{31} & J_{32} & J_{33} \end{pmatrix} \begin{pmatrix} u - u^* \\ m - m^* \\ g_a - g_a^* \end{pmatrix}, \tag{2.27}$$

where the elements of the Jacobian matrix $\mathbf{J}$ are given by

$$J_{11} \equiv \frac{\partial \dot{u}}{\partial u} = -\alpha sm(1 - \gamma) < 0, \tag{2.28}$$

$$J_{12} \equiv \frac{\partial \dot{u}}{\partial m} = -\alpha su(1 - \phi) < 0, \tag{2.29}$$

16) See Appendix A for u^* and g_a^*.

$$J_{22} \equiv \frac{\partial \dot{m}}{\partial m} = -(1 - m) < 0, \tag{2.30}$$

$$J_{23} \equiv \frac{\partial \dot{m}}{\partial g_a} = 1 - m > 0, \tag{2.31}$$

$$J_{31} \equiv \frac{\partial \dot{g}_a}{\partial u} = \frac{\beta s m g_a}{u}[\alpha(\gamma - 1) + \gamma u] \gtreqless 0, \tag{2.32}$$

$$J_{32} \equiv \frac{\partial \dot{g}_a}{\partial m} = \beta s g_a[\alpha(\phi - 1) + \phi u] \gtreqless 0, \tag{2.33}$$

$$J_{33} \equiv \frac{\partial \dot{g}_a}{\partial g_a} = -\beta g_a < 0. \tag{2.34}$$

All elements are evaluated at the long-run equilibrium, though we omit "$*$" to avoid troublesome notations. J_{31} and J_{32} can be negative when the speed of adjustment α is sufficiently large.

Let us explain the Jacobian matrix. The diagonal elements J_{11}, J_{22}, and J_{33} represent the effects of endogenous variables on themselves. They are negative, which implies that when a variable deviates from its long-run equilibrium value, it returns to the equilibrium value. This negative feedback has a stabilizing effect. However, a change in one variable affects other variables, whose effects in turn rebound on the variable in question. We take the rate of utilization for example. J_{31} shows that a rise in the rate of utilization causes an increase or a decrease in the growth rate of labor productivity. If g_a increases, then from J_{23}, it induces a rise in the profit share. From J_{12}, this rise in the profit share lowers the capacity utilization rate. To sum up, this route has negative feedback, leading to stability. In contrast, if g_a decreases in J_{31}, then from J_{23}, it induces a fall in the profit share, which raises the capacity utilization rate from J_{12}. This route has positive feedback, leading to instability.

To examine the local stability of the long-run equilibrium, we have to know the properties of the characteristic roots of the Jacobian matrix. The characteristic equation of the Jacobian matrix is given by

$$q^3 + b_1 q^2 + b_2 q + b_3 = 0, \tag{2.35}$$

where q denotes a characteristic root. Each coefficient of equation (2.35) is expressed by

$$b_1 = -\text{tr}\,\mathbf{J} = \alpha s m (1 - \gamma) + (1 - m) + \beta g_a > 0, \tag{2.36}$$

$$\begin{aligned} b_2 &= J_{22} J_{33} - J_{23} J_{32} + J_{11}(J_{22} + J_{33}) \\ &= \beta g_a \{(1 - m)(1 - s\phi u) + \alpha s[m(1 - \gamma) + (1 - m)(1 - \phi)]\} \\ &\quad + \alpha s m (1 - \gamma)(1 - m) > 0, \end{aligned} \tag{2.37}$$

$$\begin{aligned} b_3 &= -\det \mathbf{J} = -J_{11}(J_{22} J_{33} - J_{23} J_{32}) - J_{31} J_{12} J_{23} \\ &= \alpha \beta s m (1 - m) g_a[(1 - \gamma)(1 - s\phi u) + s\gamma u(1 - \phi)] > 0, \end{aligned} \tag{2.38}$$

where $-b_1 = \text{tr}\,\mathbf{J}$ denotes the trace of $\mathbf{J}$; b_2, the sum of the principal minor determinants; and $-b_3 = \det\mathbf{J}$, the determinant of $\mathbf{J}$. As shown above, all signs are positive, and consequently, necessary conditions for the local stability are satisfied. The necessary and sufficient condition for stability is that all characteristic roots of the Jacobian matrix have negative real parts, which, from Routh-Hurwitz conditions, is equivalent to $b_1 > 0$, $b_2 > 0$, $b_3 > 0$, and $b_1b_2 - b_3 > 0$.[17] We compute $b_1b_2 - b_3$ as follows:

$$
\begin{aligned}
b_1b_2 - b_3 = {} & \alpha^2 s^2 m(1 - \gamma)\{\beta g_a[m(1 - \gamma) + (1 - m)(1 - \phi)] + m(1 - \gamma)(1 - m)\} \\
& + \beta^2 g_a^2\{(1 - m)(1 - s\phi u) + \alpha s[m(1 - \gamma) + (1 - m)(1 - \phi)]\} \\
& + (1 - m)^2[\beta g_a(1 - s\phi u) + \alpha sm(1 - \gamma)] \\
& + \alpha\beta s(1 - m)g_a[2m(1 - \gamma) + (1 - \phi)\underbrace{(1 - m - msu\gamma)}_{\equiv\Theta}].
\end{aligned}
\tag{2.39}
$$

The sign of $b_1b_2 - b_3$ seems to be indeterminate. However, we obtain the following proposition:

Proposition 2.1. *Suppose that α or β is sufficiently close to zero. Then, the long-run equilibrium is locally stable.*

Proof. When α is equal to zero, we have

$$
b_1b_2 - b_3 = \beta g_a(1 - m)(1 - s\phi u)[\beta g_a + (1 - m)] > 0.
\tag{2.40}
$$

Because $b_1b_2 - b_3$ is a continuous, quadratic function of α, even if $\alpha > 0$, $b_1b_2 - b_3 > 0$ is satisfied when α is sufficiently close to zero. Therefore, when α is sufficiently close to zero, the necessary and sufficient conditions for the local stability of the long-run equilibrium, that is, $b_1 > 0$, $b_2 > 0$, $b_3 > 0$, and $b_1b_2 - b_3 > 0$ are all satisfied. When β is sufficiently close to zero, the same argument holds. ∎

Proposition 2.1 means that if the speed of adjustment of the goods market or the speed of adjustment of the labor markets is slow, the long-run equilibrium is locally stable.

Note that in equation (2.39), all parts except the part defined as Θ is positive. From this, we obtain the following proposition:

Proposition 2.2. *Suppose that the long-run equilibrium value of the profit share is less than or equal to $1/2$. Then, the long-run equilibrium is locally stable irrespective of the sizes of α and β.*

Proof. Θ is given by

$$
\Theta \equiv 1 - m - msu\gamma.
\tag{2.41}
$$

_____

17) See Gandolfo (1996) for details.

First, when s, u, and γ are close to zero, Θ will be positive because $msu\gamma$ in Θ will be sufficiently small. Second, when s, u, and γ are close to unity, Θ approaches

$$\Theta = 1 - m - m = 1 - 2m. \tag{2.42}$$

From this, if $m^* \leq 1/2$, that is, the equilibrium profit share is less than or equal to $1/2$, then $\Theta > 0$, and consequently, $b_1 b_2 - b_3 > 0$. Therefore, if $m^* \leq 1/2$, the necessary and sufficient conditions for the local stability of the long-run equilibrium are all satisfied.   ∎

In general, the profit share in the real world is considered to be smaller than $1/2$, and thus, the condition $m^* \leq 1/2$ is not so unrealistic. For example, Bernanke and Gürkaynak (2001) report that during the period 1973–1992, the average profit share was 0.26 in France, 0.31 in Germany, 0.32 in Japan, 0.33 in Netherlands, 0.25 in the U.K., and 0.26 in the U.S. These empirical findings support the validity of Proposition 2.

Note, however, that $m^* \leq 1/2$ is a sufficient and not a necessary condition for $b_1 b_2 - b_3 > 0$. Moreover, note that m^* depends on the parameters of the model.[18]

2.4   Numerical examples

This section presents numerical examples to show that the economically meaningful long-run equilibrium actually exists under plausible parameter settings and that each variable converges to its long-run equilibrium value from an arbitrary initial value. Considering the shape of the investment function, we investigate two cases in what follows: $\phi < \gamma$ (Case 1) and $\phi > \gamma$ (Case 2).

To begin with, we set parameters and initial conditions common to Cases 1 and 2 as follows:

$\alpha = 1$, $\beta = 0.5$, $A = 0.3$, $s = 0.8$, $\theta = 0.4$, $m_f = 0.3$, $m_w = 0.2$, $n = 0.04$,
$u(0) = 0.6$, $m(0) = 0.4$, $g_a(0) = 0.15$.

Next, we set the parameters of the investment function as follows:

$$\text{Case 1}: \phi = 0.2, \ \gamma = 0.3,$$
$$\text{Case 2}: \phi = 0.3, \ \gamma = 0.2.$$

The numerical examples above satisfy the conditions C1 through C4: in Case 1, C1 :

---

18) The condition for $m^* \leq 1/2$ is given by

$$G_m(1/2) \geq F_m(1/2) \implies \frac{1}{2} + n \geq A^{\frac{1}{1-\gamma}} s^{-\frac{\gamma}{1-\gamma}} \left(\frac{1}{2}\right)^{\frac{\phi-\gamma}{1-\gamma}} + B.$$

$0.20 > 0$, C2 : $0.60 > 0$, C3 : $1.81 > 0$, C4 : $0.20 > 0$; and in Case 2, C1 : $0.20 > 0$, C2 : $0.57 > 0$, C3 : $1.54 > 0$, C4 : $0.16 > 0$.

Table 2.1 shows the equilibrium values for Cases 1 and 2. From this, we see that u^*, m^*, and g_a^* all take reasonable values.

Table 2.1: Equilibrium values for Cases 1 and 2

	u^*	m^*	g_a^*
Case 1	0.658742	0.422827	0.182827
Case 2	0.64025	0.410004	0.170004

Figures 2.3–2.8 show the time path (up to $t = 100$) of each variable. Every variable converges to its equilibrium value. In these numerical examples, Cases 1 and 2 show similar dynamics.

In the above examples, we set the speed of adjustment of the goods market, that is, α to 1. If we use α that is larger or smaller than 1, the speed of convergence gets faster or slower. Nonetheless, each variable converges to its long-run equilibrium value.

We set the elasticity of the growth rate of labor productivity with respect to the employment rate, that is, β to 0.5. As can be seen from equation (2.18), β also represents the speed of adjustment of g_a. As is the case with α, even if we use β that is larger or smaller than 0.5, each variable converges to its equilibrium value.

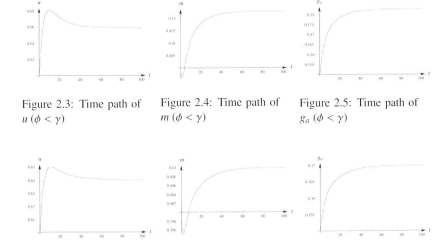

Figure 2.3: Time path of u ($\phi < \gamma$)

Figure 2.4: Time path of m ($\phi < \gamma$)

Figure 2.5: Time path of g_a ($\phi < \gamma$)

Figure 2.6: Time path of u ($\phi > \gamma$)

Figure 2.7: Time path of m ($\phi > \gamma$)

Figure 2.8: Time path of g_a ($\phi > \gamma$)

Figure 2.9 depicts the transitional dynamics of the profit share and the capital accumulation rate from the initial point to the long-run equilibrium in Case 1. The figure shows that the economy experiences the following three phases: the profit share decreases while the capital accumulation rate increases (Phase I); both the profit share and the capital accumulation rate increases (Phase II); and the profit share increases while the capital accumulation rate decreases (Phase III). These phases apparently correspond to the wage-led growth, profit-led growth, and wage-led growth regimes, in order. When $\phi < \gamma$, as will be stated in Section 5 in detail, we have a wage-led growth regime in long-run equilibrium. However, along the transitional dynamics, we can have an apparent profit-led growth regime like Phase II.[19] This phenomenon suggests that even if the data of the real economy show Phase II, it is not necessarily a true profit-led growth regime.[20]

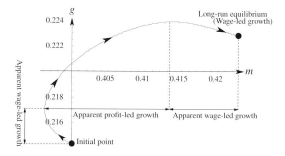

Figure 2.9: Transitional dynamics of the profit share and the capital accumulation rate in Case 1

As an example, we take the Japanese economy. Figure 2.10 shows the time-series data of the real GDP growth rate and the profit share during the period 1990–2007.[21] Except for the periods 1993–1995 and 2004–2006, the real GDP growth rate and the profit share move in the same direction, from which we might conclude that the Japanese economy experienced profit-led growth. However, as stated above, this empirical finding might show an apparent profit-led growth. Therefore, we need a detailed empirical analysis to conclude which regime the real economy belongs to.

---

19) Using a demand-led growth model that is different from ours, Bhaduri (2008) also points out that it is possible that one obtains a profit-led regime out of equilibrium but a wage-led regime in equilibrium.

20) In Case 2, naturally, we have similar phenomena. When $\phi > \gamma$, we have a profit-led growth regime in the long-run equilibrium. However, along the transitional dynamics, we can have an apparent wage-led growth regime. Moreover, similar arguments hold for the relationship between the profit share and the capacity utilization rate.

21) The real GDP growth rate is a proxy variable for the rate of capital accumulation. The profit share is obtained by subtracting the wage share from unity, and the wage share is obtained by dividing employee compensation by nominal national income.

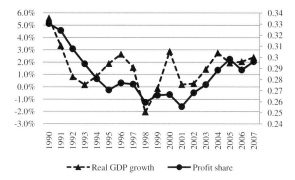

Figure 2.10: Real GDP growth and profit share during the period 1990–2007 in Japan. Source: National Accounts of Japan

2.5 Comparative statics analysis

This section investigates the effects of shifts in parameters on the long-run equilibrium. Table 2.2 summarizes the results of comparative statics analysis. These results are obtained under the assumption that the long-run equilibrium is stable. In addition, $m_f - m_w > 0$ is assumed in the analysis. It is reasonable to assume that firms attempt to set m_f as high as possible, whereas workers attempt to set m_w as low as possible. Hence, the assumption $m_f - m_w > 0$ can be justified.[22] Given that $m_f > m_w$, a rise in θ, m_f, and m_w leads to a rise in B.

Note that g_a^* and e^* are dealt with in the same row of Table 2.2 because these two variables move in the same direction (see equation (2.12)).

A parameter, Ω, which will appear below, is defined as

$$\Omega \equiv 1 - \frac{(\phi - \gamma)su}{1 - \gamma}. \tag{2.43}$$

When $\phi < \gamma$, we have $\Omega > 0$. When $\phi > \gamma$, $0 < (\phi - \gamma)/(1 - \gamma) < 1$ because $0 < \phi < 1$. Since $0 < s < 1$ and $0 < u < 1$, we have $\Omega > 0$ when $\phi > \gamma$. Therefore, we always have $\Omega > 0$ irrespective of $\phi < \gamma$ or $\phi > \gamma$.

Note, finally, that $g^* = g_a^* + n$ and $g_a^* = m^* - B$ hold in the long-run equilibrium, which are used in the following analysis.

---

22) If $m_f = m_w$, that is, the target profit shares of both classes are exactly equal, then the term B leads to $B = m_f = m_w$, and consequently, it is independent of θ. Therefore, the relative bargaining power θ does not affect the long-run equilibrium values. That is, if the demands of both classes are perfectly matched, the long-run equilibrium is independent of the bargaining power.

Table 2.2: Results for comparative statics
analysis

	s	n	$\theta^{\dagger}$	$m_f, m_w{}^{\dagger}$	A
u^*	$-$	$+$	$-$	$-$	$+$
m^*	$-$	$-$	$+$	$+$	$+$
g_a^*, e^*	$-$	$-$	$-/+^{\ddagger}$	$-/+^{\ddagger}$	$+$
g^*	$-$	$+/-^{\ddagger}$	$-/+^{\ddagger}$	$-/+^{\ddagger}$	$+$

† We assume $m_f > m_w$.
‡ When $\phi < \gamma$, the left-hand sign applies, and
when $\phi > \gamma$, the right-hand sign applies.

■ Saving rate
An increase in the saving rate decreases the capacity utilization rate, the profit
share, and the rate of capital accumulation.

$$\frac{du^*}{ds} = -\frac{A^{\frac{1}{1-\gamma}} s^{\frac{\gamma-2}{1-\gamma}} m^{\frac{\phi-1}{1-\gamma}} (1 - \phi su)}{(1 - \gamma)\Omega} < 0, \tag{2.44}$$

$$\frac{dm^*}{ds} = \frac{dg_a^*}{ds} = \frac{dg^*}{ds} = -\frac{\gamma mu}{(1 - \gamma)\Omega} < 0. \tag{2.45}$$

Hereafter, all endogenous variables are evaluated at the long-run equilibrium. The
negative effect on the growth rate is known as "the paradox of thrift." An increase in
the saving rate decreases the employment rate, thereby increasing the unemployment
rate. In Stockhammer (2004), the long-run equilibrium rate of unemployment consists
of the exogenous natural rate of growth and parameters of the investment and income
distribution functions, and does not depend on the saving rate. Consequently, a change
in the saving rate never affects the unemployment rate. In our model, on the other
hand, g_a^* and the natural rate of growth are endogenously determined, and accordingly,
a change in the saving rate affects the unemployment rate.
■ Labor supply growth
A rise in the growth rate of labor supply increases the capacity utilization rate and
decreases the profit share.

$$\frac{du^*}{dn} = \frac{(1 - \phi)A^{\frac{1}{1-\gamma}} s^{-\frac{1}{1-\gamma}} m^{\frac{\phi+\gamma-2}{1-\gamma}}}{(1 - \gamma)\Omega} > 0, \tag{2.46}$$

$$\frac{dm^*}{dn} = -\frac{1}{\Omega} < 0. \tag{2.47}$$

This mechanism is as follows. A rise in n creates excess supply in the labor market,
thereby depressing the employment rate. Because the growth rate of labor productivity depends positively on the employment rate, the depressing effect on the employment rate also decreases labor productivity, which also decreases the profit share from
equation (2.20). This decrease in the profit share leads to an increase in the capacity

utilization rate through equation (2.22). The conventional Kaleckian model cannot investigate the effect of supply side factors on equilibrium values. In contrast, our model can investigate this effect.

Let us turn to the effect on the employment rate. A rise in the growth rate of labor supply decreases the equilibrium employment and thus, increases the equilibrium unemployment rate.

$$\frac{dg_a^*}{dn} = \frac{dm^*}{dn} = -\frac{1}{\Omega} < 0. \tag{2.48}$$

Because the relation $g_a^* = sm^*u^* - n$ holds in the long-run equilibrium, a rise in n has three different effects on g_a^*: it directly decreases g_a^* with the coefficient of n being -1; it indirectly decreases g_a^* through m^* with m^* decreasing in n; and it indirectly increases g_a^* through u^* with u^* increasing in n. In total, the two negative effects outweigh the one positive effect, which leads to a decrease in g_a^* and e^* with an increase in n. Stockhammer (2004) also concludes that an increase in the growth rate of labor supply leads to a rise in unemployment in the profit-led growth regime where the long-run equilibrium is stable.[23]

Finally, a rise in the growth rate of labor supply either increases or decreases the capital accumulation rate depending on the sizes of the two elasticities of the investment function.

$$\frac{dg^*}{dn} = \frac{(\gamma - \phi)su}{(1 - \gamma)\Omega}. \tag{2.49}$$

To understand this, we need to remind ourselves that from equation (2.3), $g^* = A(m^*)^\phi(u^*)^\gamma$ holds in the long-run equilibrium. As stated above, a rise in n decreases m^* and increases u^*. When $\phi < \gamma$, the positive effect of u^* exceeds the negative effect of m^*, and consequently, in total, g^* increases with a rise in n. When $\phi > \gamma$, the converse holds.

■ Bargaining power

An increase in θ, which corresponds to an increase in the relative bargaining power of firms, brings about a decrease in the capacity utilization rate and an increase in the profit share.

$$\frac{du^*}{dB} = -\frac{(1 - \phi)A^{\frac{1}{1-\gamma}}s^{-\frac{1}{1-\gamma}}m^{\frac{\phi+\gamma-2}{1-\gamma}}}{(1 - \gamma)\Omega} < 0, \tag{2.50}$$

$$\frac{dm^*}{dB} = \frac{1}{\Omega} > 0. \tag{2.51}$$

The effect on the employment rate is worth considering. A rise in θ either increases or decreases the employment rate according to the sizes of ϕ and γ. The employment

---

23) Rowthorn (1999) reaches a similar conclusion using a different model, in which trade unions and firms are engaged in Nash bargaining for wages.

rate decreases when $\phi < \gamma$, while it increases when $\phi > \gamma$.

$$\frac{dg_a^*}{dB} = \frac{(\phi - \gamma)su}{(1 - \gamma)\Omega}.$$ (2.52)

A rise in θ has two different effects on g_a and e: it indirectly increases g_a and e through its positive effect on m; and it indirectly decreases g_a and e through its negative effect on u. Whether or not the rise in θ leads to an increase in g_a and e depends on which effect dominates, which in turn depends on the sizes of the elasticities of the investment function. When $\phi < \gamma$, the negative effect of capacity utilization dominates the positive effect of the profit share, thereby leading to a decrease in the growth rate of labor productivity and the employment rate. When $\phi > \gamma$, in contrast, the positive effect of the profit share dominates the negative effect of capacity utilization, thereby leading to an increase in the growth rate of labor productivity and the employment rate.

Stockhammer (2004) also investigates the relationship between bargaining power and unemployment. He concludes that in the profit-led growth regime, a decrease in the bargaining power of workers leads to higher employment and lower unemployment. This result is consistent with ours. However, in the wage-led growth regime of Stockhammer's model, the long-run equilibrium is necessarily unstable, and hence, we cannot investigate the relationship between bargaining power and unemployment. In our model, in contrast, the-long run equilibrium of the wage-led growth regime can be stable. In this case, we reach the opposite conclusion that an increase in the bargaining power of workers leads to higher employment and lower unemployment. This result is consistent with the empirical result of Storm and Naastepad (2007). Using data for 20 OECD countries during the period 1984–1997, they show that an increase in the bargaining power of firms due to labor market deregulation raises the unemployment rate in contrast to the view of the mainstream NAIRU model.[24]

■ Target profit share

The effect of an increase in the target profit share m_f or m_w is similar to that of an increase in θ discussed above because of the structure of the model. An important issue in the Kaleckian model is that different regimes arise due to the specification of the investment function. According to Blecker's (2002) classification, the wage-led demand (profit-led demand) regime is a situation where an increase in the profit share decreases (increases) the capacity utilization rate. The wage-led (profit-led) growth regime is a situation where an increase in the profit share decreases (increases) the rate of capital accumulation. The profit share in our model is not an exogenous but an endogenous variable, and thus, we cannot apply Blecker's classification to the model as it is. However, because the actual profit share m is closely related to the target profit shares m_f and m_w, these variables can be a proxy variable for the actual profit share. An increase in m_f and m_w leads to a decrease in the capacity utilization rate, which corresponds to the wage-led demand regime. In addition, an increase in m_f and m_w

---

24) Similar empirical results are obtained in Storm and Naastepad (2008).

raises the capital accumulation rate when $\phi > \gamma$ while it lowers the growth rate when $\phi < \gamma$: the former case corresponds to the profit-led growth regime, while the latter case corresponds to the wage-led growth regime.

$$\frac{dg^*}{dB} = \frac{dg_a^*}{dB} = \frac{(\phi - \gamma)su}{(1 - \gamma)\Omega}. \tag{2.53}$$

■ Autonomous investment

We can regard parameter A of the investment function as expressing a demand policy. Setterfield (2009), for instance, relates a constant term of the investment function to a fiscal policy and discusses the effectiveness of output targeting and inflation targeting. An increase in A in our model raises all equilibrium values: stimulating effective demand lowers the unemployment rate even in the long run. This implication makes a marked contrast to the implication of the mainstream NAIRU theory.

$$\frac{du^*}{dA} = \frac{s^{\frac{1}{1-\gamma}}A^{\frac{\gamma}{1-\gamma}}m^{\frac{\phi-1}{1-\gamma}}(1 - su)}{(1 - \gamma)\Omega} > 0, \tag{2.54}$$

$$\frac{dm^*}{dA} = \frac{dg_a^*}{dA} = \frac{dg^*}{dA} = \frac{smu}{A(1 - \gamma)\Omega} > 0. \tag{2.55}$$

2.6 Concluding remarks

This chapter has developed a Kaleckian growth model in which the rate of technological change and the employment rate are endogenously determined. The model is based on the Kaleckian model with the theory of conflicting-claims inflation, and extended to incorporate endogenous technological change. Our model responds to the criticism that in the usual Kaleckian model, technological change is not considered and the long-run employment rate is not constant.

Using the model, we have analyzed how the relative bargaining power of workers and firms affects the long-run equilibrium employment rate. The relationship between the bargaining power and the employment rate differs depending on the regime in which the long-run equilibrium lies. If the long-run equilibrium is characterized as a wage-led growth regime, a rise in the relative bargaining power of firms increases the unemployment rate. If, on the other hand, the long-run equilibrium is characterized as a profit-led growth regime, a rise in the relative bargaining power of workers increases the unemployment rate. The latter result is also obtained in the mainstream NAIRU model, but the former result is never obtained in the mainstream model. Note, however, that in a wage-led growth regime, a fall in the firms' bargaining power, that is, a rise in the workers' bargaining power, leads to higher employment, but it simultaneously leads to lower profit share: workers' interests interfere with firms' interests. For this reason, it may be difficult to implement an economic policy intended to adjust the bargaining power of both classes. Even in this case, nonetheless, demand stimulation policy is effective. As discussed in the text, stimulation of effective demand brings about higher employment and accordingly lower unemployment. This policy implication is never obtainable from the mainstream NAIRU theory.

Which regime is obtained in the long-run equilibrium is independent of bargaining power because of the structure of the model and depends only on the sizes of the elasticities of the investment function. In reality, however, demand-oriented policies are likely to affect the bargaining power of both classes. For example, less progressive income tax increases the bargaining power of capitalists, which can lead the economy to a profit-led growth. For this reason, it is important to investigate how demand-oriented policies affect bargaining power and how the resultant change in the bargaining power affects economic regimes.

Our way of introducing of technological change is very simple. Rowthorn (1981) states that technical progress influences an economy in two ways. First, technical progress makes existing equipment obsolete, and thus, it will affect the rate of depreciation. Second, technical progress stimulates firms that undertake innovations to invest more by bringing extra profits to them, and thus, the form of investment function will be modified. In Cassetti (2003), these effects are taken into account, while in the present chapter, these issues are not dealt with for the purpose of emphasizing the role of endogenous technological change in the Kaleckian model of growth. For the same purpose, target rates of workers and firms are not endogenized. It is evident that technological change influences the target rates if these are endogenized.

Appendix 2.A: Determination of the equilibrium capacity utilization rate

Eliminating m and g_a from equations (2.19), (2.20), and (2.21), we obtain the following equation for u:

$$A(B - n)^{\phi-1}u^{\gamma-1} = s(1 - su)^{\phi-1}. \tag{2.56}$$

Both sides are functions of u. Thus, we can rewrite them as follows:

$$\text{LHS} \equiv F_u(u) = A(B - n)^{\phi-1}u^{\gamma-1}, \tag{2.57}$$

$$\text{RHS} \equiv G_u(u) = s(1 - su)^{\phi-1}. \tag{2.58}$$

The intersection of these curves determines u^*. For $u^* \in (0, 1)$, we need $F_u(1) < G_u(1)$, from which we obtain C3: $s(1 - s)^{\phi-1} - A(B - n)^{\phi-1} > 0$.

Appendix 2.B: Determination of the equilibrium growth rate of labor productivity

Eliminating u and m from equations (2.19), (2.20), and (2.21), we obtain the following equation for g_a:

$$A^{\frac{1}{1-\gamma}} s^{-\frac{\gamma}{1-\gamma}} (g_a + B)^{\frac{\phi-\gamma}{1-\gamma}} = g_a + n. \qquad (2.59)$$

Both hands are functions of g_a. Thus, we can rewrite them as follows:

$$\text{LHS} \equiv F_{g_a}(g_a) = A^{\frac{1}{1-\gamma}} s^{-\frac{\gamma}{1-\gamma}} (g_a + B)^{\frac{\phi-\gamma}{1-\gamma}}, \qquad (2.60)$$

$$\text{RHS} \equiv G_{g_a}(g_a) = g_a + n. \qquad (2.61)$$

The intersection of these curves determines g_a^*. For $g_a^* > 0$, we need $F_{g_a}(0) > n$, from which we obtain C4: $A^{\frac{1}{1-\gamma}} s^{-\frac{\gamma}{1-\gamma}} B^{\frac{\phi-\gamma}{1-\gamma}} - n > 0$.

Chapter 3

Cyclical Growth in a Goodwin-Kalecki-Marx Model

3.1 Introduction

This chapter introduces a labor market and endogenous technical change to a Kaleckian model, which is a kind of disequilibrium macrodynamic model; investigates how output, income distribution, and employment are determined; and examines the stability of the long-run equilibrium.

To date, a number of models of growth cycles have been developed. This chapter focuses on endogenous growth cycles. Mainstream theories of growth cycles show that even under dynamic optimization, cyclical fluctuations can be produced endogenously.[1] In what follows, we consider two examples.

The first example is from Benhabib and Nishimura (1979). In dynamic optimization models with one state variable, a steady state equilibrium is a saddle point; consequently, cyclical fluctuations do not occur. However, in dynamic optimization models with more than two state variables, cyclical fluctuations can occur. The authors reveal this fact by using the Hopf bifurcation theorem.[2]

The second example is a model of growth cycles with innovation. Furukawa (2007) extends a variety expansion model à la Romer (1990) and shows that cyclical fluctuations occur endogenously. Specifically, he assumes that there is a lag between the invention of new products and their diffusion. This time lag produces period-by-period indeterminacy of expectations, leading to growth cycles. Similar models of growth cycles that emphasize innovation include Evans et al. (1998), variety expansion; Francois and Lloyd-Ellis (2003), quality ladder à la Grossman and Helpman (1991); and Wälde (2005), creative destruction à la Aghion and Howitt (1992).

These models assume the full utilization of capital and the full employment of labor. That is, although the time path of each endogenous variable shows cyclical

---

1) Here, we do not consider the real business cycle theory in which business cycles are produced through a stochastic shock.

2) For a detailed analysis of this line of research, see Dockner and Feichtinger (1991).

fluctuations, the economy as a whole is always in equilibrium. However, after examining data for a real economy, it is plausible that the economy is in a situation in which capital is not fully utilized and labor is not fully employed, even in the long run. For example, Zipperer and Skott (2011) present long-run cyclical trends for the capacity utilization rate and employment rate (and profit share) in the OECD that support the above assertion.[3]

These empirical findings suggest that disequilibrium macrodynamic models, rather than equilibrium macrodynamic models, are well suited to explain such long-run cyclical trends. A typical example of a disequilibrium macrodynamic model is that of Goodwin (1967). Goodwin's model shows that with full capacity utilization, there are clockwise cyclical fluctuations along closed orbits in the (e, m)-plane, where e and m denote the employment rate and profit share, respectively.[4] The empirical studies mentioned above show that in most countries, clockwise cycles are actually observed. That is, it is safe to say that clockwise cycles in the (e, m)-plane is a consensus. However, Goodwin's model assumes the validity of Say's law, which states that the goods market is always in equilibrium. Goodwin's model does not consider the disequilibrium of goods markets and hence cannot explain cyclical fluctuations of capacity utilization.

In contrast, Keynesian macrodynamic models that are founded on the principle of effective demand consider the disequilibrium of both the labor and goods markets. Because we are investigating output as well as employment, we also consider Keynesian macrodynamic models. Several types of Keynesian models have been produced for the purpose of analysis. For example, Yoshida (1999) and Sportelli (2000) built Harrodian models, while Skott (1989) presented a Kaldorian model.

In this chapter, we consider the Kaleckian model (a class of Keynesian macrodynamic models),[5] specifically the Kaleckian model that incorporates the theory of conflicting-claims inflation, because it emphasizes the importance of income distribution between classes.[6] In the Kaleckian model incorporating conflicting-claims inflation, both the capacity utilization rate and income distribution (wage share and profit share) are endogenously determined through the conflict between workers and firms.

However, even such extended models do not consider the labor market satisfacto-

---

3) Other empirical findings that support the above assertion include Barbosa-Filho and Taylor (2006), long-run trends for the capacity utilization rate in the US; Mohun and Veneziani (2008), long-run trends for the rate employment in the US; and Harvie (2000), long-run trends for the employment rate in the OECD.

4) For extensions of Goodwin's model, see Pohjola (1981), Wolfstetter (1982), Sato (1985), Foley (2003), Ryzhenkov (2009), Shah and Desai (1981), van der Ploeg (1987), Sportelli (1995), and Choi (1995).

5) Kaleckian models have the following four characteristics (Lavoie 1992): (1) they comprise the investment function; (2) the prices relative to direct costs are influenced by a broad range of factors, often summarized by the phrase "degree of monopoly"; (3) marginal costs are assumed to be constant up to full capacity; and (4) the capacity utilization rate is assumed to be generally below unity.

6) The theory of conflicting-claims inflation was originally developed by Rowthorn (1977). For Kalecki's theory, see Kalecki (1971). For Kaleckian models with conflicting-claims inflation, see also Lavoie (1992) and Cassetti (2003).

rily.[7] The existing Kaleckian growth models assume an unlimited labor supply and that firms employ as many workers as they desire at the given wage rate. If, however, the labor supply grows at an exogenously given rate, there is no guarantee that the endogenously determined employment growth will equal the exogenous labor supply growth. If the labor supply grows faster than the employment demand, then the rate of unemployment continues to rise; this is an unrealistic finding. Hence, such a model cannot suitably investigate long-run unemployment.

On the basis of the above observation, we present a Kaleckian model in which excess capacity is retained and cyclical growth never disappears, not even in the long run.[8] For this purpose, we endogenize the labor-saving technical progress. By this extension, we demonstrate the existence of a situation in which the economy experiences endogenous and perpetual growth cycles.

We assume that the growth rate of labor productivity positively depends on the employment rate. This assumption is based on Bhaduri (2006), Dutt (2006), and Flaschel and Skott (2006). Given the level of output, an increase in labor productivity lowers employment and thus gives rise to the Marxian concept of the reserve army of labor, that is, the unemployed. Because, from our specification, the growth rate of labor productivity increases with the employment rate, a counterbalancing effect that lowers the increased employment rate is exerted. We call this effect the "reserve army creation effect."[9] Marx emphasizes the role of labor-saving technological progress in the creation of the reserve army of labor (Marx, 1976; chs. 10, 13, and 23). We use this term to distinguish it from the "reserve army effect": that the growth rate of wages increases as the employment rate increases. We show that the interaction between reserve army effect and reserve army creation effect produces limit cycles.

Contrary to general belief, few studies simultaneously consider the three variables: capacity utilization rate, employment rate, and profit share. According to the findings of Zipperer and Skott (2011), in the US economy, clockwise cycles consistently exist in the (u, m)- and (e, u)-planes as well as in the (e, m)-plane, where u denotes the capacity utilization rate. In relation to this finding, Skott and Zipperer (2010) develop a three-dimensional Kaldorian model that explains clockwise cycles in the three planes.

However, as Zipperer and Skott (2011) correctly state, counterclockwise cycles in the (u, m)- and (e, u)-planes are also observed, except in the US. Figures 3.1–3.3 show time-connected scatterplots of the employment rate, capacity utilization rate, and profit share by using quarterly data for Japan during the period 1960–2007.[10]

---

7) Dutt (1992) is a rare case. He introduced the labor market into a Kaleckian model and investigated growth with business cycle. For Kaleckian models with a labor market, see also Lima (2004) and Velupillai (2006).

8) Raghavendra (2006) proves the existence of endogenous and perpetual business cycles in a Kaleckian model. However, his model is a short-run model that does not consider the labor market and economic growth.

9) For Kaleckian models with the reserve army creation effect, see also Sasaki (2010, 2011).

10) The data for the employment rate are taken from the Labour Force Survey, those for the profit share from the Financial Statements Statistics of Corporation by Industry, and those for the capacity utilization rate from the Indices of Industrial Production. These quarterly data are smoothed by the Hodrick-Prescott

The dotted circles in Figures 3.1–3.3 correspond to counterclockwise cycles. From these figures, we see that unlike in the US, clockwise cycles are not always dominant in Japan. Therefore, the directions of cycles can differ for countries and periods. Our model produces clockwise cycles in the (e, m)-plane but counterclockwise cycles in the (u, m)- and (e, u)-planes. In this sense, the model is consistent with some empirical findings.

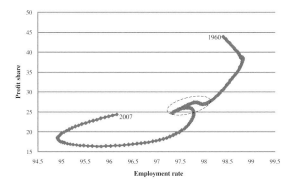

Figure 3.1: Smoothed cycle in the (e, m)-plane in Japan

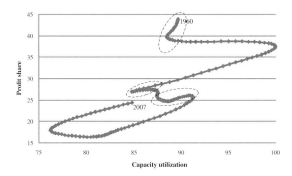

Figure 3.2: Smoothed cycle in the (u, m)-plane in Japan

Since our model incorporates certain elements from Goodwin (the dynamics of the employment rate and income distribution), Kalecki (an investment function independent of savings and mark-up pricing in oligopolistic goods markets), and Marx (the reserve army and reserve army creation effects). For this reason, we call our model a Goodwin-Kalecki-Marx model.

filter with a smoothing parameter $\lambda = 1600$.

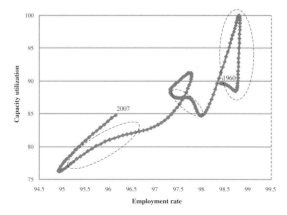

Figure 3.3: Smoothed cycle in the (e, u)-plane in Japan

The remainder of the chapter is organized as follows. Section 2 presents the framework of the model and derives the fundamental equations for the analysis. Section 3 analyzes the long-run equilibrium, shows that a limit cycle can occur, and conducts a comparative statics analysis. Section 4 shows the existence of limit cycles through the use of numerical simulations. Section 5 concludes the chapter.

3.2   Basic framework of the model

Consider an economy with workers and capitalists. Suppose that workers spend all their wages and capitalists save a constant fraction s of their profits. Let r and K be the rate of profit and capital stock, respectively. Then, the real savings are given by $S = srK$, and accordingly, the ratio of real savings to capital stock, $g_s = S/K$, yields

$$g_s = sr. \qquad (3.1)$$

We ignore capital depreciation for simplicity.

Suppose that the firms operate with the following fixed coefficients production function:

$$Y = \min\{aL, (u/k)K\}, \qquad (3.2)$$

where Y denotes real output; L, employment; and $a = Y/L$, the level of labor productivity. The capacity utilization rate is defined as $u = Y/Y^*$, where Y^* denotes the potential output. The coefficient $k = K/Y^*$ denotes the ratio of capital stock to potential output, which is assumed to be constant. This assumption implies that both K and

Y^* grow at the same rate. Moreover, when the capacity utilization rate is constant, the growth rates of capital stock and actual output are the same. Accordingly, the actual output and potential output grow at the same rate in the long-run equilibrium. To simplify the analysis, we assume $k = 1$ in what follows. The main results in this chapter do not change as long as k is assumed to be constant. From this, we have $r = mu$, where m denotes the profit share.

Based on the argument of Marglin and Bhaduri (1990), we specify the ratio of real investment I to capital stock K, $g_d = I/K$, as a function that is increasing in both the profit share and the capacity utilization rate.[11] In particular, following Blecker (2002), we specify the investment function as follows:

$$g_d = \psi m^\beta u^\gamma, \quad \psi > 0, \ \beta \in (0, 1), \ \gamma \in (0, 1), \tag{3.3}$$

where ψ denotes a constant; β, the elasticity of the investment rate with respect to the profit share; and γ, the elasticity of the investment rate with respect to the capacity utilization rate. Equation (3.3) implies that the desired investment rate of firms is increasing in both the profit share and the capacity utilization rate. The parameter restriction $0 < \gamma < 1$ ensures that, evaluated at the equilibrium, investment is less sensitive than saving to variations in the rate of utilization.[12] Because the investment function is not linear but Cobb-Douglas, as will be shown later, different regimes can be produced by changing the sizes of β and γ. When $\beta < \gamma$, the long-run equilibrium is wage-led growth, whereas when $\beta > \gamma$, it is profit-led growth. The equilibrium is said to be wage-led (profit-led) growth if a rise in the profit share leads to a fall (rise) in the rate of capital accumulation.[13]

An equation of motion for the capacity utilization rate is given by

$$\dot{u} = \alpha(g_d - g_s), \quad \alpha > 0, \tag{3.4}$$

where α denotes the speed of adjustment of the goods market. Equation (3.4) shows that excess demand leads to a rise in the capacity utilization rate, while excess supply leads to a decline in the capacity utilization rate.

From the definition of profit share, we have $m = 1 - (wL/pY)$, from which we

---

11) The reason for this is as follows. The profit rate is equal to the product of the profit share and the capacity utilization rate, that is, $r = mu$. Thus, it is plausible that a combination of high capacity utilization and a low profit share and a combination of low capacity utilization and a high profit share will produce different levels of investment even when the rate of profit is held constant at a given level.

12) However, there is a view that the long-run parameter restrictions in the Kaleckian investment function have neither theoretical nor empirical support. See Skott (2010).

13) In this chapter, the profit share is an endogenous variable, not an exogenous variable. Thus, we cannot define $\partial g^*/\partial m$ at the equilibrium. Accordingly, we use the relationship between g^* and the parameter m_f (the target profit share of firms introduced later). Hence, the equilibrium is wage-led growth if $\partial g^*/\partial m_f < 0$ and profit-led growth if $\partial g^*/\partial m_f > 0$. As seen from equation (3.67), the sign of $\partial g^*/\partial m_f$ depends on the relative sizes of β and γ. If $\beta > 1$ in this specification, we have a profit-led demand regime in which an increase in the profit share leads to a rise in the capacity utilization rate. However, $\beta > 1$, as Blecker (2002) points out, is an extreme case. Hence, we assume $0 < \beta < 1$ in the following analysis.

obtain the following relation:[14]

$$\frac{\dot{m}}{1-m} = \frac{\dot{p}}{p} - \frac{\dot{w}}{w} + \frac{\dot{a}}{a}, \tag{3.5}$$

where w denotes the money wage and p, the price. To know the dynamics of m, we have to specify the dynamics of p, w, and a.

We specify the dynamics of the money wage and price by using the theory of conflicting-claims inflation. First, suppose that the growth rate of the money wage that workers manage to negotiate depends on the discrepancy between their target profit share and the actual profit share. Second, suppose that the firms set their price to close the gap between their target profit share and the actual profit share. From these considerations, the dynamics of the money wage and price can be described, respectively, as follows:

$$\frac{\dot{w}}{w} = \theta_w(m - m_w), \quad \theta_w > 0, \ m_w \in (0, 1), \tag{3.6}$$

$$\frac{\dot{p}}{p} = \theta_f(m_f - m), \quad \theta_f > 0, \ m_f \in (0, 1), \tag{3.7}$$

where θ_w and θ_f denote the speed of adjustment; m_w, the target profit share set by workers; and m_f, the target profit share set by firms. In equations (3.6) and (3.7), expected price- and wage inflations are not explicitly considered. However, even if inflationary expectations are introduced, we obtain similar results given perfect foresight (see Dutt, 1992). Therefore, the present simple specification suffices for our purpose. In equation (3.7), it is assumed that firms are unable to set the markup at the level that they consider optimal. According to Lavoie (1992), in historical time, prices do not always follow wages. For example, firms have to publish price lists before wage bargaining is over. In addition, firms face constraints on prices that are not considered in the present model, such as foreign competition. Hence, it is difficult for firms to set the optimal markup.

We can interpret θ_w and θ_f as the bargaining powers of the workers and firms, respectively.[15] We assume $\theta_f + \theta_w = 1$ and define $\theta_f \equiv \theta$ because bargaining power is a relative concept. Then, we have $\theta_w = 1 - \theta$, where $0 < \theta < 1$.[16] For example, we consider an increase in the unionization rate as a factor in increasing the bargaining power of workers (i.e., a decrease in θ), and an increase in the market power of oligopolistic firms as a factor in increasing the bargaining power of firms (i.e., an increase in θ).

14) Cassetti (2003) derives an equation of motion for the profit share by specifying a price-setting equation of firms and differentiating it with respect to time. However, this procedure is unnecessary for deriving the dynamics of the profit share, and our procedure is easier than his. Under the conflicting-claims inflation theory, the price-setting equation in Cassetti's model plays the role of determining the mark-up rate, and not the price level.

15) This interpretation is also adopted in Lavoie (1992, p. 393) and Cassetti (2003, p. 453).

16) The constraints $0 < \theta_w, \theta_f < 1$ are also adopted by Dutt and Amadeo (1993), who, however, do not assume $\theta_f + \theta_w = 1$. Even if we impose only $0 < \theta_w, \theta_f < 1$ and not $\theta_f + \theta_w = 1$, we can obtain similar results.

We assume that the workers' target m_w depends negatively on the employment rate, e.

$$m_w = m_w(e), \quad m'_w < 0, \tag{3.8}$$

Here, $e = L/N$ and $N = N_0 e^{nt}$ denotes the exogenous labor supply, where N_0 is the initial value of labor supply and $n > 0$ is the exogenously given growth rate of N. As the employment rate increases, workers' demands in the bargaining are likely to increase, which leads workers to set a higher target wage share, and accordingly, set a lower target profit share. We consider equation (3.8) as expressing the "reserve-army effect."[17] On the other hand, for simplicity, we consider the firms' target profit share m_f as exogenously given.[18] Notice the difference between θ and equation (3.8). The parameter θ represents the relative bargaining power of firms (workers) and reflects the power to realize their demands. In contrast, equation (3.8) reflects their demands in the bargaining. To what extent their demands can be realized depends on θ.

From equation (3.2), the employment rate is given by $e = uK/(aN)$, and hence, the rate of change in the employment rate yields

$$\frac{\dot{e}}{e} = \frac{\dot{u}}{u} + g_d - g_a - n, \tag{3.9}$$

where n is the growth rate of N and given exogenously, and $g_a = \dot{a}/a$.

As stated above, we assume that the growth rate of labor productivity depends positively on the employment rate.[19]

$$g_a = g_a(e), \quad g'_a > 0, \ g_a > 0. \tag{3.10}$$

This equation includes the reserve-army-creation effect.[20] Based on Marx's idea, Bhaduri (2006) states that this formulation captures the view that technological change is driven by inter-class conflict over income distribution between workers and capitalists. Dutt (2006) says that as the labor market tightens and labor shortage becomes clearer, the bargaining power of workers increases, which exerts an upward pressure on wages, leading capitalists to adopt labor-saving technical changes. The view that increases in wages induce labor-saving technical progress is consistent with an em-

---

17) Cassetti (2003) also considers such a reserve-army effect in the Kaleckian framework.

18) We can endogenize the target profit share of firms. Lima (2004) assumes that m_f is an increasing function of u.

19) The adoption of a new technology entails cost. The purpose of this chapter is to analyze the effect of induced technical progress arising from demand factors on the stability of the economy, and not to investigate the consequences of resource allocation to R&D sectors. Therefore, we neglect the adoption cost of technology.

20) We can also interpret that equation (3.10) is obtained through the learning-by-doing effect à la Arrow (1962). If the level of labor productivity is increasing in the production experience and the experience is measured by the cumulative sums of the employment rate, then the growth rate of labor productivity is increasing in the employment rate. Moreover, this specification apparently relates to both Verdoorn's law and Okun's law. In this chapter, however, we emphasize that a rise in the employment rate makes firms adopt labor-saving technology.

pirical study by Marquetti (2004), who investigates the co-integration between real wages and labor productivity and conducts Granger non-causality tests by using US data. He shows that Granger non-causality tests support unidirectional causation from real wage to labor productivity. In determining technical change, mainstream growth theory emphasizes supply side factors such as R&D investment and human capital accumulation. In contrast, this chapter emphasizes the demand side factors contributing to technical change: changes in aggregate demand cause changes in employment, which leads to technical change.

In general, the natural rate of growth is defined as a sum of the growth rates of labor productivity and labor supply. Although the growth rate of labor supply in our model is exogenously given, the growth rate of labor productivity is endogenously determined. Under our specification, therefore, the natural rate of growth increases when business is good (i.e., when the employment rate is high) and it decreases when business is bad (i.e., when the employment rate is low). The assumption that the natural rate of growth is endogenously determined is consistent with the empirical studies of León-Ledesma and Thirlwall (2002) and Libânio (2009).[21]

We now focus on the derivation of the system of differential equations. First, substituting equations (3.1) and (3.3) in equation (3.4), we obtain the dynamics of u. Second, substituting equations (3.6) and (3.7) in equation (3.5), and substituting equations (3.8) and (3.10) in the resulting expression, we obtain the dynamics of m. Finally, substituting the dynamics of u, equation (3.3), and equation (3.10) in equation (3.9), we obtain the dynamics of e.

$$\dot{u} = \alpha(\psi m^\beta u^\gamma - smu), \tag{3.11}$$

$$\dot{m} = -(1 - m)[m - \theta m_f - (1 - \theta)m_w(e) - g_a(e)], \tag{3.12}$$

$$\dot{e} = e[\alpha(\psi m^\beta u^{\gamma-1} - sm) + \psi m^\beta u^\gamma - g_a(e) - n]. \tag{3.13}$$

We now provide an explanation with regard to the structure of our model. If we introduce $m_w = m_w(e)$ with g_a as exogenously given, we find that the employment rate is endogenously determined whereas the natural rate of growth is exogenous. If we, on the other hand, introduce $g_a = g_a(e)$ with m_w as exogenously given, we find that both the employment rate and the natural rate of growth are endogenously determined. Hence, to endogenize both the employment rate and the natural rate of growth, we do not need to specify m_w as a function of e. Nevertheless, we use both $g_a(e)$ and $m_w(e)$. This is because we intend to capture the interaction between the reserve-army and reserve-army-creation effects.

---

21) León-Ledesma and Thirlwall (2002) empirically investigate whether the natural growth rate is exogenous or endogenous to demand and whether it is input growth that causes output growth or vice versa. This question lies at the heart of the debate between neoclassical growth economists and economists in the Keynesian/post-Keynesian tradition. Using the same method, Libânio (2009) empirically investigates Latin America and reaches similar conclusions.

3.3   Long-run equilibrium analysis

3.3.1   Existence of the long-run equilibrium

The long-run equilibrium is a situation where $\dot{u} = \dot{m} = \dot{e} = 0$. Here, we have the following three equations:

$$\psi m^\beta u^\gamma - smu = 0, \tag{3.14}$$

$$m - \theta m_f - (1 - \theta)m_w(e) - g_a(e) = 0, \tag{3.15}$$

$$\psi m^\beta u^\gamma - g_a(e) - n = 0. \tag{3.16}$$

These equations show that the equilibrium values do not depend on the speed of adjustment, α. From equation (3.14), we obtain

$$u = \left(\frac{\psi}{s}\right)^{\frac{1}{1-\gamma}} m^{\frac{\beta-1}{1-\gamma}}. \tag{3.17}$$

Substituting equation (3.17) in equation (3.16), we find that the resulting expression will be an equation of m and e. Combining this equation with equation (3.15), we can obtain the equilibrium values of m and e, which are substituted in equation (3.17) to find the equilibrium value of u. In the following analysis, we assume that there are unique long-run equilibrium values (u^*, m^*, e^*) that satisfy equations (3.14), (3.15), and (3.16) simultaneously. In addition, we assume $u^*, m^*, e^* \in (0, 1)$. Hereafter, the long-run equilibrium values are denoted with "$*$."

3.3.2   Local stability of the long-run equilibrium

To investigate the local stability of the long-run equilibrium, we linearize the system of differential equations (3.11), (3.12), and (3.13) around the equilibrium.

$$\begin{pmatrix} \dot{u} \\ \dot{m} \\ \dot{e} \end{pmatrix} = \begin{pmatrix} J_{11} & J_{12} & 0 \\ 0 & J_{22} & J_{23} \\ J_{31} & J_{32} & J_{33} \end{pmatrix} \begin{pmatrix} u - u^* \\ m - m^* \\ e - e^* \end{pmatrix}, \tag{3.18}$$

where the elements of the Jacobian matrix $\mathbf{J}$ are given by

$$J_{11} \equiv \frac{\partial \dot{u}}{\partial u} = -\alpha s(1 - \gamma)m < 0, \tag{3.19}$$

$$J_{12} \equiv \frac{\partial \dot{u}}{\partial m} = -\alpha s(1 - \beta)u < 0, \tag{3.20}$$

$$J_{22} \equiv \frac{\partial \dot{m}}{\partial m} = -(1 - m) < 0, \tag{3.21}$$

$$J_{23} \equiv \frac{\partial \dot{m}}{\partial e} = (1 - m)\underbrace{[(1 - \theta)m'_w(e) + g'_a(e)]}_{\equiv \Gamma(e,\theta)} = (1 - m)\Gamma(e, \theta) \gtrless 0, \tag{3.22}$$

$$J_{31} \equiv \frac{\partial \dot{e}}{\partial u} = sme \left[\frac{\alpha(\gamma - 1) + \gamma u}{u} \right] \gtrless 0, \tag{3.23}$$

$$J_{32} \equiv \frac{\partial \dot{e}}{\partial m} = se[\alpha(\beta - 1) + \beta u] \gtrless 0, \tag{3.24}$$

$$J_{33} \equiv \frac{\partial \dot{e}}{\partial e} = -eg'_a(e) < 0. \tag{3.25}$$

All elements are evaluated at the long-run equilibrium; we omit "∗" to avoid trouble-some notations.

The term $\Gamma(e, \theta) \equiv (1 - \theta)m'_w(e) + g'_a(e)$ in equation (3.22) consists of the following three elements: the relative bargaining power of firms θ, the extent of the reserve-army effect m'_w, and the extent of the reserve-army-creation effect g'_a. Because $m'_w < 0$ and $g'_a > 0$, Γ can be positive or negative. When the reserve-army effect is strong (i.e., the absolute value of m'_w is large), and the bargaining power of firms and the reserve-army-creation effect are weak (i.e., θ and g'_a, respectively, are small), we have $\Gamma < 0$. However, when the reserve-army effect is weak, and the bargaining power of firms and the reserve-army-creation effect are strong, we have $\Gamma > 0$. The sign of Γ plays an important role in both the stability of the equilibrium and the comparative statics analysis below.

The signs of equations (3.23) and (3.24) are indeterminate. When α is sufficiently large, these signs are likely to be negative.

The characteristic equation of the Jacobian matrix (3.18) is given by

$$\lambda^3 + a_1\lambda^2 + a_2\lambda + a_3 = 0, \tag{3.26}$$

where λ denotes a characteristic root. Each coefficient of equation (3.26) is given by

$$a_1 = -\text{tr}\,\mathbf{J} = -(J_{11} + J_{22} + J_{33}), \tag{3.27}$$

$$a_2 = \begin{vmatrix} J_{22} & J_{23} \\ J_{32} & J_{33} \end{vmatrix} + \begin{vmatrix} J_{11} & 0 \\ J_{31} & J_{33} \end{vmatrix} + \begin{vmatrix} J_{11} & J_{12} \\ 0 & J_{22} \end{vmatrix} = J_{22}J_{33} - J_{23}J_{32} + J_{11}J_{33} + J_{11}J_{22}, \tag{3.28}$$

$$a_3 = -\det\mathbf{J} = -J_{11}J_{22}J_{33} + J_{11}J_{23}J_{32} - J_{31}J_{12}J_{23}, \tag{3.29}$$

where $-a_1 = \text{tr}\,\mathbf{J}$ denotes the trace of $\mathbf{J}$; a_2, the sum of the principal minors' determinants; and $-a_3 = \det\mathbf{J}$, the determinant of $\mathbf{J}$.

The necessary and sufficient condition for local stability is that all characteristic roots of the Jacobian matrix have negative real parts, which, from the Routh-Hurwitz condition, is equivalent to

$$a_1 > 0, \; a_2 > 0, \; a_3 > 0, \; a_1a_2 - a_3 > 0. \tag{3.30}$$

Let us examine whether these inequalities hold. We arrange the coefficients with re-spect to α.

First, a_1 is a linear function of α.

$$a_1 \equiv a_1(\alpha) = \underbrace{s(1-\gamma)m}_{\equiv A>0}\,\alpha + \underbrace{(1-m) + eg_a'(e)}_{\equiv B>0} = \underset{+}{A}\alpha + \underset{+}{B}. \qquad (3.31)$$

Therefore, we can confirm that $a_1 > 0$. This implies that $\mathrm{tr}\,\mathbf{J} < 0$, which is a necessary condition for the local stability of the equilibrium.

Second, a_2 is a linear function of α.

$$a_2 \equiv a_2(\alpha) = \underbrace{\{s(1-\gamma)m[1-m+eg_a'(e)] + s(1-\beta)e(1-m)\Gamma(e,\theta)\}}_{\equiv C \gtreqless 0}\,\alpha$$

$$+ \underbrace{e(1-m)[(1-\beta su)g_a'(e) - s\beta(1-\theta)um_w'(e)]}_{\equiv D>0} = \underset{+/-}{C}\,\alpha + \underset{+}{D}. \qquad (3.32)$$

If $\Gamma > 0$, we always have $C > 0$. Hence, we obtain $a_2 > 0$. If, however, $\Gamma < 0$, we do not always have $C > 0$.

Third, a_3 is a linear function of α.

$$a_3 \equiv a_3(\alpha) = s(1-\gamma)em(1-m)\underbrace{\left[g_a'(e) - \frac{s(\beta-\gamma)}{1-\gamma}u\Gamma(e,\theta)\right]}_{\equiv \Theta}\,\alpha$$

$$= \underbrace{s(1-\gamma)em(1-m)\Theta}_{\equiv E}\,\alpha = E\alpha. \qquad (3.33)$$

Finally, $a_1a_2 - a_3$ is a quadratic function of α.

$$a_1a_2 - a_3 \equiv \phi(\alpha) = (AC)\alpha^2 + (AD + BC - E)\alpha + \underbrace{BD}_{+}. \qquad (3.34)$$

At this stage, we cannot confirm whether this parabola is convex upward or convex downward. However, when $\alpha = 0$, we have $\phi(0) = BD > 0$, which shows that there is an α such that $a_1a_2 - a_3 > 0$ for $\alpha > 0$.

Observing equations (3.31) through (3.34), we obtain the following proposition:

Proposition 3.1. *Suppose that $\Gamma > 0$. Suppose also that the equilibrium profit share m^* is less than or equal to $1/2$. Then, the long-run equilibrium is locally stable irrespective of the size of α.*

Proof. If $\Gamma > 0$, and consequently $C > 0$, $\phi(\alpha)$ becomes a parabola that is convex downward. Here, we focus on the coefficient of α in $\phi(\alpha)$, that is, $AD + BC - E$. Expanding this coefficient, we have

$$AD + BC - E = \underbrace{s(1-\gamma)m[1-m+eg_a'(e)]^2}_{+}$$

$$+ \underbrace{s(1-\beta)e(1-m)}_{+}\Gamma[\underbrace{eg'_a(e)}_{+} + \underbrace{(1-m-s\gamma um)}_{\equiv\Lambda}]. \qquad (3.35)$$

When s, γ, and u are close to zero, $\Lambda \equiv 1 - m - s\gamma um$ will be positive because $s\gamma um$ will be sufficiently small. In contrast, when s, γ, and u are close to unity, Λ approaches $\Lambda = 1 - 2m$. From this, if $m^* \leq 1/2$, we have $\Lambda \geq 0$. When $\Lambda \geq 0$, we have $AD + BC - E > 0$, and consequently, we obtain $\phi(\alpha) > 0$ for $\alpha > 0$. Therefore, if $\Gamma > 0$ and if $m^* \leq 1/2$, then the necessary and sufficient conditions for local stability, that is, $a_1 > 0$, $a_2 > 0$, $a_3 > 0$, and $a_1 a_2 - a_3 > 0$, are all satisfied. ∎

Proposition 3.1 is obtained when the reserve-army effect is weak, and the relative bargaining power of firms and the reserve-army-creation effect are strong. In general, the profit share in the real world is considered to be less than $1/2$, and hence, condition $m^* \leq 1/2$ is plausible. Note, however, that $m^* \leq 1/2$ is a sufficient and not a necessary condition for $a_1 a_2 - a_3 > 0$. Moreover, m^* depends on the parameters of the model.

Here, we introduce the following assumption:

Assumption 3.1. *The sign of* Θ *in equation* (3.33) *is positive.*

The sign of a_3 depends on the sign of Θ. If $\Theta > 0$, we have $E > 0$, and consequently, $a_3 > 0$. This implies that $\det \mathbf{J} < 0$, which is a necessary condition for the local stability of the equilibrium. When $\beta > \gamma$, we always have $\Theta > 0$ irrespective of the sign of Γ.[22] However, when $\beta < \gamma$, we do not always have $\Theta > 0$. When $\beta < \gamma$, we always have $\Theta > 0$ if $\Gamma > 0$. Even if $\Gamma < 0$, we can have $\Theta > 0$.

From this, we obtain the following proposition:

Proposition 3.2. *Suppose that the speed of adjustment of the goods market* α *is sufficiently close to zero. Then, the long-run equilibrium is locally stable.*

Proof. From the above discussion, we have $a_1 > 0$ and $a_3 > 0$. When $\alpha = 0$, we have $\phi(0) = BD > 0$, that is, $a_1 a_2 - a_3 > 0$. If $a_1 > 0$, $a_3 > 0$, and $a_1 a_2 - a_3 > 0$, then $a_2 > 0$ is necessarily satisfied. Hence, if $\alpha = 0$, the necessary and sufficient conditions given by (3.30) are all satisfied. Because $\phi(\alpha)$ is a continuous function of α, even if $\alpha > 0$, $a_1 a_2 - a_3 > 0$ is satisfied when α is sufficiently close to zero. Therefore, when α is sufficiently close to zero, the necessary and sufficient conditions given by (3.30) are all satisfied. ∎

Proposition 3.2 is obtained regardless of whether $\Gamma > 0$ or $\Gamma < 0$. That is, if the speed of adjustment of the goods market is very slow, the long-run equilibrium

---

22) Expanding Θ, we obtain

$$\Theta = \left(1 - su\frac{\beta-\gamma}{1-\gamma}\right)g'_a(e) - su\frac{\beta-\gamma}{1-\gamma}(1-\theta)m'_w(e).$$

When $\beta > \gamma$, $(\beta - \gamma)/(1 - \gamma)$ is larger than zero and smaller than unity. From this, the first term of the right-hand side is positive. The second term of the right-hand side is positive because $m'_w < 0$. Therefore, when $\beta > \gamma$, we have $\Theta > 0$ irrespective of the sign of Γ.

is locally stable irrespective of the size of the relative bargaining power of firms, the reserve-army effect, and the reserve-army-creation effect.

3.3.3   Existence of closed orbits

As explained above, if $\Gamma < 0$, it is possible that $C < 0$, which implies that the system is locally unstable. However, the instability of the steady state does not necessarily mean that the system will explode. If there is a limit cycle, it is possible that the economy converges to a cyclical path.

Proposition 3.3. *Suppose that $C < 0$. Then, a limit cycle occurs when the speed of adjustment of the goods market lies within some range.*

Proof. If $C < 0$, $a_2(\alpha)$ becomes a straight line whose slope is negative and intercept is positive. This implies that there exists $\bar{\alpha} > 0$ such that $a_2(\bar{\alpha}) = 0$. Moreover, if $C < 0$, Descartes' rule of signs assures that the quadratic equation $\phi(\alpha) = 0$ has one negative real root and one positive root. Since only the positive root has economic meaning, we let $\underline{\alpha}$ denote the positive root. Let us investigate which is larger, $\bar{\alpha}$ or $\underline{\alpha}$. From $a_2(\bar{\alpha}) = 0$, we obtain $\bar{\alpha} = -D/C > 0$. Substituting $\bar{\alpha}$ in $\phi(\alpha)$, we obtain

$$\phi(\bar{\alpha}) = \frac{DE}{C} < 0 \tag{3.36}$$

because $C < 0$. This implies that $\underline{\alpha} < \bar{\alpha}$. From this, we get that $a_1 > 0$, $a_2 > 0$, $a_3 > 0$, and $a_1 a_2 - a_3 > 0$ within the range $\alpha \in (0, \underline{\alpha})$, while $a_1 > 0$, $a_2 > 0$, $a_3 > 0$, and $a_1 a_2 - a_3 < 0$ within the range $\alpha \in (\underline{\alpha}, \bar{\alpha})$. Consequently, a Hopf bifurcation occurs at $\underline{\alpha}$. Indeed, at $\alpha = \underline{\alpha}$, we obtain

$$a_1 > 0, \ a_2 > 0, \ a_3 > 0, \ a_1 a_2 - a_3 = 0, \ \left.\frac{\partial(a_1 a_2 - a_3)}{\partial \alpha}\right|_{\alpha = \underline{\alpha}} \neq 0. \tag{3.37}$$

That is, all conditions for the occurrence of the Hopf bifurcation are satisfied.[23] Therefore, when $C < 0$, there is a continuous family of non-constant, periodic solutions of the system around $\alpha = \underline{\alpha}$. ∎

We obtain $C < 0$ when g_a' and θ are small, and the absolute value of m_w' is large. These conditions are similar to the conditions for $\Gamma < 0$. Indeed, $\Gamma < 0$ is a necessary condition for $C < 0$. From this, we can obtain Proposition 3.3 when the reserve-army effect is strong, and the relative bargaining power of firms and the reserve-army-creation effect are weak.

As explained above, the long-run equilibrium can be both stable and unstable. Let us briefly explain this mechanism. Here, we focus on the capacity utilization rate.

---

23) For the Hopf bifurcation theorem, see Gandolfo (1996). The last condition in equation (3.37), that is, $\partial(a_1 a_2 - a_3)/\partial \alpha|_{\alpha = \underline{\alpha}} \neq 0$, is equivalent to the condition that the derivatives of the real parts of the characteristic roots with respect to α are not zero when evaluated at $\alpha = \underline{\alpha}$. For details, see Asada and Semmler (1995, pp. 634–635).

Suppose that the capacity utilization rate exceeds its equilibrium value for some reason. Then, as long as the speed of adjustment of the goods market is not extremely large, the increase in the capacity utilization rate induces the employment rate to increase through equation (3.23). This increase in the employment rate changes the profit share through equation (3.22). The direction of the change in the profit share depends on the sign of Γ.

If $\Gamma > 0$, that is, the power of firms is relatively strong, then the profit share increases. This increase in the profit share has two opposing effects. (1) The increase in the profit share stimulates the investment of firms, which increases the output. (2) The increase in the profit share increases the savings of capitalists, which decreases the output. Because the adjustment process of the goods market is stable, the latter negative effect on the output is stronger than the former positive effect, and as a result, the output and the capacity utilization rate decrease (see equation (3.20)). Therefore, here, a negative feedback effect acts on the capacity utilization rate, and accordingly, the long-run equilibrium will be stable.

If, however, $\Gamma < 0$, that is, the power of workers is relatively strong, then the profit share declines, which increases the capacity utilization rate through equation (3.20). Therefore, here, a positive feedback effect acts on the capacity utilization rate, and accordingly, the long-run equilibrium will be unstable.

$$u \uparrow \Longrightarrow e \uparrow \text{ (when } \alpha \text{ is not so large)} \Longrightarrow \begin{cases} m \uparrow & (\Gamma > 0) \implies u \downarrow \quad \text{(stabilizing)} \\ m \downarrow & (\Gamma < 0) \implies u \uparrow \quad \text{(destabilizing)} \end{cases}.$$

Finally, we refer to the roles of the reserve-army and reserve-army-creation effects. When only the reserve-army-creation effect exists, that is, $m'_w = 0$, we always have $\Gamma = g'_a > 0$. In this case, from Proposition 3.1, the long-run equilibrium is locally stable given that $m^* \leq 1/2$, and accordingly, the Hopf bifurcation never occurs. Therefore, the reserve-army-creation effect has a stabilizing effect.

In contrast, when only the reserve-army effect exists, that is, $g'_a = 0$, we always have $\Gamma = (1 - \theta)m'_w < 0$. In this case,

$$\Theta = -\frac{s(\beta - \gamma)}{1 - \gamma} u(1 - \theta)m'_w. \tag{3.38}$$

If $\beta > \gamma$, then $\Theta > 0$ necessarily holds. However, if $\beta < \gamma$, then $\Theta < 0$ necessarily holds, which contradicts Assumption 3.1, and consequently, the long-run equilibrium becomes unstable. This implies that the long-run equilibrium in a wage-led growth regime is always unstable, and also that the Hopf bifurcation never occurs. Therefore, the reserve-army effect has a destabilizing effect.

From the above reasoning, the interaction between the reserve-army effect and the reserve-army-creation effect plays an important role in stabilizing both the wage-led and profit-led growth regimes, and in the occurrence of the Hopf bifurcation.

3.3.4   Comparative statics analysis

This section investigates the effects of shifts in the parameters on the long-run equilibrium. To conduct a comparative statics analysis, we need the stability of the equilibrium. For this reason, we assume $\Theta > 0$ in the following analysis. As discussed above, the long-run equilibrium can be unstable. Therefore, we confine ourselves to the case where the long-run equilibrium is stable.

Table 3.1 summarizes the results of comparative statics in four cases.[24] In Table 3.1, the "+" sign indicates that the corresponding variable increases with the parameter, while the "−" sign indicates that the corresponding variable decreases with the parameter. The signs "+/−" and "−/+" indicate that an increase in the parameter either increases or decreases the corresponding variable. The mark "†" shows that the left-hand sign applies when $\Gamma < 0$, while the right-hand sign applies when $\Gamma > 0$.

Moreover, for the effect of θ, we assume that $m_f - m_w(e) > 0$. Firms attempt to set their target profit share as high as possible, whereas workers attempt to set their target profit share as low as possible. Therefore, this assumption is reasonable.

Table 3.1: Results of comparative statics analysis

$\beta < \gamma$	s	n	θ	m_f	ψ
u^*	$-$	$-/+^\dagger$	$-$	$-$	$+^\ddagger$
m^*	$+/-^\dagger$	$+/-^\dagger$	$+$	$+$	$-/+^\dagger$
e^*, g_a^*	$-$	$-$	$-$	$-$	$+$
g^*	$-$	$-/+^\dagger$	$-$	$-$	$+$
$\beta > \gamma$	s	n	θ	m_f	ψ
u^*	$-$	$-/+^\dagger$	$-$	$-$	$+^\ddagger$
m^*	$+/-^\dagger$	$+/-^\dagger$	$+$	$+$	$-/+^\dagger$
e^*, g_a^*	$-$	$-$	$+$	$+$	$+$
g^*	$-$	$+/-^\dagger$	$+$	$+$	$+$

† When $\Gamma < 0$, the left-hand sign applies, and when $\Gamma > 0$, the right-hand sign applies.
‡ These signs are obtained by numerical calculations.

Let us explain the results in Table 3.1. Because of the limitations of space, we focus especially on the employment rate.

■ Savings rate

An increase in the savings rate of capitalists decreases the capacity utilization rate and the rate of capital accumulation. This negative effect on the growth rate is known as the "paradox of thrift." A rise in the savings rate decreases the employment rate. Stockhammer (2004) also investigates the employment rate in a Kaleckian framework.

---

24) See Appendix for details.

In Stockhammer's model, the long-run equilibrium value of the employment rate consists of the exogenous natural rate of growth and the parameters of the investment function and the income distribution function, and does not depend on the savings rate. Hence, a change in the savings rate never affects the employment rate. In our model, however, the natural rate of growth is endogenously determined, and accordingly, the change in the savings rate affects the employment rate.

■ Labor supply growth

Previous Kaleckian models cannot investigate the effect of supply side factors on equilibrium values. In contrast, our model can investigate these. In either case, an increase in n lowers the employment rate. Because the relation $g_a^* = sm^*u^* - n$ holds in the long-run equilibrium, an increase in n has three different effects on g_a^* and consequently, on e^*: it directly decreases g_a^* with the coefficient of n being -1; it indirectly affects g_a^* through m^*, which is positive when $\Gamma < 0$ and negative when $\Gamma > 0$; and it indirectly affects g_a^* through u^*, which is negative when $\Gamma < 0$ and positive when $\Gamma > 0$. In total, the two negative effects outweigh the one positive effect, which leads to a decline in g_a^* and e^*. Stockhammer (2004) also concludes that an increase in labor supply growth leads to a decrease in the employment rate in the profit-led growth regime ($\beta > \gamma$ in our model), in which the long-run equilibrium is stable. Yet, the wage-led growth regime in Stockhammer's model ($\beta < \gamma$ in our model) is unstable, and thus, one cannot conduct a comparative statics analysis. In contrast, even the wage-led growth regime can be stable in our model.

■ Relative bargaining power

An increase in the relative bargaining power of firms either increases or decreases the employment rate depending on the size of the two elasticities of the investment function. The employment rate decreases when $\beta < \gamma$, whereas it increases when $\beta > \gamma$. An increase in θ has two different effects on g_a and e: it indirectly increases g_a and e through its positive effect on m and it indirectly decreases g_a and e through its negative effect on u. Whether or not the increase in θ leads to an increase in g_a and e depends on which effect dominates, which in turn depends on the size of the elasticities of the investment function. When $\beta < \gamma$, the negative effect of the capacity utilization dominates the positive effect of the profit share, thereby leading to a decrease in the growth rate of labor productivity and the employment rate. When $\beta > \gamma$, in contrast, the positive effect of the profit share dominates the negative effect of the capacity utilization, thereby leading to an increase in the growth rate of labor productivity and the employment rate.

Stockhammer (2004) also investigates the relationship between bargaining power and unemployment. He concludes that in a profit-led growth regime, a decrease in the bargaining power of workers leads to higher employment and lower unemployment. This result is consistent with our results. However, in the wage-led growth regime of Stockhammer's model, the long-run equilibrium is unstable, and consequently, one cannot investigate the relationship between bargaining power and unemployment. In our model, in contrast, the-long run equilibrium of a wage-led growth regime can be stable. In this case, we reach the opposite conclusion that an increase in the bargaining power of workers leads to higher employment and lower unemployment. This result is consistent with the empirical result of Storm and Naastepad (2007). Using data for 20 OECD countries during 1984–1997, they show that an increase in the bargaining power of firms because of labor market deregulation increases the unemployment rate; this is in contrast to the view of mainstream theory.

3.4 Numerical simulations

In this section, we present numerical examples to show that, under plausible settings, an economically meaningful long-run equilibrium actually exists and limit cycles really occur. Note, however, that the results of numerical simulations depend on the specification of the functional form and the numerical values of the parameters.

For the numerical simulation, we have to specify the functional forms of equations (3.8) and (3.10). We specify these functions as follows:

$$m_w(e) = \delta(1 - e), \quad \delta > 0, \tag{3.39}$$

$$g_a(e) = \eta e, \quad \eta > 0. \tag{3.40}$$

In this case, Γ and Θ are respectively given by

$$\Gamma = \eta - (1 - \theta)\delta, \tag{3.41}$$

$$\Theta = \eta - \frac{s(\beta - \gamma)}{1 - \gamma}[\eta - (1 - \theta)\delta]u. \tag{3.42}$$

The equilibrium profit share m^* satisfies the following equation:

$$\Gamma\psi^{\frac{1}{1-\gamma}}s^{-\frac{\gamma}{1-\gamma}}m^{\frac{\beta-\gamma}{1-\gamma}} - \eta m + \eta[\theta m_f + (1 - \theta)\delta] - \Gamma n = 0. \tag{3.43}$$

From this, we obtain m^*, which we substitute in equation (3.17) to determine u^*. Furthermore, we substitute m^* in the following equation to determine e^*:

$$e^* = \frac{m^* - [\theta m_f + (1 - \theta)\delta]}{\Gamma}. \tag{3.44}$$

We consider two cases depending on which is larger, β or γ given that $\Gamma < 0$ is negative.[25]

3.4.1 Case 1 (wage-led growth): $\beta < \gamma$, $\Gamma < 0$

Case 1 corresponds to the case where the elasticity of the investment rate with respect to the profit share is smaller than the elasticity of the investment rate with respect to the capacity utilization rate, the reserve-army effect is strong, and the relative bargaining power of firms and the reserve-army-creation effect are weak. We set the parameters as follows:

$$\beta = 0.2, \ \gamma = 0.4, \ \psi = 0.15, \ s = 0.6, \ \eta = 0.1, \ \delta = 0.5, \ \theta = 0.25, \ m_f = 0.3, \ n = 0.015. \tag{3.45}$$

In this case, the long-run equilibrium values, Γ and Θ, yield the following:[26]

$$u^* = 0.74642, \ m^* = 0.220134, \ e^* = 0.835875, \ \Gamma = -0.275 < 0, \ \Theta = 0.0589496 > 0. \tag{3.46}$$

These equilibrium values are economically meaningful. In addition, $\Theta > 0$ is satisfied.

Figure 3.4 displays the solution path when the initial values and the speed of adjustment are set as $u(0) = 0.7$, $m(0) = 0.21$, $e(0) = 0.8$, and $\alpha = 4$. The figure shows a cyclical fluctuation. In Figure 3.4, we draw the solution path from $t = 100$ to $t = 200$, and upon performing the calculations further, we find that the solution path is not a perfect closed orbit and that it converges to the long-run equilibrium with rotation. Moreover, if we set the initial conditions further away from the long-run equilibrium, we find that the solution path diverges from the equilibrium. From these observations, we confirm that in this numerical example, the subcritical Hopf bifurcation occurs and the periodic solution is unstable.

Figure 3.5 projects the three-dimensional dynamics on the (u, e)-plane. The solution path starting from point P converges to the long-run equilibrium with rotation. In contrast, the solution path starting from point Q diverges from the long-run equilibrium with rotation. These phenomena correspond to the "corridor stability" of Leijonhufvud (1973).

Figure 3.6 shows the graphs of $a_2(\alpha)$ and $\phi(\alpha)$. We find that $\bar{\alpha} = 4.61097$ and $\underline{\alpha} = 4.02288$. In Figure 3.4, we use $\alpha = 4$, from which we have $4 < \underline{\alpha}$. Therefore, the subcritical Hopf bifurcation certainly occurs in this case.[27] Moreover, if we choose α larger than $\underline{\alpha}$, we find that the solution path diverges irrespective of the initial conditions. This confirms that the subcritical Hopf bifurcation occurs at $\underline{\alpha}$.

Note, however, that the Hopf bifurcation that occurs in case 1 is not always the subcritical Hopf bifurcation. We can find a numerical example wherein the supercritical Hopf bifurcation occurs in case 1.[28]

Finally, Figures 3.7, 3.8, and 3.9 show cyclical patterns in the (e, m)-, (u, m)-, and

26) From these numerical settings, we obtain two values of m within the range $m \in (0, 1)$: $m_1^* = 0.220134$ and $m_2^* = 0.0516332$. However, from m_2^*, we obtain $u^* = 5.16014$ and $e^* = 1.44861$, which are unrealistic. For this reason, we do not adopt m_2^*.

27) In this numerical example, the range of α is such that both $a_2(\alpha) > 0$ and $\phi(\alpha) < 0$ are narrow. However,

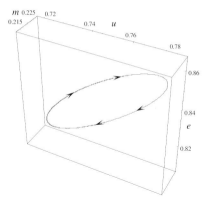

Figure 3.4: Solution path in case 1 ($\alpha = 4$)

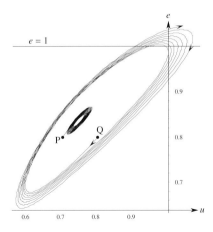

Figure 3.5: Solution paths starting from different initial values in case 1 ($\alpha = 4$)

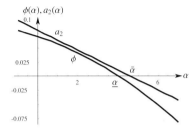

Figure 3.6: Graphs of $a_2(\alpha)$ and $\phi(\alpha)$ in case 1

(e, u)-planes. In the (e, m)-plane, clockwise cycles emerge whereas in the (u, m)- and (e, u)-planes, counterclockwise cycles emerge. These cyclical patterns are consistent with some empirical findings stated in Section 3.1. Therefore, the type of cyclical fluctuations produced by our model matches empirical findings.

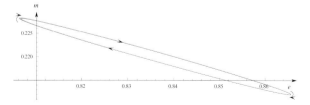

Figure 3.7: Clockwise cycles in the (e, m)-plane in case 1

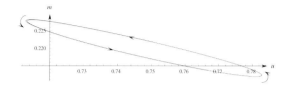

Figure 3.8: Counterclockwise cycles in the (u, m)-plane in case 1

3.4.2   Case 2 (profit-led growth): $\beta > \gamma$, $\Gamma < 0$

Case 2 corresponds to the case where the elasticity of the investment rate with respect to the profit share is larger than the elasticity of the investment rate with respect to the capacity utilization rate, the reserve-army effect is strong, and the relative bargaining power of firms and the reserve-army-creation effect are weak. We set the parameters as follows:

$$\beta = 0.4, \ \gamma = 0.2, \ \psi = 0.2, \ s = 0.6, \ \eta = 0.1, \ \delta = 1, \ \theta = 0.25, \ m_f = 0.3, \ n = 0.016.$$
$$(3.47)$$

Here, the long-run equilibrium values, Γ and Θ, yield the following:

$$u^* = 0.741857, \ m^* = 0.238619, \ e^* = 0.902125, \ \Gamma = -0.65 < 0, \ \Theta = 0.172331 > 0.$$
$$(3.48)$$

---

we can widen the range by choosing different parameter settings.

28) Under the parameters $\beta = 0.4$, $\gamma = 0.41$, $\psi = 0.2$, $s = 0.6$, $\eta = 0.1$, $\delta = 1$, and $\theta = 0.25$, the Hopf bifurcation point leads to $\underline{\alpha} = 2.56626$, and there is a stable limit cycle at $\alpha > \underline{\alpha}$.

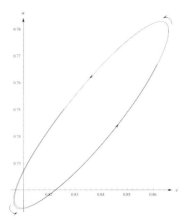

Figure 3.9: Counterclockwise cycles in the (e, u)-plane in case 1

These equilibrium values are economically meaningful. In addition, $\Theta > 0$ is satisfied.

Figure 3.10 displays the solution path when $u(0) = 0.7$, $m(0) = 0.2$, $e(0) = 0.9$, and $\alpha = 2$. The figure shows a cyclical fluctuation. Using various initial values, we find that in this case, a stable limit cycle emerges: any initial point converges to the limit cycle with rotation. Therefore, the supercritical Hopf bifurcation occurs in case 2.

Figure 3.11 shows the graphs of $a_2(\alpha)$ and $\phi(\alpha)$. We find that $\bar{\alpha} = 2.34506$ and $\underline{\alpha} = 1.95504$. In Figure 3.10, we use $\alpha = 2$, from which we have $\underline{\alpha} < 2$. Therefore, the supercritical Hopf bifurcation certainly occurs in this case.[29]

In case 2 as in case 1, though we do not present figures because of limitation of space, we obtain clockwise cycles in the (e, m)-plane and counterclockwise cycles in the (u, m)- and (e, u)-planes.[30]

3.5   Concluding remarks

In this chapter, we have developed a demand-led growth model that considers elements from Goodwin, Kalecki, and Marx. More specifically, we have presented a Kaleckian model that describes a labor-constrained economy. In the model, we have considered

---

29) In this case, as in case 1, the range of α is such that both $a_2(\alpha) > 0$ and $\phi(\alpha) < 0$ are narrow. However, we can widen the range by choosing different parameter settings. Note that we were unable to find a numerical example that produced subcritical Hopf bifurcation.

30) Depending on conditions, our model produces clockwise cycles in the all three planes as observed in the US by Zipperer and Skott (2011). For example, if the long-run equilibrium exhibits a profit-led demand regime, if the reserve army creation effect is weak, and if the reserve army effect is strong, then clockwise cycles can occur.

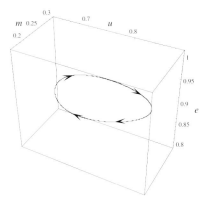

Figure 3.10: Solution path in case 2 ($\alpha = 2$)

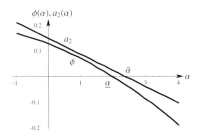

Figure 3.11. Graphs of $a_2(\alpha)$ and $\phi(\alpha)$ in case 2

the two opposing effects caused by an increase in the employment rate. One is the reserve-army effect: as the labor market tightens and labor shortage becomes clearer, the bargaining power of workers increases, which exerts an upward pressure on wages. The other is the reserve-army-creation effect: such an upward pressure on wages leads firms to adopt labor-saving technical changes to intentionally create the reserve-army of labor.

We have presented the two cases that produce limit cycles according to the size of parameters of the investment function, the relative bargaining power of firms, the reserve-army effect, and the reserve-army-creation effect. These two cases correspond to the case where the relative bargaining power of firms is weak, the reserve-army effect is strong, and the reserve-army-creation effect is weak. Our theoretical analysis and numerical examples show that limit cycles occur in both wage-led growth and profit-led growth, which implies that perpetual business cycles are inherent in capitalist economies.

Using the model, we have analyzed how the relative bargaining power of workers and firms affects the long-run equilibrium employment rate. The relationship between the bargaining power and the employment rate differs depending on the regime of the long-run equilibrium. If the long-run equilibrium is characterized as a wage-led growth regime, a rise in the relative bargaining power of workers increases the employment rate. If, however, the long-run equilibrium is characterized as a profit-led growth regime, a rise in the relative bargaining power of workers decreases the employment rate.

Note, however, that in a wage-led growth regime, an increase in the workers' bargaining power leads to higher employment, but it simultaneously leads to lower profit share: the workers' interests interfere with firms' interests. For this reason, it may be difficult to implement an economic policy intended to adjust the bargaining power of both classes. Even in this case, nonetheless, the demand stimulation policy is effective. The stimulation of effective demand brings about higher employment and accordingly, lower unemployment.

Appendix 3.A: Effects of a rise in parameters on the long-run equilibrium values

The effects of a rise in parameters on the long-run equilibrium values are as follows.
■ The capacity utilization rate

$$\frac{du^*}{ds} = \frac{u^*[s\beta u^*(1 - \theta)m'_w(e^*) - (1 - s\beta u^*)g'_a(e^*)]}{s(1 - \gamma)\Theta} < 0, \tag{3.49}$$

$$\frac{du^*}{dn} = \frac{(1 - \beta)u^*\Gamma}{(1 - \gamma)m^*\Theta} \gtrless 0, \tag{3.50}$$

$$\frac{du^*}{d\theta} = -\frac{(1-\beta)u^*g_a'(e^*)[m_f - m_w(e^*)]}{(1-\gamma)m^*\Theta} < 0, \qquad (3.51)$$

$$\frac{du^*}{dm_f} = -\frac{\theta(1-\beta)u^*g_a'(e^*)}{(1-\gamma)m^*\Theta} < 0, \qquad (3.52)$$

$$\frac{du^*}{d\psi} = \frac{u^*[(1-\gamma)\Theta - s(1-\beta)m^*\Gamma]}{\psi(1-\gamma)^2\Theta}. \qquad (3.53)$$

■ The profit share

$$\frac{dm^*}{ds} = -\frac{\gamma u^* m^* \Gamma}{(1-\gamma)\Theta} \gtrless 0, \qquad (3.54)$$

$$\frac{dm^*}{dn} = -\frac{\Gamma}{\Theta} \gtrless 0, \qquad (3.55)$$

$$\frac{dm^*}{d\theta} = \frac{g_a'(e^*)[m_f - m_w(e^*)]}{\Theta} > 0, \qquad (3.56)$$

$$\frac{dm^*}{dm_f} = \frac{\theta g_a'(e^*)}{\Theta} > 0, \qquad (3.57)$$

$$\frac{dm^*}{d\psi} = \frac{sm^*u^*\Gamma}{\psi(1-\gamma)\Theta} \gtrless 0. \qquad (3.58)$$

■ The employment rate

$$\frac{de^*}{ds} = -\frac{\gamma u^* m^*}{(1-\gamma)\Theta} < 0, \qquad (3.59)$$

$$\frac{de^*}{dn} = -\frac{1}{\Theta} < 0, \qquad (3.60)$$

$$\frac{de^*}{d\theta} = \frac{s(\beta-\gamma)u^*[m_f - m_w(e^*)]}{(1-\gamma)\Theta} \gtrless 0, \qquad (3.61)$$

$$\frac{de^*}{dm_f} = \frac{\theta s(\beta-\gamma)u^*}{(1-\gamma)\Theta} \gtrless 0, \qquad (3.62)$$

$$\frac{de^*}{d\psi} = \frac{sm^*u^*}{\psi(1-\gamma)\Theta} > 0. \qquad (3.63)$$

■ The rate of capital accumulation

$$\frac{dg^*}{ds} = -\frac{\gamma m^* u^* g_a'(e^*)}{(1-\gamma)\Theta} < 0, \qquad (3.64)$$

$$\frac{dg^*}{dn} = -\frac{s(\beta-\gamma)u^*\Gamma}{(1-\gamma)\Theta} \gtrless 0, \qquad (3.65)$$

$$\frac{dg^*}{d\theta} = \frac{s(\beta-\gamma)u^*g_a'(e^*)[m_f - m_w(e^*)]}{(1-\gamma)\Theta} \gtrless 0, \qquad (3.66)$$

$$\frac{dg^*}{dm_f} = \frac{\theta s(\beta - \gamma)u^* g_a'(e^*)}{(1 - \gamma)\Theta} \gtrless 0, \tag{3.67}$$

$$\frac{dg^*}{d\psi} = \frac{sm^* u^* g_a'(e^*)}{\psi(1 - \gamma)\Theta} > 0. \tag{3.68}$$

Part 2: Long-run Kaleckian Models

Chapter 4

Conflict, Growth, Distribution, and Employment: A Long-run Kaleckian Model

4.1 Introduction

This chapter develops a Kaleckian growth model in which the employment rate is endogenously determined. Using the model, we investigate the medium-run and long-run equilibria.

Thus far, a number of Kaleckian models have been developed and improved upon.[1] Kaleckian models have the following four characteristics (Lavoie 1992, 1995): (1) the investment function; (2) prices relative to direct costs are influenced by a broad range of factors, often summarized under the phrase 'degree of monopoly'; (3) marginal costs are assumed to be constant up to full capacity; and (4) the capacity utilization rate is assumed to be generally below unity. In early Kaleckian models, the capacity utilization rate and the capital accumulation rate are determined with income distribution given exogenously. New Kaleckian models were then proposed in which income distribution is endogenously determined with the theory of conflicting-claims inflation.[2]

However, Marxists and Sraffians criticize the Kaleckian model, claiming that the Kaleckian model is a short-run or medium-run model and not a long-run model (Auerbach and Skott 1988; Duménil and Lévy 1999; Park 1997). In the Kaleckian model, the equilibrium capacity utilization rate diverges from the normal capacity utilization rate. Critics assert that this divergence does not last and should vanish in the long run; accordingly, the Kaleckian model lacks logical consistency. For Marxists and Sraffians, the long-run equilibrium is a state where all variables are fully adjusted.

In contrast, Lavoie (1995, 2002, 2003) and Cassetti (2006) introduce the adjustment process of the normal capacity utilization rate in the long run.[3] They show

---

1) See Kalecki (1971) for his economic theory. For the framework of the Kaleckian model, see Rowthorn (1981), Lavoie (1992), Foley and Michl (1999, ch. 10), Blecker (2002), and Taylor (2004, ch. 5).

2) The theory of conflicting-claims inflation is developed by Rowthorn (1977). For Kaleckian models with conflicting-claims inflation, see Dutt (1987) and Cassetti (2002, 2003, 2006).

3) Ohno (2009) presents a long-run Kaleckian model which considers capital-labor substitution and in-

that even in the long-run equilibrium where the actual capacity utilization rate and the normal capacity utilization rate are equalized, 'the paradox thrift' and 'the paradox of cost' hold, which are important characteristics of the Kaleckian model. Here, the paradox of thrift means that an increase in capitalists' propensity to save lowers the rate of capital accumulation. The paradox of cost means that an increase in the real wage leads to an increase in the realized profit rate.

However, even such extended models miss an important point, that is, the determination of the employment rate, which we focus on in this chapter. Conventional Kaleckian growth models assume that labor supply is unlimited and that firms employ as many workers as they desire at given wages. If, however, the labor supply grows at an exogenously given rate, there is no guarantee that the endogenously determined growth employment rate would be equal to the growth rate of labor supply. Thus, if the growth of labor supply steadily exceeds that of the labor demand, then the rate of unemployment will keep on increasing; however, this is unrealistic.[4]

Therefore, we extend the Kaleckian model to determine the employment rate, and to investigate how changes in parameters affect the employment rate.

This chapter is not an initial attempt to explicitly consider the determination of the employment rate in the Kaleckian model. Stockhammer (2004) presents an augmented Kaleckian model that incorporates equations that determine employment and income distribution, and investigates the employment rate in the long-run equilibrium. However, the notion of the long run in Stockhammer (2004) is different from that in the present chapter. The long run in Stockhammer's model corresponds to the medium run in our model. Moreover, we determine employment and income distribution differently, and thus, we obtain different results than Stockhammer.

To determine the employment rate, we endogenize the growth rate of labor productivity, which is given exogenously in conventional Kaleckian models.[5] We assume that the growth rate of labor productivity depends positively on the employment rate. Such a formulation is also proposed by Bhaduri (2006) and Dutt (2006). Based on Marx's idea, Bhaduri states that this captures a view that technological change is driven by inter-class conflict over income distribution between workers and capitalists. Dutt says that as the labor market tightens and a labor shortage becomes clear, the bargaining power of workers increases, which exerts an upward pressure on wages, leading capitalists to adopt labor-saving technical changes.[6] Bhaduri's (2006) model is not Kaleckian because income distribution is not determined by mark-up pricing.

creasing returns to scale in the production function. In the long-run equilibrium, the desired capital-labor ratio and the actual capital-labor ratio are equalized.

4) Cassetti (2002, pp. 205–206) also points out that the long-run employment rate in the conventional Kaleckian models is not constant.

5) Rowthorn (1981), Lavoie (1992, p. 322), You (1994), Cassetti (2003), and Stockhammer and Onaran (2004) also endogenize technical progress in the Kaleckian model through use of Kaldorian technical progress functions. Lima (2004) develops a Kaleckian model with endogenous technical progress in which the growth rate of labor productivity depends non-linearly on the wage share.

6) The view that increases in wages induce labor-saving technical change is consistent with an empirical study by Marquetti (2004), who investigates the co-integration between real wages and labor productivity by using US data.

However, it bears similarity to the Kaleckian model in that effective demand plays a crucial role in determining output. In contrast, Dutt's (2006) model can be said to be Kaleckian, but it does not deal with issues such as income distribution or inflation because its purpose is to present a simple growth model that integrates the roles of aggregate demand and supply.

In determining technological change, mainstream growth theory emphasizes supply side factors such as R&D investment and human capital accumulation. In contrast, we emphasize the demand side factors contributing to technological change: changes in aggregate demand cause changes in employment, which lead to technological change. Under our formulation, 'the natural rate of growth' becomes an endogenous variable. Here, we define the natural rate of growth as the sum of the growth rate of labor productivity and that of labor supply. Although the growth rate of labor supply in our model is exogenously given, the growth rate of labor productivity is endogenously determined, and consequently, the natural rate of growth is an endogenous variable. Our formulation suggests that the natural rate of growth increases when business is good (i.e., when the employment rate is high), while it decreases when business is bad (i.e., when the employment rate is low). This property is consistent with empirical studies by León-Ledesma and Thirlwall (2002), Libânio (2009), and Vogel (2009). Therefore, our formulation of technological change is reasonable in that it describes an important feature of the real world.

Our model's framework is based on Cassetti (2006). He introduces the theory of conflicting-claims inflation into the Kaleckian model and analyzes the medium-run and long-run equilibria. We introduce the above mentioned endogenous technical change into Cassetti's (2006) model and analyze the medium-run and long-run equilibria. In the medium run, the capacity utilization rate, the profit share, and the employment rate are adjusted. In the long run, the normal capacity utilization rate and the expected capital accumulation rate are adjusted.

The remainder of the chapter is organized as follows. Section 2 presents our model's framework and analyzes the medium-run equilibrium. Section 3 conducts a long-run analysis and presents numerical examples. Section 4 concludes the chapter.

4.2   Medium-run analysis

4.2.1   Framework of the model

Consider an economy with workers and capitalists. Suppose that workers consume all their wages and capitalists save a fraction s of their profits. Then, the ratio of the real saving S to the capital stock K, that is, $g_s = S/K$ leads to

$$g_s = sr, \tag{4.1}$$

where r denotes the rate of profit.

Suppose that firms operate with the following fixed coefficients production function:

$$Y = \min\{aE, (u/k)K\}, \tag{4.2}$$

where Y denotes real output; E, employment; and $a = Y/E$, the level of labor productivity.[7] The capacity utilization rate is defined as $u = Y/Y^*$, where Y^* denotes the potential output. The coefficient $k = K/Y^*$ denotes the ratio of the capital stock to the potential output, which is assumed to be constant. This assumption means that both K and Y^* grow at the same rate. Moreover, when the capacity utilization rate is constant, the growth rate of capital stock and that of the actual output will be the same. Accordingly, the actual output and the potential output grow at the same rate in the equilibrium where the capacity utilization rate is constant. To simplify the analysis, we assume $k = 1$ in what follows. From this, we have $r = mu$, where m denotes the profit share.

Let us introduce the investment function. Following Amadeo (1986) and Lavoie (2006), we specify the ratio of the real investment I to the capital stock, $g_d = I/K$, as follows:

$$g_d = \gamma + \varepsilon(u - u_n), \quad \gamma > \varepsilon u_n, \tag{4.3}$$

where γ denotes a constant term capturing the expected rate of growth; ε, a positive parameter; and u_n, a normal capacity utilization rate. Firms determine the normal capacity utilization rate through convention, historical experience, and strategic considerations. Equation (4.3) states that investment responds to the gap between the actual capacity utilization rate and the normal capacity utilization rate.[8] If the actual capacity utilization rate is equal to the normal capacity utilization rate, firms expand plants at the same pace as the expected rate of growth. If, however, the actual capacity utilization rate falls short of the normal capacity utilization rate, firms consider themselves as facing excess capacity, and they decrease the rate of capital accumulation. If, however, the actual capacity utilization rate exceeds the normal capacity utilization rate, firms increase the capital accumulation rate faster than the expected rate of

---

7) Given the fixed coefficients production function, a cost minimizing firm operates at a point on isoquant curves such that $aE = (u/k)K$, from which we obtain $a = Y/E$.

8) Cassetti (2006) uses an investment function that contains the rate of profit as an endogenous variable in addition to the capacity utilization rate. To simplify the analysis, our model uses an investment function that contains only the capacity utilization rate. Introducing the rate of profit as a second variable does not change the main results in this chapter. For the specification of the investment function, see also Marglin and Bhaduri (1990). They assert that the profit share, not the rate of profit, should be a variable in the investment function. In this case, according to the shape of the investment function, we obtain various equilibrium regimes. For this issue, see also Bhaduri and Marglin (1990) and Blecker (2002). Agliardi (1988) and Mott and Slattery (1994) disagree with the logic of Bhaduri and Marglin (1990). Using Marglin and Bhaduri's (1990) investment function, Sasaki (2010) presents a Kaleckian growth model in which the employment rate is endogenously determined as in the present chapter. He shows that whether or not an increase in the relative bargaining power of workers raises the equilibrium employment rate depends on which regime is realized in the equilibrium.

growth. Finally, the constraint $\gamma > \varepsilon u_n$ means that $g_d > 0$ even when $u = 0$.

4.2.2   Dynamics of the capacity utilization rate, the profit share, and the employment rate

In the medium run, the capacity utilization rate, the profit share, and the employment rate are adjusted.

An equation of motion for the capacity utilization rate can be formulated by

$$\dot{u} = \alpha(g_d - g_s), \quad \alpha > 0, \tag{4.4}$$

where α denotes the speed of adjustment of the goods market. Equation (4.4) shows that excess demand leads to a rise in the capacity utilization rate, while excess supply leads to a decline in the capacity utilization rate.

From the definition of the profit share, we have $m = 1 - (wE/pY)$, from which we obtain the following relationship:[9]

$$\frac{\dot{m}}{1-m} = \frac{\dot{p}}{p} - \frac{\dot{w}}{w} + \frac{\dot{a}}{a}. \tag{4.5}$$

To know the dynamics of the profit share, we have to specify the dynamics of the price, the money wage, and labor productivity.

We specify the dynamics of the money wage and price by using the theory of conflicting-claims inflation. First, suppose that the growth rate of the money wage that workers manage to negotiate depends on the discrepancy between their target profit share and the actual profit share. Second, suppose that firms set their price to close the gap between their target profit share and the actual profit share. From these considerations, the dynamics of the money wage and price can be described, respectively, as follows:

$$\frac{\dot{w}}{w} = \theta_w(m - m_w), \quad \theta_w > 0,\ 0 < m_w < 1, \tag{4.6}$$

$$\frac{\dot{p}}{p} = \theta_f(m_f - m), \quad \theta_f > 0,\ 0 < m_f < 1, \tag{4.7}$$

where θ_w and θ_f are the speed of adjustment, m_w is the target profit share set by workers, and m_f is the target profit share set by firms. In our model, the target profit shares are exogenously given. However, we can endogenize them. For example, Dutt (1992) and Cassetti (2002, 2003) assume that the workers' target depends negatively on the employment rate, that is, $m_w = m_w(e)$, where $m'_w(e) < 0$. In this case, combining

---

9) Cassetti (2002, 2003, 2006) derives an equation of motion for the profit share by specifying a price-setting equation of firms and differentiating it with respect to time. However, this procedure is unnecessary for deriving the equation of motion for the profit share; plus, our procedure is easier than his procedure. With the conflicting-claims inflation theory, the price-setting equation in Cassetti's model plays the role of determining the mark-up rate rather than the price level.

equation (4.6) with equation (4.7), we obtain a real-wage Phillips curve such that the growth rate of the real wage rate depends positively on the employment rate. With this Phillips curve, we can build a Kaleckian model in which the equilibrium employment rate is endogenously determined.[10] As stated in Section 4.1, we use a different way to endogenize the equilibrium employment rate.

In the following analysis, we assume that $m_f > m_w$. Firms attempt to set their targets as high as possible whereas workers attempt to set their targets as low as possible. Therefore, the assumption $m_f > m_w$ is reasonable. We can interpret θ_w and θ_f as the bargaining power of workers and that of firms, respectively (Lavoie 1992, p. 393; Cassetti 2002, p. 192; Cassetti 2003, p. 453). We assume $\theta_f + \theta_w = 1$ and define $\theta_f \equiv \theta$ because bargaining power is a relative concept. We then obtain $\theta_w = 1 - \theta$, where $0 < \theta < 1$.[11] For example, we can consider an increase in the unionization rate as a factor for raising the bargaining power of workers (i.e., a decrease in θ), and an increase in the market power of oligopolistic firms as a factor for raising the bargaining power of firms (i.e., an increase in θ).

We now turn to the specification of endogenous technological change. As stated above, we assume that the growth rate of labor productivity $g_a = \dot{a}/a$ depends positively on the employment rate e.

$$g_a(e) = \lambda e^{\psi}, \quad \lambda > 0, \ \psi > 0, \tag{4.8}$$

where $e = E/N$ denotes the employment rate; N, the exogenous labor supply; λ, a positive constant; and ψ, the elasticity of the growth rate of labor productivity with respect to the employment rate. We use the above specification to conduct numerical simulations in what follows. Note, however, that our results do not depend on this specification as long as the growth rate of labor productivity is an increasing function of the employment rate. In addition, the non-linearity of equation (4.8), when $\psi \neq 1$, has no effect on the local stability of equilibrium and the results of comparative statics analysis. Nevertheless, the non-linearity can affect the global behavior of each endogenous variable.

Let us explain the difference between equation (4.8) and specifications of Bhaduri (2006) and Dutt (2006). Equation (4.8) and their specifications bear similarities but differ in some respects. In Bhaduri's (2006) model, a change in the growth rate of la-

---

10) If we introduce both the real-wage Phillips curve and equation (4.8) below into our model, the medium-run equilibrium can be stable or unstable depending on which effect dominates, the effect of the real-wage Phillips curve or the effect of equation (4.8). However, as long as the medium-run equilibrium is stable, results of comparative statics analysis are the same as those of our model. Moreover, we can assume that the target profit share of workers depends negatively on the growth rate of labor productivity while the target profit share of firms depends positively on the growth rate of labor productivity. Because the growth rate of labor productivity is an increasing function of the employment rate, it amounts to saying that the workers' target is a decreasing function of the employment rate while the firms' target is an increasing function of the employment rate. In this case also, as long as the medium-run equilibrium is stable, similar arguments hold. For details, see section A of the Appendix.

11) The constraint $0 < \theta_w, \theta_f < 1$ is also adopted by Dutt and Amadeo (1993), who, however, do not assume $\theta_f + \theta_w = 1$. Even if we impose only $0 < \theta_w, \theta_f < 1$ and not $\theta_f + \theta_w = 1$, we obtain similar results.

bor productivity ($\dot{g}_a$) depends positively on the rate of change in the employment rate ($\dot{e}/e$). Dutt (2006) presents two kinds of specifications. In Dutt's (2006) first model, the rate of change in the growth rate of labor productivity ($\dot{g}_a/g_a$) depends positively on the rate of change in the employment rate ($\dot{e}/e$). In these specifications, it is the growth rate of labor productivity, not the employment rate that is endogenously determined. In this chapter, to examine how the employment rate is determined, we relate the growth rate of labor productivity (g_a) to the employment rate (e). In Dutt's (2006) second model, the rate of change in the growth rate of labor productivity ($\dot{g}_a/g_a$) depends negatively on the employment rate (e). In addition, when the employment rate is equal to its natural rate e_N, the rate of change in the growth rate of labor productivity will be zero. From this, the steady-state employment rate is equal to the natural rate. The natural rate e_N is exogenously given, and then, it does not depend on other parameters of the model. In our model, both the growth rate of labor productivity and the employment rate are simultaneously determined, and moreover, the employment rate depends on parameters.

Substituting equations (4.6), (4.7), and (4.8) in equation (4.5), we obtain an equation of motion for the profit share:

$$\dot{m} = -(1 - m)[m - A - g_a(e)], \tag{4.9}$$

where $A \equiv \theta m_f + (1 - \theta)m_w$. We assume that $A > n$, which means that a weighted average of the two groups' target profit shares is larger than the growth rate of labor supply. Given that the size of n is about 10 percent at most, this assumption is plausible.

Let us derive an equation of motion for the employment rate. From equation (4.2), the rate of change in the employment rate is given by $e = uK/(aN)$, from which the rate of change of e leads to

$$\frac{\dot{e}}{e} = \frac{\dot{u}}{u} + g_d - g_a(e) - n, \tag{4.10}$$

where n is the growth rate of N and given exogenously.

4.2.3   Medium-run equilibrium

From the above analysis, in the medium run, we obtain the following system of three differential equations with respect to u, m, and e:

$$\dot{u} = \alpha[\gamma + \varepsilon(u - u_n) - smu], \tag{4.11}$$

$$\dot{m} = -(1 - m)[m - A - g_a(e)], \tag{4.12}$$

$$\dot{e} = e\left\{ \frac{\alpha[\gamma + \varepsilon(u - u_n) - smu]}{u} + \gamma + \varepsilon(u - u_n) - g_a(e) - n \right\}. \tag{4.13}$$

Let us find the medium-run equilibrium. Using $\dot{u} = \dot{m} = \dot{e} = 0$, we obtain the following quadratic equation for the profit share:

$$sm^2 - \Theta m + \varepsilon(A - n) = 0, \tag{4.14}$$

where $\Theta \equiv s(\gamma - \varepsilon u_n) + s(A - n) + \varepsilon > 0$.

From equation (4.14), we obtain two real and distinct roots. However, the larger root corresponds to the medium-run equilibrium value.[12]

$$m^* = \frac{\Theta + \sqrt{\Theta^2 - 4s\varepsilon(A - n)}}{2s}. \tag{4.15}$$

Hereafter, medium-run equilibrium values are denoted with '$*$.' Using equation (4.15), we obtain the rates of employment, capacity utilization, and capital accumulation in the medium-run equilibrium.

$$e^* = \left(\frac{m^* - A}{\lambda}\right)^{1/\psi}, \tag{4.16}$$

$$u^* = \frac{\gamma - \varepsilon u_n}{sm^* - \varepsilon}, \tag{4.17}$$

$$g^* = \frac{s(\gamma - \varepsilon u_n)m^*}{sm^* - \varepsilon}. \tag{4.18}$$

Because we assume $\gamma > \varepsilon u_n$, we need $sm^* - \varepsilon > 0$ to obtain the positive values of u^* and g^*.

To analyze the local stability of the medium-run equilibrium, we linearize equations (4.11), (4.12), and (4.13) around the equilibrium, and investigate the corresponding Jacobian matrix. From this procedure, we obtain the following proposition:

Proposition 4.1. *Suppose that the medium-run equilibrium value of the profit share is less than or equal to $1/2$. Then, the medium-run equilibrium is locally stable if ε is less than or equal to $1/2$.*

Proof. See Appendix 4.C.   ∎

Proposition 4.1 means that if the sensitivity of investment with respect to the capacity utilization rate ε is small, the medium-run equilibrium can be locally stable. In general, the profit share in the real world is considered to be less than $1/2$, and thus, the condition $m^* \leq 1/2$ is not so unrealistic. In the following analysis, we assume both $m^* \leq 1/2$ and $\varepsilon \leq 1/2$.

4.2.4   Comparative statics in the medium-run equilibrium

Table 4.1 summarizes the results of comparative statics in the medium-run equilibrium.[13]

---

12) For details, see Appendix 4.B.
13) For details of comparative statics analysis, see Appendix 4.D.

Table 4.1: Results for medium-run comparative statics analysis

	A	s	n
m^*	+	−	−
e^*	−	−	−
u^*	−	−	+
g^*	−	−	+

Note that an increase in A means an increase in θ.[14] An increase in the bargaining power of firms decreases the capacity utilization rate and the employment rate. This implies that a policy for weakening the bargaining power of workers cannot lower the rate of unemployment. Stockhammer (2004) also investigates the relationship between bargaining power and unemployment. He concludes that in a profit-led growth regime, a decline in the bargaining power of workers leads to lower unemployment. However, in a wage-led growth regime of Stockhammer's model, the equilibrium is unstable, and consequently, we cannot investigate the relationship between bargaining power and unemployment.[15] In our model, in contrast, the medium-run equilibrium is stable even though it is wage-led growth. The reason for this stability is a stabilizing effect of the endogenous labor-saving technological change. Our result is consistent with the empirical result of Storm and Naastepad (2007, 2008). Using data for 20 OECD countries during the period 1984–1997, they show that an increase in the bargaining power of firms due to labor market deregulation raises the rate of unemployment in contrast to the view of mainstream theory.

An increase in the saving rate decreases the capacity utilization rate and the employment rate. In Stockhammer (2004), the equilibrium employment rate consists of the exogenous natural rate of growth and parameters of the investment function and the income distribution function, and does not depend on the saving rate. Hence, a change in the saving rate never affects the employment rate. In our model, in contrast, the natural rate of growth is endogenously determined and a change in the saving rate affects the employment rate accordingly.

The effect of an increase in the target profit shares m_f and m_w is similar to that of an increase in θ discussed above. An important issue in the Kaleckian tradition is what regime is obtained in the equilibrium. Classification of regimes is based on the relationship between the profit share, the capacity utilization rate and the rate of capital accumulation. Note, however, that the profit share in the medium-run equilibrium is not an exogenous but an endogenous variable. Nevertheless, because m_f and m_w change in the same direction as m^*, we can use these variables as a proxy for the

14) Recall that we assume that $m_f > m_w$. With this assumption, an increase in A corresponds to an increase in θ.
15) Stockhammer (2004) uses a Marglin and Bhaduri (1990) type of investment function, thereby leading to both wage-led growth and profit-led growth in the equilibrium.

actual profit share. An increase in m_f or m_w leads to a decline in both u^* and g^*. From this, we can conclude that the medium-run equilibrium corresponds to both a wage-led demand regime and a wage-led growth regime, which are typical of the Kaleckian model.[16]

4.3   Long-run analysis

4.3.1   Dynamics of the normal capacity utilization rate and the expected rate of growth

In the long run, the medium-run equilibrium is always attained and the normal capacity utilization rate and the expected rate of growth are adjusted. Therefore, in the long run, planned investment and saving are always equalized. We follow Lavoie (1996), Dutt (1997), Lavoie et al. (2004), and Cassetti (2006) to describe the long-run dynamics.[17]

First, we introduce the following adjustment equation for the normal capacity utilization rate:

$$\dot{u}_n = \phi(u^* - u_n), \quad \phi > 0, \tag{4.19}$$

where ϕ denotes the speed of adjustment. Equation (4.19) states that the normal capacity utilization rate is adjusted according to the gap between the actual capacity utilization rate and the normal capacity utilization rate. Note that we have $u^* = u^*(u_n, \gamma)$ from the medium-run analysis.

Second, we introduce the following adjustment equation for the expected rate of capital accumulation:

$$\dot{\gamma} = \eta(g^* - \gamma), \quad \eta > 0, \tag{4.20}$$

where η denotes the speed of adjustment. Equation (4.20) shows that the expected rate of growth is adjusted according to the gap between the actual growth rate and the expected rate of growth, which corresponds to adaptive expectations. Because we have $g^* = \gamma + \varepsilon(u^* - u_n)$, we can rewrite equation (4.20) as follows:

$$\dot{\gamma} = \eta\varepsilon(u^* - u_n). \tag{4.21}$$

The empirical validity of simultaneous adjustments of u_n and γ is discussed by Lavoie et al. (2004). They empirically test four kinds of investment functions—the

---

16) Our classification of regimes is based on Blecker (2002). A wage-led demand regime contrasts with a profit-led demand regime and a wage-led growth regime contrasts with a profit-led growth regime.

17) Cassetti (2006) develops a model in which, in addition to the normal capacity utilization rate and the expected rate of capital accumulation, the normal rate of profit and the drop-out ratio of capital equipment are also adjusted in the long run.

French Marxist equation, the naive Kaleckian equation, the American Marxist equation, and the hysteresis Kaleckian equation—by using data from the Canadian manufacturing sector and the total industrial sector during the period 1960–2000. Their results show that the hysteresis Kaleckian equation performs better than the other three specifications. In contrast, Skott (2008) criticizes Lavoie et al. (2004): their estimated empirical hysteresis Kaleckian equation bears no relation to the theoretical model. In either case, because we cannot directly observe the normal capacity utilization rate, we need to devise methods for an empirical study.[18] In addition, because Lavoie et al. (2004) and Skott (2008) use only Canadian data, we also need to investigate other countries to ascertain the validity of the hysteresis Kaleckian investment function.

4.3.2   Long-run equilibrium

We derive the long-run equilibrium. A system of differential equations composed of equations (4.19) and (4.21) takes a special form called a zero-root system, in which one eigenvalue of the Jacobian matrix is zero.[19]

In the long-run equilibrium, we obtain $u^* = u_n$, which yields the following relationship between u_n and γ:[20]

$$\gamma = \frac{s(A - n)u_n}{1 - su_n}. \tag{4.22}$$

This is an upward-sloping curve through the origin with $u_n = 1/s$ being an asymptote. Points on this curve correspond to the long-run equilibria. Note, however, that not all the points on this curve are long-run equilibria and some constraints are imposed. To begin with, the capacity utilization rate has to be smaller than unity. This constraint is located to the left of the asymptote $u_n = 1/s$ because $0 < s < 1$. Next, we have $\gamma > \varepsilon u_n$. This constraint means that the long-run equilibria have to be located above the straight line $\gamma = \varepsilon u_n$. Finally, we have $sm^* - \varepsilon > 0$ from the medium-run analysis. This constraint means that the long-run equilibria have to be larger than $\gamma = [\varepsilon - s(A - n)]/s$.

From equations (4.19) and (4.21), we obtain the relationship $\dot{\gamma} = (\eta\varepsilon/\phi)\dot{u}_n$, from which we have the constant ratio $\gamma = (\eta\varepsilon/\phi)u_n$ along the transitional process. Hence, the transitional process is given by the following upward sloping straight line:[21]

$$\gamma(t) = \frac{\eta\varepsilon}{\phi} u_n(t) + \gamma(0) - \frac{\eta\varepsilon}{\phi} u_n(0), \tag{4.23}$$

18) Lavoie et al. (2004) apply the Hodrick-Prescott filter to the actual series of capacity utilization to obtain the series of normal rates of capacity utilization. Skott (2008) uses the Koyck transformation to delete the normal capacity utilization rate from the estimated equation, and accordingly, he dispenses with unobservable variables.

19) The other eigenvalue is the trace of the Jacobian matrix.

20) For the derivation of equation (4.22), see Appendix 4.E.

21) For the solution method below, see Giavazzi and Wyplosz (1985) and van de Klundert and van Schaik (1990).

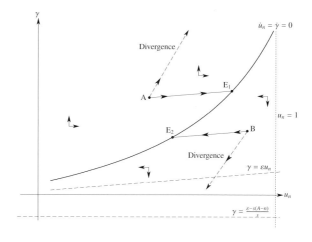

Figure 4.1: Transitional dynamics to the long-run equilibrium

where $\gamma(0)$ and $u_n(0)$ are initial conditions. The intersection of equations (4.23) and (4.22) yields the long-run equilibrium.

The long-run equilibrium values are given by

$$g^{**} = \gamma^{**}, \tag{4.24}$$

$$g_a^{**} = \gamma^{**} - n, \tag{4.25}$$

$$m^{**} = \gamma^{**} + A - n, \tag{4.26}$$

$$u^{**} = \frac{\gamma^{**}}{s(\gamma^{**} + A - n)}, \tag{4.27}$$

$$e^{**} = \left(\frac{\gamma^{**} - n}{\lambda}\right)^{1/\psi}. \tag{4.28}$$

The long-run equilibrium values are denoted with '**.' Given initial conditions, we can determine the long-run value of γ^{**}, which determines equations (4.24) through (4.28). What is important here is that different initial conditions produce different long-run values of γ^{**}. Therefore, the long-run equilibrium shows path-dependency.

Figure 4.1 shows the long-run phase diagram. As stated above, the locus of $\dot{\gamma} = \dot{u}_n = 0$ is an upward-sloping curve. The constraints $\gamma = \varepsilon u_n$ and $\gamma = [\varepsilon - s(A - n)]/s$ are also drawn in Figure 4.1.[22] The solution path denoted by the solid line starting

---

22) Indeed, in addition to these two constraints, there are two additional constraints: one is given by $\gamma < n + \lambda$, which represents that the long-run equilibrium employment rate is less than unity; the other is given by $\gamma < 1 - (A - n)$, which represents that the long-run equilibrium profit share is less than unity. For ease of presentation, we omit the two additional constraints.

Table 4.2: Results for long-run comparative statics analysis

	A	s	n
m^{**}	$+$	$-$	$-$
e^{**}	$-$	$-$	$-$
u^{**}	$-$	$-$	$+$
g^{**}	$-$	$-$	$+$

from point A converges to the long-run equilibrium point denoted by E_1, whereas the solution path denoted by the solid line starting from point B converges to long-run equilibrium E_2. For this reason, if the initial point is different, then the corresponding long-run equilibrium is also different.

The long-run equilibrium is not always stable. If the coefficient $\eta\varepsilon/\phi$, the slope of the solution path, is extremely large, the economy cannot reach the long-run equilibrium. This phenomenon arises when the speed of adjustment of the expected rate of growth is large, when the coefficient of the investment function is large, and when the speed of adjustment of the capacity utilization rate is small. These discussions are also shown in Figure 4.1. The solution path denoted by the broken line starting from point A crosses the locus of $\dot{\gamma} = \dot{u}_n = 0$ at a point where u_n exceeds unity, and consequently, the path is divergent. The solution path denoted by the broken line starting from point B crosses the constraint, and consequently, that path is also divergent.

Moreover, even if the slope of the solution path is small, the economy cannot reach the long-run equilibrium depending on the position of the initial value.

From these observations, it follows that both the speed of adjustment and the initial position are crucial to the stable convergence to the long-run equilibrium.

4.3.3   Comparative statics in the long-run equilibrium

Table 4.2 shows the results of comparative statics in the long-run equilibrium.

When s or A increases, the curve represented by equation (4.22) rotates counter-clockwise around the origin. Because the solution path is unaffected by the change in s or A, the intersection of the solution path and the curve moves toward the lower left. Therefore, both the normal capacity utilization rate and the expected rate of growth decrease.

When n increases, the curve rotates clockwise, and hence, the long-run equilibrium values of u^{**} and γ^{**} increase.

The results in Table 4.2 are the same as those in Table 4.1. In the long run, an increase in the bargaining power of firms also lowers the employment rate.

Let us compare our results with those of Dutt (2006). In the long run of Dutt's model, the growth rate of labor productivity and the autonomous rate of growth (i.e.,

the expected rate of growth in our model) are adjusted. The adjustment of labor productivity growth is equivalent to the adjustment of the employment rate because in
Dutt's model, productivity growth is an increasing function of the employment rate.
The long-run equilibrium has a path-dependent property and depends on the saving
rate, the growth rate of labor supply, and the coefficient of the capacity utilization rate
in the investment function. An increase in the saving rate lowers the employment rate
and the rate of capital accumulation. An increase in the growth rate of labor supply
lowers the employment rate and raises the rate of capital accumulation. These results
are the same as our results. A rise in the coefficient of the capacity utilization rate
in the investment function increases both the employment rate and the rate of capital
accumulation. In our model, in contrast, a change in the coefficient in the investment
function does not affect the long-run equilibrium value: in the long-run equilibrium,
the actual capacity utilization rate and the normal capacity utilization rate are equalized, and accordingly, the effect of the capacity utilization rate on investment vanishes.
Our model extends Dutt's (2006) results in that (i) unlike Dutt's model, long-run income distribution is endogenously determined and (ii) our model can investigate the
effect of the bargaining power on the employment rate.

How are our results modified if we do not consider the adjustment process of the
expected rate of growth and if we consider only the adjustment process of the normal
capacity utilization rate? This corresponds to considering γ as a parameter rather than
an endogenous variable. In this case, the adjustment process of u_n is stable and the
long-run equilibrium values are given by equations (4.24) through (4.28) with γ being
a parameter. It follows from this that the long-run equilibrium values of the rate of
capital accumulation, the growth rate of labor productivity, and the employment rate
do not depend on relative bargaining power.

In contrast, how are our results modified if we do not consider the adjustment
process of the normal capacity utilization rate and if we consider only the adjustment
process of the expected rate of growth? In this case, the adjustment process of γ is
unstable: if there is any divergence from the long-run equilibrium, then the divergence
continues to expand cumulatively. This reminds us of Harrod's instability principle
(Lavoie 1995, p. 806).

Summarizing these discussions, we can understand that because we allow both the
normal capacity utilization rate and the expected rate of growth to adjust simultaneously, the long-run equilibrium will be stable and depend on bargaining power.

The adjustment process of the expected rate of growth also concerns the long-run
equilibrium regime. As is the case with the medium-run equilibrium, we investigate
the relationship between m_f or m_w, and u^{**} and g^{**}. An increase in m_f or m_w lowers
the long-run equilibrium value of the capacity utilization rate, irrespective of whether
the expected rate of growth is endogenous or exogenous. This means that the long-run
equilibrium is a wage-led demand regime. If the expected rate of growth is endogenous, then an increase in m_f or m_w lowers the long-run equilibrium value of the rate of
capital accumulation, which shows that the long-run equilibrium is a wage-led growth

Table 4.3: Results of numerical simulations for the five-dimensional dynamical system

	Initial values: Case 1	Equilibrium: Case 1	Initial values: Case 2	Equilibrium: Case 2
u	0.6	0.39	0.7	0.69
m	0.2	0.26	0.3	0.37
e	0.7	0.14	0.8	0.93
u_n	0.7	0.39	0.8	0.69
γ	0.1	0.08	0.2	0.19

regime. However, if the expected rate of growth is exogenous, then changes in m_f and m_w do not affect the long-run equilibrium value of the rate of capital accumulation.

4.3.4   Numerical examples

In the foregoing analysis, we separate the medium run and the long run. In this sub-section, we consider the adjustment processes of the five endogenous variables all together: the capacity utilization rate, profit share, employment rate, normal capacity utilization rate, and expected rate of growth. The property of the equilibrium is identical in both the model in which the two runs are distinguished and the five-variable model. However, the transitional dynamics toward equilibrium can differ between the two models. For this purpose, we need to analyze the system of five differential equations that consists of equations (4.11), (4.12), (4.13), (4.19), and (4.21). Note that in this case, u^* of equations (4.19) and (4.21) should be replaced with u. Whereas analytical treatment of high-order differential equations is troublesome, numerical analysis is relatively easy, which we now turn to.[23]

For numerical simulations, we set parameters as follows:

$$\theta = 0.3, \ m_f = 0.3, \ m_w = 0.2, \ s = 0.75, \ n = 0.05, \ \varepsilon = 0.08, \ \alpha = 1,$$
$$\lambda = 0.15, \ \psi = 0.9, \ \phi = 1, \ \eta = 1.$$

If the five-dimensional model exhibits path-dependency, different initial conditions must produce different steady-state values under exactly the same parameter settings. Table 4.3 shows the results of this numerical analysis.

The initial values in Case 1 are smaller than those in Case 2. From Table 4.3, we find that if we change initial conditions, we obtain different long-run equilibrium values. Therefore, in this five dimensional dynamical system, we also have path dependency.[24]

Moreover, non-monotonic dynamics emerge in the five-dimensional system. Pa-

---

23) For numerical computation, we use *Mathematica* 7. The *Mathematica* code used is available on request.
24) For the time paths for Cases 1 and 2, see Appendices 4.F and 4.G.

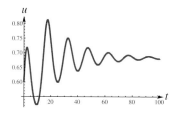

Figure 4.2: Dynamics of u in the five-dimensional system

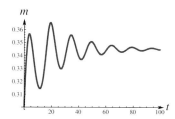

Figure 4.3: Dynamics of m in the five-dimensional system

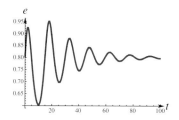

Figure 4.4: Dynamics of e in the five-dimensional system

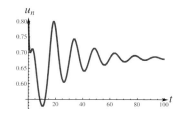

Figure 4.5: Dynamics of u_n in the five-dimensional system

rameters and initial values are set as follows:

$$\theta = 0.3, \; m_f = 0.3, \; m_w = 0.2, \; s = 0.7, \; n = 0.05, \; \varepsilon = 0.3, \; \alpha = 7,$$
$$\lambda = 0.15, \; \psi = 1.2, \; \phi = 1, \; \eta = 1,$$
$$u(0) = 0.6, \; m(0) = 0.3, \; e(0) = 0.8, \; u_n(0) = 0.8, \; \gamma(0) = 0.2.$$

Note that in this case, ε, that is, the sensitivity of investment to the capacity utilization, and α, that is, the adjustment speed of the goods market, are larger than those in Cases 1 and 2. Larger ε and α are destabilizing factors. The time path of each variable is drawn in Figures 4.2–4.6, from which we can see that each variable converges to its long-run equilibrium with oscillation.

We note that in the five-dimensional system, u_n and γ synchronize as in the model in section 4.3. Hence, if we plot the dynamics of u_n and γ on the u_n-γ plane, we obtain a solution path as per the one in Figure 4.1.

4.4   Conclusion

In this chapter, we have developed a Kaleckian model that considers the determination of the employment rate. For this purpose, we have introduced endogenous technolog-

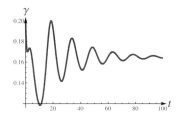

Figure 4.6: Dynamics of γ in the five-dimensional system

ical change into a Kaleckian model with conflicting-claims inflation. We have also discussed how the endogenous variables in our model are determined in the long run where the normal capacity utilization rate and the expected rate of growth are adjusted. This is an answer to the criticism that the Kaleckian model lacks logical consistency in the long run. We have shown that the results in the medium-run equilibrium are carried over to the long-run equilibrium. In this sense, the Kaleckian model can be used for long-run analysis.

In our model, both the medium-run and the long-run employment rate depend on the relative bargaining power between workers and capitalists. A rise in the bargaining power of capitalists increases the unemployment rate, which is contrary to the assertion of mainstream theory. As long as the medium-run and the long-run regime experience wage-led growth, a policy intended to raise the bargaining power of capitalists is unfavorable for a reduction in the unemployment rate.

Long-run equilibrium values have path-dependent properties. As such, slightly different initial conditions are likely to produce large differences in both the transitional path to the long-run equilibrium and the position of the long-run equilibrium itself, which can account for cross-country differences in the long-run unemployment rate.

Appendix 4.A: Endogenizing the target profit shares of workers and firms

We explain how our results are modified if we endogenize the workers' target and the firms' target.

First, we assume that the target profit share of workers is a decreasing function of the growth rate of labor productivity.

$$m_w = m_w(g_a), \quad m_w'(g_a) < 0. \tag{4.29}$$

Because $g_a = g_a(e)$ and $g'_a(e) > 0$, we can rewrite it as follows:

$$m_w = m_w(g_a(e)) = m_w(e), \quad m'_w(e) < 0. \tag{4.30}$$

This equation relates the fruit of labor productivity gains to a wage claim.

Second, we assume that the target profit share of firms is an increasing function of the growth rate of labor productivity.

$$m_f = m_s(g_a), \quad m'_f(g_a) > 0. \tag{4.31}$$

Because $g_a = g_a(e)$ and $g'_a(e) > 0$, we can rewrite it as follows:

$$m_f = m_f(g_a(e)) = m_f(e), \quad m'_f(e) > 0. \tag{4.32}$$

This equation relates the fruit of labor productivity gains to a profit claim.

Using these equations, we obtain the following equation of motion for the profit share.

$$\dot{m} = -(1-m)[m - \theta m_f(e) - (1-\theta)m_w(e) - g_a(e)], \tag{4.33}$$

where the sign below the variables denotes the sign of the corresponding partial derivative of the variable. In this case, J_{23} of the Jacobian matrix is modified as follows:

$$J_{23} = \frac{\partial \dot{m}}{\partial e} = (1-m)[\theta m'_f(e) + (1-\theta)m'_w(e) + g'_a(e)], \tag{4.34}$$

which is evaluated at the medium-run equilibrium.

When we do not endogenize the targets, the first and second terms in the square bracket of the right-hand side will be zero, which yields $J_{23} > 0$ with $g'_a(e) > 0$, as in the text.

When we endogenize the targets, the first term is positive and the second term is negative. If the negative effect of $m'_w(e) < 0$ is smaller than the other two positive effects, we have $J_{23} > 0$, and accordingly, the foregoing analysis remains unchanged. If, however, the negative effect of $m'_w(e) < 0$ is larger than the other two positive effects, we have $J_{23} < 0$, which has a destabilizing effect on the medium-run equilibrium.

If the medium-run equilibrium is stable, that is, $J_{23} > 0$, results of comparative statics analysis remain unchanged. For example, the effect of a rise in the bargaining power of firms leads to

$$\frac{de}{d\theta} = \frac{m_f(e) - m_w(e)}{\dfrac{g'_a(e)}{g'(m)} - [\theta m'_f(e) + (1-\theta)m'_w(e) + g'_a(e)]} = \frac{m_f(e) - m_w(e)}{\dfrac{g'_a(e)}{g'(m)} - \dfrac{J_{23}}{1-m}}. \tag{4.35}$$

Here, we assume $m_f(e) > m_w(e)$ as in the text. Then, the numerator of the right-hand side is positive. In our model, we have $g'(m) < 0$. From $g'_a(e) > 0$ and $J_{23} > 0$, the denominator of the right-hand side is negative. It follows that we have $de/d\theta < 0$: a rise in the bargaining power of firms lowers the equilibrium employment rate, which is the same as that in the text. Similar arguments hold for other derivatives.

Appendix 4.B: Derivation of the medium-run equilibrium profit share

We derive the profit share in the medium-run equilibrium. The discriminant of equation (4.14) in the text is given by

$$\mathcal{D} = \Theta^2 - 4s\varepsilon(A - n) = s^2(\gamma - \varepsilon u_n)^2 + [s(A - n) - \varepsilon]^2 + 2s(\gamma - \varepsilon u_n)[s(A - n) + \varepsilon] > 0. \tag{4.36}$$

Hence, the quadratic equation (4.14) has the two real and distinct roots, m_1 and m_2. Let $m_1 < m_2$. We have

$$m_1 + m_2 = \frac{s(\gamma - \varepsilon u_n) + s(A - n) + \varepsilon}{s} > 0, \tag{4.37}$$

$$m_1 m_2 = \frac{(A - n)\varepsilon}{s} > 0. \tag{4.38}$$

and thus, both m_1 and m_2 are positive. Rearranging the condition $sm - \varepsilon > 0$, we obtain $m > \varepsilon/s$. Accordingly, m has to satisfy this inequality. Let the left-hand side of equation (4.14) be $f(m)$. Because $f(\varepsilon/s) = -(\gamma - \varepsilon u_n) < 0$, m_1 is smaller than $m = \varepsilon/s$, and m_2 is larger than $m = \varepsilon/s$. Therefore, m_2 is the medium-run equilibrium value of the profit share.

Appendix 4.C: Local stability of the medium-run equilibrium

To investigate the local stability of the medium-run equilibrium, we linearize the system of differential equations (4.11), (4.12), and (4.13) around the equilibrium.

$$\begin{pmatrix} \dot{u} \\ \dot{m} \\ \dot{e} \end{pmatrix} = \begin{pmatrix} J_{11} & J_{12} & 0 \\ 0 & J_{22} & J_{23} \\ J_{31} & J_{32} & J_{33} \end{pmatrix} \begin{pmatrix} u - u^* \\ m - m^* \\ e - e^* \end{pmatrix},$$

where the elements of the Jacobian matrix $\mathbf{J}$ are given by

$$J_{11} \equiv \frac{\partial \dot{u}}{\partial u} = -\alpha(sm - \varepsilon) < 0,$$

$$J_{12} \equiv \frac{\partial \dot{u}}{\partial m} = -\alpha su < 0,$$

$$J_{22} \equiv \frac{\partial \dot{m}}{\partial m} = -(1 - m) < 0,$$

$$J_{23} \equiv \frac{\partial \dot{m}}{\partial e} = (1 - m)g'_a(e) > 0,$$

$$J_{31} \equiv \frac{\partial \dot{e}}{\partial u} = -\frac{\alpha e(sm - \varepsilon)}{u} + \varepsilon e,$$

$$J_{32} \equiv \frac{\partial \dot{e}}{\partial m} = -\alpha s e < 0,$$

$$J_{33} \equiv \frac{\partial \dot{e}}{\partial e} = -e g'_a(e) < 0.$$

All elements are evaluated at the medium-run equilibrium value; we omit '*' to avoid troublesome notations.

The characteristic equation of $\mathbf{J}$ is given by

$$q^3 + a_1 q^2 + a_2 q + a_3 = 0, \tag{4.39}$$

where q denotes a characteristic root. Each coefficient of equation (4.39) is given by

$$a_1 = -\operatorname{tr} \mathbf{J} = -(J_{11} + J_{22} + J_{33}),$$

$$a_2 = \begin{vmatrix} J_{22} & J_{23} \\ J_{32} & J_{33} \end{vmatrix} + \begin{vmatrix} J_{11} & 0 \\ J_{31} & J_{33} \end{vmatrix} + \begin{vmatrix} J_{11} & J_{12} \\ 0 & J_{22} \end{vmatrix} = J_{22}J_{33} - J_{23}J_{32} + J_{11}(J_{33} + J_{22}),$$

$$a_3 = -\det \mathbf{J} = -J_{11}(J_{22}J_{33} - J_{23}J_{32}) - J_{31}J_{12}J_{23},$$

where $-a_1 = \operatorname{tr} \mathbf{J}$ denotes the trace of $\mathbf{J}$; a_2, the sum of the principal minors' determinants; and $-a_3 = \det \mathbf{J}$, the determinant of $\mathbf{J}$.

The necessary and sufficient condition for the local stability is that all characteristic roots of $\mathbf{J}$ have negative real parts, which leads to $a_1 > 0$, $a_2 > 0$, $a_3 > 0$, and $a_1 a_2 - a_3 > 0$. Accordingly, we need to examine these inequalities.

$$a_1 = \underbrace{(sm - \varepsilon)}_{\equiv b_1 > 0} \alpha + \underbrace{(1 - m) + e g'_a(e)}_{\equiv b_2 > 0} = \underset{+}{b_1 \alpha} + \underset{+}{b_2} > 0,$$

$$a_2 = \underbrace{\{(sm - \varepsilon)[(1 - m) + e g'_a(e)] + s(1 - m)e g'_a(e)\}}_{\equiv b_3 > 0} \alpha + \underbrace{(1 - m)e g'_a(e)}_{\equiv b_4 > 0}$$

$$= \underset{+}{b_3 \alpha} + \underset{+}{b_4} > 0,$$

$$a_3 = \underbrace{(1 - m)e g'_a(e)[(sm - \varepsilon) + \varepsilon s u]}_{\equiv b_5 > 0} \alpha = \underset{+}{b_5 \alpha} > 0,$$

$$a_1 a_2 - a_3 = \underbrace{b_1 b_3}_{+} \alpha^2 + (b_1 b_4 + b_2 b_3 - b_5)\alpha + \underbrace{b_2 b_4}_{+} .$$

Here, we have

$$b_1b_4 + b_2b_3 - b_5 = \underbrace{(sm - \varepsilon)[(1 - m) + eg_a'(e)]^2}_{+} + \underbrace{s(1 - m)eg_a'(e)}_{+}[eg_a'(e) + \underbrace{1 - m - \varepsilon u}_{\equiv \Lambda}].$$

The part Λ will be positive if ε is not so large. The profit share in the real world is considered to be less than $1/2$ and the capacity utilization rate is less than unity. In this case, we have $\Lambda = (1/2) - \varepsilon$, and accordingly, we have $\Lambda \geq 0$ if $\varepsilon \leq 1/2$. When $\Lambda \geq 0$, we have $b_1b_4 + b_2b_3 - b_5 > 0$, from which we obtain $a_1a_2 - a_3 > 0$. Therefore, the necessary and sufficient conditions for local stability are all satisfied.

Appendix 4.D: Medium-run comparative statics analysis

We conduct a comparative statics analysis in the medium-run equilibrium.

4.4.1 A rise in A

The effect of a rise in A on m is as follows. Totally differentiating the equilibrium conditions, we have

$$\frac{dm}{dA} = \frac{1}{1 - (\partial g/\partial m)}. \tag{4.40}$$

From $\dot{u} = 0$, we have $\partial g/\partial m < 0$, and consequently, this derivative is positive. Therefore, a rise in A increases the profit share.

The effect of a rise in A on e is as follows:

$$\frac{de}{dA} = \frac{\dfrac{\partial g/\partial m}{1 - (\partial g/\partial m)}}{g_a'(e)}. \tag{4.41}$$

The denominator is positive and the numerator is negative, and consequently, this derivative is negative. Therefore, a rise in A decreases the employment rate.

The effect of a rise in A on u is opposite to the effect of a rise in A on m because u is decreasing in m.

4.4.2 A rise in s

The effect of a rise in s on m is as follows:

$$\frac{dm}{ds} = \frac{\partial g/\partial s}{1 - (\partial g/\partial m)}. \tag{4.42}$$

The denominator is positive and the numerator is negative, and consequently, this derivative is negative. Therefore, a rise in s decreases the profit share.

The effect of a rise in s on e is as follows:

$$\frac{de}{ds} = \frac{dm/ds}{g_a'(e)}. \tag{4.43}$$

The denominator is positive and the numerator is negative, and consequently, this derivative is negative. Therefore, a rise in s decreases the employment rate.

4.4.3   A rise in n

The effect of a rise in n on m is as follows:

$$\frac{dm}{dn} = -\frac{1}{1 - (\partial g/\partial m)}. \tag{4.44}$$

The denominator is positive, and consequently, this derivative is negative. Therefore, a rise in n decreases the profit share.

The effect of a rise in n on e is as follows:

$$\frac{de}{dn} = \frac{dm/dn}{g_a'(e)}. \tag{4.45}$$

The denominator is positive and the numerator is negative, and consequently, this derivative is negative. Therefore, a rise in n decreases the employment rate.

The effect of a rise in n on u is opposite to the effect of a rise in n on m because u is decreasing in m.

Appendix 4.E: Derivation of equation (4.22)

We derive equation (4.22) in the text. In the long-run equilibrium, u^* and u_n are equalized, and accordingly, u_n and γ satisfy the following relation:

$$\frac{\gamma - \varepsilon u_n}{sm^*(u_n, \gamma) - \varepsilon} = u_n. \tag{4.46}$$

Because we know that the long-run equilibrium value of the profit share is given by $m^{**} = \gamma + A - n$, we can replace m^* with m^{**} as follows:

$$\frac{\gamma - \varepsilon u_n}{s(\gamma + A - n) - \varepsilon} = u_n. \tag{4.47}$$

The long-run equilibrium values of u_n and γ have to satisfy equation (4.47), which is a rewritten form of equation (4.22). Substituting equation (4.15) in the text into m^* of equation (4.46), we obtain

$$\cfrac{\gamma - \varepsilon u_n}{\cfrac{[s(\gamma - \varepsilon u_n) + s(A - n) + \varepsilon] + \sqrt{[s(\gamma - \varepsilon u_n) + s(A - n) + \varepsilon]^2 - 4s\varepsilon(A - n)}}{2} - \varepsilon} = u_n.$$

(4.48)

Using numerical simulations, we confirm that equation (4.47) yields exactly the same results as equation (4.48).

Appendix 4.F: Convergence and path-dependency in the five-dimensional system with relatively small initial values (Case 1)

Time paths of the five variables in Case 1 of Table 4.3 are as follows:

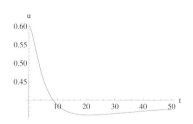

Figure 4.7: Time path of u in Case 1

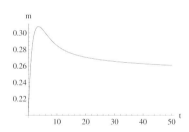

Figure 4.8: Time path of m in Case 1

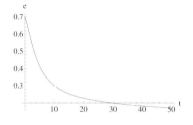

Figure 4.9: Time path of e in Case 1

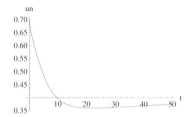

Figure 4.10: Time path of u_n in Case 1

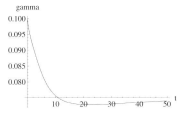

Figure 4.11: Time path of γ in Case 1

Appendix 4.G: Convergence and path-dependency in the five-dimensional system with relatively large initial values (Case 2)

Time paths of the five variables in Case 2 of Table 4.3 are as follows:

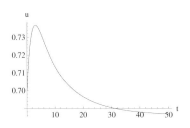

Figure 4.12: Time path of u in Case 2

Figure 4.13: Time path of m in Case 2

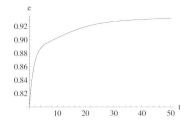
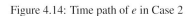
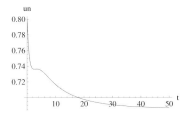

Figure 4.14: Time path of e in Case 2

Figure 4.15: Time path of u_n in Case 2

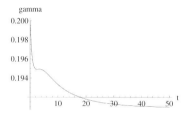

Figure 4.16: Time path of γ in Case 2

Is the Long-run Equilibrium Wage-led or Profit-led? A Kaleckian Approach

5.1   Introduction

This chapter builds medium-run and long-run Kaleckian models and investigates the employment rate in the medium-run and long-run equilibria and identifies which regime is realized in the long-run equilibrium.

Thus far, a number of Kaleckian models have been developed and improved to investigate the relationship between income distribution and growth.[1] At the same time, however, there are criticisms of the Kaleckian models, especially regarding the long-run concept of Kaleckian models.

Critics claim that the Kaleckian model is a short-run/medium-run model and not a long-run model (Auerbach and Skott, 1988; Duménil and Lévy, 1999; Park, 1997; Skott, 2010). They assert that in the long run, the divergence between the actual capacity utilization rate and the normal (desired) capacity utilization rate should vanish: all variables are fully adjusted; consequently, we have a return to classical economics.

In contrast, Lavoie (1996, 2010), Dutt (1997), and Cassetti (2006) introduce the long-run adjustment process of the normal capacity utilization rate in the Kaleckian model.[2] In such extended models, Kaleckian results are obtained even in the long run. For example, "the paradox of thrift" and "the paradox of cost" hold even in the long run. Here, the paradox of thrift means that an increase in the capitalists' savings rate lowers the rate of capital accumulation. The paradox of cost means that an increase in the real wage leads to an increase in the realized profit rate.

However, even these extended models miss an important point, that is, they do not explicitly consider capital accumulation, which should be considered in the long-run growth model. As will be explained later, considering capital accumulation is equivalent to considering the adjustment of the employment rate. The existing Kaleckian models do not satisfactorily investigate the employment rate. These models consider

---

1) For Kaleckian model framework, see Rowthorn (1981) and Lavoie (1992). For various regimes in the Kaleckian model, see Marglin and Bhaduri (1990), Bhaduri and Marglin (1990), and Blecker (2002).

2) See also Lavoie (1995, 2003) and Hein, Lavoie and van Treeck (2010, 2011).

the labor supply to be unlimited and the firms to employ as many workers as they desire at the given wages. However, it is reasonable to think that labor supply is constrained in the long run. In this case, the equalization of labor demand growth and labor supply growth is an accidental occurrence. Thus, if the labor supply growth steadily exceeds the labor demand growth, then the employment rate will be zero; however, this is unrealistic. Therefore, to determine the long-run employment rate, we need a model in which the economically meaningful employment rate is endogenously determined.

This chapter is not the first to explicitly consider the determination of the employment rate in the Kaleckian model. Lima (2004) and Sasaki (2010), for example, present Kaleckian models in which the employment rate is endogenously determined.

Stockhammer (2004) presents an augmented Kaleckian model that incorporates equations that determine employment and income distribution, and investigates the non-accelerating inflation rate of unemployment (NAIRU). However, our model differs considerably from Stockhammer's model in the determination of employment and income distribution. Stockhammer (2004) uses an employment determination equation such that a change in the unemployment rate is given by the difference between the growth rate of exogenous labor supply and the rate of capital accumulation, and an income distribution determination equation such that the profit share depends on the unemployment rate.

In contrast, we use an employment determination equation such that the growth rate of labor productivity depends positively on the employment rate, and an income distribution equation that results from the theory of conflicting-claims inflation. For the endogenization of labor productivity growth, we introduce into the Kaleckian model a specification relating the employment rate with the growth rate of labor productivity, as in Bhaduri (2006), Dutt (2006), and Flaschel and Skott (2006). We assume that the growth rate of labor productivity depends positively on the employment rate.

Furthermore, our model is different from Stockhammer's model in terms of the variables used in the investment function and in terms of whether technological progress is exogenous or endogenous. With these differences, we obtain different results. In Stockhammer's model, the capital accumulation rate (and accordingly, the capacity utilization rate) and the profit share are adjusted in the short run, while the unemployment rate is adjusted in the long run. However, employment (and accordingly, unemployment) necessarily changes with changes in the capacity utilization rate. Hence, it is reasonable to assume that these three variables—the capacity utilization rate, the profit share, and the employment rate—are adjusted at the same time. Therefore, we simultaneously analyze the adjustment of these three variables.

Dutt (1992) is also a rare case. He introduced the labor market into a Kaleckian model and investigated growth with business cycles. He simultaneously considered two situations: a situation where the capacity of firms is not fully utilized and a situation where the capacity of firms is fully utilized. Accordingly, his model comprises two equilibria: the excess-capacity equilibrium and the full-capacity equilibrium. The excess-capacity equilibrium is a saddle-point while the full capacity equilibrium is a locally stable focus. Hence, depending on the initial condition, the economy converges to the full-capacity equilibrium with oscillations and cyclical growth occurs along the transition process. Moreover, the business cycle disappears when the economy reaches the long-run equilibrium. However, in reality, we seldom observe a full-capacity situation even if we observe an economy for a very long period of time. In our model, in contrast, the capacity of firms is not fully utilized even in the long run.

This chapter presents a Kaleckian model that considers both the adjustment of the normal capacity utilization rate and the adjustment of the employment rate. In our analysis, we introduce Marglin and Bhaduri's (1990) investment function (hereafter, the MB-type investment function) and investigate which regime is realized in the long-run equilibrium. It is well known that in the short-run/medium-run analysis, the use of an MB-type investment function produces various regimes depending on the conditions. In the MB-type investment function, the profit share and the capacity utilization rate determine investment. However, existing long-run Kaleckian models use only the Kalecki-type investment function and do not use the MB-type investment function. Introducing the MB function into long-run analysis makes it possible to classify the long-run regime. In addition, for comparison, we also use the conventional Kalecki-type investment function, in which the profit rate and the capacity utilization rate determine investment. It is known that in the short-run/medium-run equilibrium with the Kalecki-type investment function, both a wage-led demand regime and a wage-led growth regime hold. However, the long-run equilibrium with the Kalecki-type investment function has not been discussed in detail.[3] To sum up, this chapter contributes to the long-run regime analysis.

Through an analysis of our model, in the long run, we show (1) whether the paradox of thrift is obtained or not, (2) which regime is obtained, and (3) the relationship between the employment rate and the bargaining power of workers/firms.

The remainder of the chapter is organized as follows. Section 2 conducts a medium-run analysis. In the medium run, the capacity utilization rate, the profit share, and the employment rate are adjusted and endogenously determined. Section 3 conducts a long-run analysis. In the long-run, the normal capacity utilization rate and the expected rate of growth are adjusted and endogenously determined. Moreover, this section investigates which regime is obtained in the long-run equilibrium. Section 4 concludes the chapter.

5.2   Medium-run equilibrium

Consider an economy with workers and capitalists. Suppose that the workers consume all their wages and the capitalists save a fraction s of their profit. Then, the ratio of

---

3) Cassetti (2006) uses the Kalecki-type investment function in the long-run analysis.

real savings S to the capital stock K, that is, $g_s = S/K$ leads to

$$g_s = sr, \quad 0 < s \leq 1, \tag{5.1}$$

where r denotes the profit rate.

Suppose that the firms operate with the following fixed coefficient production function:

$$Y = \min\{aL, (u/k)K\}, \tag{5.2}$$

where Y denotes the real output; L, employment; and $a = Y/L$, the level of labor productivity. The capacity utilization rate u is defined as $u = Y/Y^*$, where Y^* denotes the potential output. The coefficient $k = K/Y^*$ denotes the ratio of the capital stock to the potential output, which is assumed to be constant. This assumption implies that both K and Y^* grow at the same rate. Moreover, when the capacity utilization rate is constant, the growth rate of capital stock and that of the actual output will be the same. Accordingly, the actual output and the potential output grow at the same rate in the equilibrium where the capacity utilization rate is constant. To simplify the analysis, in what follows, we assume that $k = 1$. From this, we have $r = mu$, where m denotes the profit share.

Let us specify the firms' planned investment. As stated above, we introduce two kinds of investment function.

For the Kalecki-type investment function, we specify the ratio of the real investment I to the capital stock, $g_d = I/K$ as follows:

$$\text{Kalecki-type}: \ g_d = \gamma + \delta r + \varepsilon(u - u_n), \quad \gamma \in (0,1), \ \delta \in (0,1), \ \varepsilon \in (0,1), \ \gamma > \varepsilon u_n, \tag{5.3}$$

where γ denotes a constant term capturing the expected rate of growth, and u_n, the normal capacity utilization rate. Note that the investment function is increasing in both the profit rate and the gap between the actual capacity utilization rate and the normal capacity utilization rate. The specification that $u - u_n$ is an explanatory variable is adopted by Amadeo (1986) and Lavoie (2006). If the actual capacity utilization rate is equal to the normal capacity utilization rate ($u = u_n$), the firms expand plants at the rate of $g_d = \gamma + \delta r$. If, however, the actual capacity utilization rate is less than the normal capacity utilization rate ($u < u_n$), the firms consider themselves as facing excess capacity, and they decrease the capital accumulation rate to a level lower than in the case of $u = u_n$. If, however, the actual capacity utilization rate exceeds the normal capacity utilization rate, the firms increase the capital accumulation rate to a level higher than in the case of $u = u_n$. Finally, the constraint $\gamma > \varepsilon u_n$ means that $g_d > 0$ even if both u and r are zero.

For the MB-type investment function, we specify g_d as follows:

MB-type : $g_d = \gamma + \delta m + \varepsilon(u - u_n), \quad \gamma \in (0, 1), \; \delta \in (0, 1), \; \varepsilon \in (0, 1), \; \gamma > \varepsilon u_n.$
$$(5.4)$$

Marglin and Bhaduri (1990) state that it is not the profit rate but the profit share that should be an explanatory variable of the investment function. In this case, it is well known that we obtain different regimes in the equilibrium depending on which effect dominates, the effect of the profit share or the effect of the capacity utilization rate.

Now that we present the basic framework of the model, we turn to the derivation of the dynamic equations for the medium-run analysis.

To begin with, we specify the adjustment of the capacity utilization rate. In the goods market, excess demand leads to a rise in the capacity utilization rate while excess supply leads to a decline in the capacity utilization rate.

$$\dot{u} = \alpha(g_d - g_s), \quad \alpha > 0, \qquad (5.5)$$

where α denotes the speed of adjustment of the goods market. The typical Kaleckian model assumes that quantity adjustment in the goods market is very rapid, that is, $g_d = g_s$ is instantaneously attained. However, in reality, quantity adjustment takes time and hence, we assume the slow adjustment of the goods market, which is reflected in equation (5.5).

From the definition of the profit share, we have $m = 1 - (wL/pY)$, where w denotes the money wage, and p, the price of goods. Differentiating the profit share with respect to time, we obtain the following relationship

$$\frac{\dot{m}}{1 - m} = \frac{\dot{p}}{p} - \frac{\dot{w}}{w} + \frac{\dot{a}}{a}. \qquad (5.6)$$

To know the dynamics of the profit share, we must specify the dynamics of p, w, and a of equation (5.6).

We specify the dynamics of the money wage and price by using the theory of conflicting-claims inflation.[4] First, suppose that the growth rate of the money wage that the workers manage to negotiate depends on the discrepancy between their target profit share and the actual profit share. Second, suppose that the firms set their price to close the gap between their target profit share and the actual profit share.[5] From

---

4) The theory of conflicting-claims inflation was originally developed by Rowthorn (1977). For Kaleckian models with conflicting-claims inflation, see also Dutt (1987), Lavoie (1992), and Cassetti (2002, 2003, 2006).

5) Some might worry about whether the mark-up pricing rule $p = (1 + \mu)(w/a)$, one of the main characteristics of the Kaleckian model, is lost when introducing equation (5.8). Here, $\mu > 0$ denotes the mark-up rate. With regard to this problem, we can use the dynamic mark-up pricing rule, that is, $\dot{p} = \rho[(1 + \mu)(w/a) - p]$, where $\rho > 0$ denotes the speed of adjustment of the price. In this case, we obtain $\dot{p}/p = \rho(1 + \mu)[(\mu/(1 + \mu)) - m]$. This equation, indeed, has the same meaning as equation (5.8), because we have the following relations: $\theta = \rho(1 + \mu)$ and $m_f = \mu/(1 + \mu)$. Therefore, essentially, equation (5.8) captures the dynamic mark-up pricing rule.

these considerations, the dynamics of the money wage and price can be described, respectively, as follows:

$$\frac{\dot{w}}{w} = (1 - \theta)(m - m_w), \quad m_w \in (0, 1), \tag{5.7}$$

$$\frac{\dot{p}}{p} = \theta(m_f - m), \quad \theta \in (0, 1), \ m_f \in (0, 1), \tag{5.8}$$

where θ is a positive parameter, which captures the bargaining power of the firms, and $1 - \theta$ is the bargaining power of the workers. The parameter m_w denotes the target profit share set by the workers, and m_f, the target profit share set by the firms.[6] In the following analysis, we assume that $m_f > m_w$. The firms attempt to set their targets as high as possible whereas the workers attempt to set their targets as low as possible. Therefore, the assumption that $m_f > m_w$ is reasonable.

We now turn to the specification of endogenous technological change. As stated above, we assume that the growth rate of labor productivity g_a depends positively on the employment rate e.

$$g_a = \lambda e^\beta, \quad \lambda > 0, \ \beta > 0, \tag{5.9}$$

where $g_a = \dot{a}/a$. The employment rate is defined as $e = L/N$, where N denotes the exogenous labor supply. The coefficient λ denotes a positive constant, and β, the elasticity of the growth rate of labor productivity with respect to the employment rate. A rise in the employment rate has an upward pressure on wages. The firms facing this upward pressure tend to adopt labor-saving techniques.[7] We use the above specification to explicitly solve for the employment rate. Note, however, that our results do not depend on this specification as long as g_a is an increasing function of e.[8]

We explain the meaning of this specification in detail.[9] Bhaduri (2006) states that this formulation captures the view that technological change is driven by inter-class conflict over income distribution between workers and capitalists. Dutt (2006) says that as the labor market tightens and labor shortage becomes clearer, the bargaining power of workers increases, which exerts an upward pressure on wages, leading

---

6) In our model, m_w and m_f are given exogenously. Naturally, we can endogenize them. For example, it is possible that m_w is a decreasing function of g_a whereas m_f is an increasing function of g_a. The former specification captures the effect wherein the labor unions attempt to reflect the fruit of an increase in labor productivity in higher wages, whereas the latter specification captures the effect wherein the firms attempt to reflect the fruit of an increase in labor productivity in higher profit. As will be shown by equation (5.9), g_a is an increasing function of e, and hence, m_w is a decreasing function of e while m_f is an increasing function of e. With these modifications, the positive effect of $m'_f(e) > 0$ has an effect of stabilizing the medium-run equilibrium while the negative effect of $m'_w(e) < 0$ has a destabilizing effect on the medium-run equilibrium.

7) For a Kaleckian model that considers such an effect, see also Sasaki (2010).

8) Indeed, the stabilization analysis and the comparative static analysis that will be shown later are conducted with the general form of $g_a = g_a(e)$.

9) This specification apparently relates to Verdoorn's law as well as to Okun's law. In this chapter, however, we emphasize the route that a rise in the employment rate makes firms adopt labor-saving technology.

capitalists to adopt labor-saving technical changes. The view that increases in wages induce labor-saving technical progress is consistent with an empirical study by Marquetti (2004), who investigates the co-integration between real wages and labor productivity and conducts Granger non-causality tests by using US data. He shows that Granger non-causality tests support unidirectional causation from real wages to labor productivity.

The specification given by equation (5.9) has the following merits. In general, the natural rate of growth is defined as a sum of the growth rates of labor productivity and labor supply. Although the growth rate of labor supply in our model is exogenously given, the growth rate of labor productivity is endogenously determined. Under our specification, therefore, the natural rate of growth increases when business is good (i.e., when the employment rate is high) and it decreases when business is bad (i.e., when the employment rate is low). The assumption that the natural rate of growth is endogenously determined and is procyclical is consistent with the empirical studies of León-Ledesma and Thirlwall (2002), Libânio (2009), Vogel (2009), and León-Ledesma and Lanzafame (2010).[10]

Let us derive an equation of motion for the employment rate. From equation (5.2), the employment rate is given by $e = uK/(aN)$, from which the rate of change in e leads to

$$\frac{\dot{e}}{e} = \frac{\dot{u}}{u} + g_d - g_a - n,\qquad(5.10)$$

where n denotes the growth rate of N and is given exogenously.

5.2.1 Medium-run with Kalecki-type investment function

In conventional Kaleckian models, the variables u and m are adjusted in the short or medium run. In our medium-run model, in contrast, the three variables u, m, and e are adjusted. Substituting equations (5.1), (5.3), (5.7), (5.8), and (5.9) in equations (5.5), (5.6), and (5.10), we obtain the following dynamic system:[11]

$$\dot{u} = \alpha[\gamma + \delta mu + \varepsilon(u - u_n) - smu],\qquad(5.11)$$

10) These studies empirically investigate whether the natural growth rate is exogenous or endogenous to demand and whether it is input growth that causes output growth or vice versa. This question lies at the heart of the debate between neoclassical growth economists and economists in the Keynesian/post-Keynesian tradition.

11) In this chapter, we separate the adjustment of the capacity utilization rate and that of the employment rate. Since we have $e = uK/(aN)$, the employment rate moves proportionately with the capacity utilization rate as long as capital stock, labor productivity, and labor supply are all constant. However, when these three variables change, the employment rate does not move proportionately with the capacity utilization rate, and accordingly, we need to separate these two adjustments. Therefore, for our purpose, we need to analyze the three dimensional dynamics. Moreover, some might think that including the employment rate and the profit share dynamics is a little unusual in Kaleckian models. However, since our model considers quantity adjustment in the goods market and the mark-up pricing rules of firms—these are very Kaleckian—, our model is a Kaleckian model. For a Keynesian model that considers the capacity utilization rate, the employment rate, and profit share dynamics, see also Chiarella and Flaschel (1998).

$$\dot{m} = -(1 - m)[m - \Gamma - g_a(e)], \quad \text{where } \Gamma \equiv \theta m_f + (1 - \theta)m_w, \tag{5.12}$$

$$\dot{e} = e \left\{ \frac{\alpha[\gamma + \delta mu + \varepsilon(u - u_n) - smu]}{u} + \gamma + \delta mu + \varepsilon(u - u_n) - g_a(e) - n \right\}. \tag{5.13}$$

Here, we assume that $\Gamma > n$. This assumption means that the weighted average of the two groups' target profit shares is larger than the growth rate of exogenous labor supply. Given that the size of n is about 10 percent at most, this assumption is plausible. Because $\Gamma = \theta m_f + (1 - \theta)m_w$, an increase in m_f or m_w corresponds to an increase in Γ. Moreover, because $m_f > m_w$, an increase in θ corresponds to an increase in Γ. Furthermore, we assume that $s > \delta$. This means that the capitalists' savings rate is larger than the sensitivity of investment with respect to the profit rate, which is called the Keynesian stability condition.

The medium-run equilibrium is a situation wherein $\dot{u} = \dot{m} = \dot{e} = 0$; using this, we obtain the following quadratic equation for the profit share:

$$(s - \delta)m^2 - \Theta m + \varepsilon(\Gamma - n) = 0, \quad \text{where } \Theta \equiv s(\gamma - \varepsilon u_n) + (s - \delta)(\Gamma - n) + \varepsilon > 0. \tag{5.14}$$

From equation (5.14), we obtain two real and distinct roots. However, the larger root corresponds to the medium-run equilibrium value.[12]

$$m^* = \frac{\Theta + \sqrt{\Theta^2 - 4\varepsilon(s - \delta)(\Gamma - n)}}{2(s - \delta)}. \tag{5.15}$$

Hereafter, the medium-run equilibrium values are denoted with "$*$." Using equation (5.15), we obtain the rates of capacity utilization and employment in the medium-run equilibrium:

$$u^* = \frac{\gamma - \varepsilon u_n}{(s - \delta)m^* - \varepsilon}, \tag{5.16}$$

$$e^* = \left(\frac{m^* - \Gamma}{\lambda} \right)^{\frac{1}{\beta}}. \tag{5.17}$$

For the capacity utilization rate to be positive, we need $(s - \delta)m^* - \varepsilon > 0$, which can be rewritten as $m^* > \varepsilon/(s - \delta)$. In addition, we assume that m^*, u^*, and e^* are larger than zero and less than unity. Note that as long as g_a is positive, the profit share in the medium-run equilibrium satisfies $m^* > \Gamma$, which leads to $e^* > 0$ from equation (5.17).

To analyze the local stability of the medium-run equilibrium, we linearize equations (5.11), (5.12), and (5.13) around the equilibrium, and investigate the corresponding Jacobian matrix. From this procedure, we obtain the following proposition:

Proposition 5.1. *Suppose that the coefficients of the investment function with respect to the profit rate and the capacity utilization rate are not extremely large. Then, the*

---

12) See Appendix 5.A.

medium-run equilibrium is locally stable.

Proof. See Appendix 5.C. ∎

In the following analysis, we assume that the coefficients of the investment function are not extremely large.

5.2.2 Medium-run analysis with MB-type investment function

Following the same procedure as in the case with the Kalecki-type investment function, we obtain the following dynamic system:

$$\dot{u} = \alpha[\gamma + \delta m + \varepsilon(u - u_n) - smu], \tag{5.18}$$

$$\dot{m} = -(1 - m)[m - \Gamma - g_a(e)], \quad \text{where } \Gamma \equiv \theta m_f + (1 - \theta)m_w, \tag{5.19}$$

$$\dot{e} = e\left\{ \frac{\alpha[\gamma + \delta m + \varepsilon(u - u_n) - smu]}{u} + \gamma + \delta m + \varepsilon(u - u_n) - g_a(e) - n \right\}. \tag{5.20}$$

The medium-run equilibrium is a situation wherein $\dot{u} = \dot{m} = \dot{e} = 0$; using this, we obtain the following quadratic equation for the profit share:

$$s(1 - \delta)m^2 - \Theta m + \varepsilon(\Gamma - n) = 0, \quad \text{where } \Theta \equiv s(\gamma - \varepsilon u_n) + s(\Gamma - n) + \varepsilon > 0. \tag{5.21}$$

From equation (5.21), we obtain two real and distinct roots. However, the larger root corresponds to the medium-run equilibrium value.[13]

$$m^* = \frac{\Theta + \sqrt{\Theta^2 - 4s\varepsilon(1 - \delta)(\Gamma - n)}}{2s(1 - \delta)}. \tag{5.22}$$

Using equation (5.22), we obtain the rates of capacity utilization and employment in the medium-run equilibrium:

$$u^* = \frac{\delta m^* + (\gamma - \varepsilon u_n)}{sm^* - \varepsilon}, \tag{5.23}$$

$$e^* = \left(\frac{m^* - \Gamma}{\lambda} \right)^{\frac{1}{\beta}}. \tag{5.24}$$

For the capacity utilization rate to be positive, we need $sm^* - \varepsilon > 0$, which can be rewritten as $m^* > \varepsilon/s$. In addition, we assume that m^*, u^*, and e^* are larger than zero and less than unity.

By examining the system of differential equations (5.18), (5.19), and (5.20), we obtain the following proposition with regard to the stability of the medium-run equilibrium.

---

13) See Appendix 5.B.

Proposition 5.2. *Suppose that the coefficient of the investment function with respect to the capacity utilization rate is not extremely large. Then, the medium-run equilibrium is locally stable.*

Proof. See Appendix 5.D.   ■

In the following analysis, we assume that the coefficient of the investment function is not extremely large.

5.2.3   Medium-run comparative statics analysis

Kalecki-type investment function

Table 5.1 summarizes the results of the comparative statics analysis in the medium-run equilibrium with the Kalecki investment function.[14] These results are the same as those obtained from the conventional Kaleckian model except for the results of the employment rate that is not analyzed in the conventional models. For example, a rise in the capitalists' savings rate lowers the rate of capital accumulation, which is also known as the paradox of thrift. In our model, the profit share is an endogenous variable, and thus, we cannot directly relate a rise in m to the changes in u and g. Accordingly, we relate a rise in m_f (m_w) to the changes in u and g. A rise in m_f (m_w) increases the profit share and lowers the rate of utilization and the rate of capital accumulation. In this sense, the medium-run equilibrium corresponds to both a wage-led demand regime and a wage-led growth regime.

Table 5.1: Medium-run comparative statics analysis—Kalecki-type investment function

	s	n	m_f, m_w, θ
u^*	−	+	−
m^*	−	−	+
e^*	−	−	−
g^*	−	+	−

We now look at the effect of a rise in θ on the employment rate. In the Kalecki-type investment function, an increase in the bargaining power of the firms decreases the employment rate in the medium-run equilibrium. In contrast, an increase in the bargaining power of the workers decreases the rate of unemployment. This result contrasts sharply with the neoclassical assertion that lowering the bargaining power of the labor union decreases the rate of unemployment.

---

14) We omit the partial derivatives because of spatial limitations.

MB-type investment function

Table 5.2 summarizes the results of the comparative statics analysis in the medium-run equilibrium with the MB-type investment function.[15] The columns that contain two opposing signs indicate that two results are obtained depending on the conditions.

Table 5.2: Medium-run comparative statics analysis—MB-type investment function

	s	n	m_f, m_w, θ
u^*	$-$	$+$	$-$
m^*	$-$	$-$	$+$
e^*	$-$	$-$	$-/+$
g^*	$-$	$+/-$	$-/+$

Using the MB-type investment function, we obtain results that are different from the results in the Kalecki-type investment function.

As in the case with the Kalecki-type investment function, we define the regime using m_f and m_w. First, a rise in m_f (m_w) decreases the capacity utilization rate, which means that the medium-run equilibrium is a wage-led demand regime.[16] Second, a rise in m_f (m_w) either decreases (a wage-led growth regime) or increases (a profit-led growth regime) the rate of capital accumulation.

When the medium-run equilibrium is a profit-led growth regime, a rise in the bargaining power of the firms increases the employment rate. In contrast, when the medium-run equilibrium is a wage-led growth, a rise in the bargaining power of the firms decreases the employment rate. Therefore, the relationship between the bargaining power and the employment rate differs between the two regimes.[17]

Stockhammer (2004) also investigates the relationship between bargaining power and unemployment. He concludes that in a profit-led growth regime, a decrease in the bargaining power of workers leads to higher employment and lower unemployment. This result is consistent with ours. However, in a wage-led growth regime of Stockhammer's model, the long-run equilibrium is necessarily unstable, and hence, we cannot investigate the relationship between bargaining power and unemployment. In our model, in contrast, the-long run equilibrium of a wage-led growth regime can be stable. In this case, we reach the opposite conclusion that an increase in the bargaining power of workers leads to higher employment and lower unemployment. This result is consistent with the empirical result of Storm and Naastepad (2007). Using data for

---

15) We omit the partial derivatives because of spatial limitations.
16) The reason why a profit-led demand regime is not obtained in the MB case is that we assume that $\gamma - \varepsilon u_n > 0$. If we assume that $\gamma - \varepsilon u_n < 0$, we can obtain a profit-led demand regime. Nevertheless, we ignore the case where $\gamma - \varepsilon u_n < 0$ because with this assumption, the term Θ in equations (5.21) and (5.22) can be negative, which complicates our analysis too much. Therefore, we restrict ourselves to the case where $\gamma - \varepsilon u_n > 0$.
17) Similar results are also obtained in Sasaki (2010).

20 OECD countries during the period 1984–1997, they show that an increase in the bargaining power of firms due to labor market deregulation raises the unemployment rate in contrast to the view of the mainstream NAIRU model.[18]

5.3   Long-run equilibrium

In the long run, the normal capacity utilization rate and the expected rate of growth are adjusted. We assume that in the long run, the medium-run equilibrium is always attained: the medium-run equilibrium values u^*, m^*, and e^* correspond to the actual values in the long run. Following Lavoie (1996, 2010), Dutt (1997), and Cassetti (2006), we describe the long-run dynamics.[19]

First, we assume that the normal capacity utilization rate is adjusted according to the gap between the actual capacity utilization rate and the normal capacity utilization rate.[20]

$$\dot{u}_n = \phi(u^* - u_n), \quad \phi > 0, \tag{5.25}$$

where ϕ denotes the speed of adjustment. Note that we have $u^* = u^*(u_n, \gamma)$ from the medium-run analysis.

Second, we assume that the expected rate of growth is adjusted according to the gap between the actual growth rate and the expected rate of growth:

$$\dot{\gamma} = \eta(g^* - g_d^*), \quad \eta > 0, \tag{5.26}$$

where η denotes the speed of adjustment. Note that when $u = u_n$, we have $g_d^* = \gamma + \delta r^*$ for the Kalecki-type investment function and $g_d^* = \gamma + \delta m^*$ for the MB-type investment function. Using this, for both the Kalecki-type and the MB-type investment functions, equation (5.26) can be rewritten as follows:

$$\dot{\gamma} = \eta\varepsilon(u^* - u_n). \tag{5.27}$$

The empirical validity of simultaneous adjustments of u_n and γ is discussed by Lavoie et al. (2004). They empirically test four kinds of investment functions—the French Marxist equation, the naive Kaleckian equation, the American Marxist equation, and the hysteresis Kaleckian equation—by using data from the Canadian manufacturing sector and the total industrial sector during the period 1960–2000. Their

---

18) Similar empirical results are obtained in Storm and Naastepad (2008).

19) According to Cassetti (2006), in the long run, in addition to the normal capacity utilization rate and the expected rate of growth, the normal profit rate and the drop-out ratio of capital equipment are also adjusted: the four variables are adjusted in the long run. In the present chapter, we consider only the adjustments of the normal capacity utilization rate and the expected growth rate because we think that these two variables are essential in the long run.

20) For debates with regard to the long-run adjustment of the normal capacity utilization rate, see also Hein, Lavoie, and van Treeck (2010, 2011), Skott (2010b), and Skott and Zipperer (2010).

results show that the hysteresis Kaleckian equation performs better than the other three specifications. In contrast, Skott (2010a) criticizes Lavoie et al. (2004), claiming that their estimated empirical hysteresis Kaleckian equation bears no relation to the theoretical model. In either case, because we cannot directly observe the normal capacity utilization rate, we need to devise methods for an empirical study.[21] In addition, because Lavoie et al. (2004) and Skott (2010a) use only Canadian data, we also need to investigate other countries to ascertain the validity of the hysteresis Kaleckian investment function

5.3.1 Kalecki-type investment function

The system of differential equations composed of equations (5.25) and (5.27) takes a special form called a zero-root system.[22] In the zero-root system, one eigenvalue of the Jacobian matrix is zero.[23]

The long-run equilibrium is a situation wherein $\dot{u}_n = \dot{\gamma} = 0$. From equations (5.25) and (5.27), we obtain $u^*(u_n, \gamma) = u_n$, which yields the following relationship between u_n and γ:[24]

$$\gamma = \frac{(s - \delta)(\Gamma - n)u_n}{1 - su_n}.$$

(5.28)

On the u_n-γ plane, this is an upward-sloping curve through the origin with $u_n = 1/s$ being an asymptote. The points on this curve correspond to the long-run equilibria. However, not all the points on this curve are long-run equilibria and some constraints are imposed.[25]

From the two adjustment equations (5.25) and (5.27), we obtain the relationship $\dot{\gamma} = (\eta\varepsilon/\phi)\dot{u}_n$, from which we have the constant ratio $\gamma = (\eta\varepsilon/\phi)u_n$ along the transitional process. Hence, with initial conditions $\gamma(0)$ and $u_n(0)$, the transitional process is given by the following upward-sloping straight line:

$$\gamma(t) = \frac{\eta\varepsilon}{\phi} u_n(t) + \gamma(0) - \frac{\eta\varepsilon}{\phi} u_n(0).$$

(5.29)

---

21) Lavoie et al. (2004) apply the Hodrick-Prescott filter to the actual series of capacity utilization to obtain the series of normal rates of capacity utilization. Skott (2010a) uses the Koyck transformation to delete the normal capacity utilization rate from the estimated equation; accordingly, he dispenses with non-observable variables.

22) For solutions to the zero-root system, see Giavazzi and Wyplosz (1985).

23) The other eigenvalue is the trace of the Jacobian matrix.

24) Using $u^*(u_n, \gamma) = u_n$ and (5.16), we obtain

$$\frac{\gamma - \varepsilon u_n}{(s - \delta)m^*(u_n, \gamma) - \varepsilon} = u_n.$$

Because $m^{**} = [s\gamma + (s - \delta)(\Gamma - n)]/(s - \delta)$ in the long-run equilibrium, by replacing $m^*(u_n, \gamma)$ with $m^{**} = [s\gamma + (s - \delta)(\Gamma - n)]/(s - \delta)$ and rearranging the resultant expression, we obtain (5.28).

25) Strictly speaking, we need additional conditions: u^*, m^*, and e^* should be more than zero and less than unity in the medium run, u_n should be more than zero and less than unity in the long run, etc. In the following analysis, we omit those conditions for the sake of simplicity.

The intersection of equations (5.28) and (5.29) yields the long-run equilibrium. It follows from this that the long-run equilibrium depends on the initial conditions $\gamma(0)$ and $u_n(0)$: different initial conditions produce different long-run equilibria. Therefore, in this sense, the long-run equilibrium shows path-dependency.

Figure 5.1 shows the long-run phase diagram. First, we consider an economy that starts from point A. In this case, the long-run equilibrium is given by point E_1. Next, we consider an economy that starts from point B. In this case, the long-run equilibrium is given by point E_2.

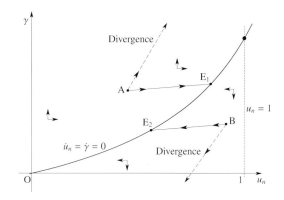

Figure 5.1: Long-run phase diagram

When γ^{**} is determined, the other long-run equilibrium values are determined as follows:

$$g^{**} = \frac{s\gamma^{**}}{s - \delta}, \tag{5.30}$$

$$g_a^{**} = \frac{s\gamma^{**} - n(s - \delta)}{s - \delta}, \tag{5.31}$$

$$m^{**} = \frac{s\gamma^{**} + (s - \delta)(\Gamma - n)}{s - \delta}, \tag{5.32}$$

$$u^{**} = \frac{\gamma^{**}}{s\gamma^{**} + (s - \delta)(\Gamma - n)}, \tag{5.33}$$

$$e^{**} = \left[\frac{s\gamma^{**} - n(s - \delta)}{\lambda(s - \delta)} \right]^{\frac{1}{\beta}}. \tag{5.34}$$

The long-run equilibrium values are denoted with "$**$." Note that in addition to $u_n(0)$ and $\gamma(0)$, γ^{**} depends on the initial conditions.

The long-run equilibrium is not always stable. If the coefficient $\eta\varepsilon/\phi$, the slope of the path, is extremely large, then the economy cannot reach the long-run equilibrium. In addition, even if the size of $\eta\varepsilon/\phi$ is modest, it is possible that the economy does not reach the long-run equilibrium depending on the initial condition. Let us return to Figure 5.1. The solution path denoted by the broken line starting from point A crosses the locus $\dot{u}_n = \dot{\gamma} = 0$ at a point where u_n exceeds unity, and consequently, the path is divergent. Moreover, the solution path denoted by the broken line starting from point B does not cross the locus $\dot{u}_n = \dot{\gamma} = 0$. Therefore, both the size of adjustment and the initial condition are crucial for stable convergence to the long-run equilibrium.

We conduct a comparative statics analysis in the long-run equilibrium by assuming that the equilibrium is stable. Here, we investigate u_n and γ. First, when s or Γ increases, the locus $\dot{u}_n = \dot{\gamma} = 0$ rotates counterclockwise around the origin. Because the solution path is unaffected by the change in s or Γ, the intersection of the solution path and the locus move toward the lower left. Therefore, both u_n^{**} and γ^{**} decrease. Second, when n increases, the locus rotates clockwise. Because the solution path is unaffected by the change in n, both u_n^{**} and γ^{**} increase. These results are summarized in table 5.3.

Table 5.3: Long-run comparative statics analysis—Kalecki-type investment function

	s	n	m_f, m_w, θ
γ^{**}	−	+	−
u^{**}	−	+	−

We investigate the regime obtained in the long-run equilibrium. As in the medium-run equilibrium, we define the regime using m_f and m_w. Depending on whether or not the expected growth rate γ is adjusted, we obtain different results.[26]

Differentiating u^{**} and g^{**} with respect to Γ, we obtain

$$\frac{du^{**}}{d\Gamma} = \frac{(s-\delta)(\Gamma-n)\frac{d\gamma^{**}}{d\Gamma} - \gamma(s-\delta)}{[s\gamma + (s-\delta)(\Gamma-n)]^2} < 0, \tag{5.35}$$

$$\frac{dg^{**}}{d\Gamma} = \frac{s}{s-\delta}\frac{d\gamma^{**}}{d\Gamma} \leq 0. \tag{5.36}$$

First, when the expected rate of growth is not adjusted, we have $d\gamma^{**}/d\Gamma = 0$, and consequently, a rise in m_f decreases the capacity utilization rate but does not affect the rate of capital accumulation. Therefore, the long-run equilibrium is a wage-led demand regime and not a wage-led growth regime or a profit-led growth regime. These results are explained as follows. When γ is not adjusted, we can regard γ as an exogenous variable. g^{**} depends on γ but γ does not depend on m_f, which implies that g^{**} does not depend on m_f. Therefore, the long-run equilibrium is neither a wage-led

---

26) When γ is fixed and only u_n is adjusted in our model, the resultant long-run equilibrium is always stable. However, when u_n is fixed and only γ is adjusted, the resultant long-run equilibrium is necessarily unstable. Therefore, we do not examine this latter case.

growth regime nor a profit-led growth regime. However, u^{**} depends on m_f through Γ. Therefore, even if γ is an exogenous variable, a rise in m_f decreases u^{**}.

Second, when the expected rate of growth is adjusted, we have $d\gamma^{**}/d\Gamma < 0$, and consequently, a rise in m_f decreases both the capacity utilization rate and the capital accumulation rate in the long-run equilibrium. Therefore, the long-run equilibrium is both a wage-led demand regime and a wage-led growth regime. In other words, if the expected rate of growth is adjusted, even in the long run, we obtain properties that are typical of the Kaleckian model. The reasoning is explained as follows. Both g^{**} and u^{**} depend on γ^{**}. When the expected rate of growth is adjusted, γ becomes an endogenous variable, and hence, γ^{**} is decreasing in m_f. Therefore, a rise in m_f leads to a decrease in γ^{**}, which leads to a decrease in both u^{**} and g^{**}.

We now focus on the effect of a rise in the capitalists' savings rate on the capacity utilization rate and the capital accumulation rate in the long-run equilibrium. Differentiating u^{**} and g^{**} with respect to s, we obtain the following equations:

$$\frac{du^{**}}{ds} = \frac{(s-\delta)(\Gamma - n)\frac{d\gamma^{**}}{ds} - \gamma[\gamma + (\Gamma - n)]}{[s\gamma + (s-\delta)(\Gamma - n)]^2} < 0, \tag{5.37}$$

$$\frac{dg^{**}}{ds} = \frac{s}{s-\delta}\frac{d\gamma^{**}}{ds} - \frac{\delta\gamma^{**}}{(s-\delta)^2} < 0. \tag{5.38}$$

While u^{**} and g^{**} depend directly on s, these values depend indirectly on s through γ^{**}. From this, we can see that both u^{**} and g^{**} are affected by a change in the savings rate irrespective of whether the expected rate of growth is adjusted or not. From equations (5.37) and (5.38), we find that a rise in s decreases both u^{**} and g^{**}. That is, a rise in the capitalists' savings rate lowers both the capacity utilization rate and the capital accumulation rate in the long-run equilibrium.[27] Therefore, even in the long run, the paradox of thrift still holds, which is a characteristic of the Kaleckian growth model.

In turn, we investigate the long-run relationship between the employment rate and bargaining power. Since, in the long-run equilibrium, the relation $g_a^{**} = g^{**} - n$ holds and g_a is increasing in e, the effect of Γ (i.e., the effect of θ) on e^{**} is the same as the effect of Γ on g^{**}. First, when the expected rate of growth is not adjusted, the bargaining power of the firms is unrelated to the employment rate because θ does not appear in equation (5.34). Second, when the expected rate of growth is adjusted, a rise in the bargaining power of the firms lowers the employment rate in the long-run equilibrium, which is the same result as that in the medium-run equilibrium.

---

27) We must pay attention to the case where the expected rate of growth is not adjusted. Note that in the present chapter, both the profit rate and the capacity utilization rate are explanatory variables of the investment function. In contrast, if the investment function includes only the capacity utilization rate as the explanatory variable, that is, if $\delta = 0$, we have $g^{**} = \gamma^{**}$. If the expected rate of growth is not adjusted, that is, if γ is fixed, then g^{**} is independent of s, and consequently, the paradox of thrift is not obtained. Therefore, the results in the present chapter depend on the specification of the investment function. The case where $\delta = 0$ is analyzed in detail by Sasaki (2011).

5.3.2 MB-type investment function

In the long-run equilibrium, both u_n and γ satisfy the following relationship:[28]

$$\gamma = \frac{(\Gamma - n)(su_n - \delta)}{1 - su_n}. \tag{5.39}$$

As in the Kalecki-type investment function, this is an upward-sloping curve.

The long-run solution path satisfies the following relationship:

$$\gamma(t) = \frac{\eta\varepsilon}{\phi} u_n(t) + \gamma(0) - \frac{\eta\varepsilon}{\phi} u_n(0). \tag{5.40}$$

This is identical to the solution path in the Kalecki-type investment function. The intersection of (5.39) and (5.40) determines the long-run equilibrium.

When γ^{**} is determined, the other long-run equilibrium values are determined as follows:

$$g^{**} = \frac{\gamma^{**} + \delta(\Gamma - n)}{1 - \delta}, \tag{5.41}$$

$$g_a^{**} = \frac{\gamma^{**} - n + \delta\Gamma}{1 - \delta}, \tag{5.42}$$

$$m^{**} = \frac{\gamma^{**} + \Gamma - n}{1 - \delta}, \tag{5.43}$$

$$u^{**} = \frac{\gamma^{**} + \delta(\Gamma - n)}{s[\gamma^{**} + (\Gamma - n)]}, \tag{5.44}$$

$$e^{**} = \left[\frac{\gamma^{**} - n + \delta\Gamma}{\lambda(1 - \delta)}\right]^{\frac{1}{\beta}}. \tag{5.45}$$

The long-run phase diagram is almost the same as that of the Kalecki-type investment function, and thus we omit it. Therefore, the long-run equilibrium is stable in some cases and unstable in others. Table 5.4 shows the results of the long-run comparative statics analysis given the stability of the long-run equilibrium. The reasons why we obtain such results are the same as those in the Kalecki-type investment function case. A rise in s or Γ rotates the locus of $\dot{u}_n = \dot{\gamma} = 0$ counterclockwise, and a rise in n rotates the locus clockwise. In either case, the solution path does not shift. Therefore, we obtain the results shown in Table 5.4.

Let us investigate the long-run equilibrium regime. Differentiating u^{**} and g^{**} with respect to Γ, we obtain

$$\frac{du^{**}}{d\Gamma} = \frac{s(1 - \delta)(1 - n)\frac{d\gamma^{**}}{d\Gamma} - s\gamma(1 - \delta)}{[s\gamma + s(\Gamma - n)]^2} < 0, \tag{5.46}$$

$$\frac{dg^{**}}{d\Gamma} = \frac{1}{1 - \delta}\left(\frac{d\gamma^{**}}{d\Gamma} + \delta\right). \tag{5.47}$$

---

28) Equation (5.39) can be obtained by the procedure detailed in footnote 24).

Table 5.4: Long-run comparative statics analysis—MB-type investment function

	s	n	m_f, m_w, θ
γ^{**}	−	+	−
u^{**}	−	+	−

First, we consider the case where the expected rate of growth is not adjusted. Since γ is fixed and constant in this case, we obtain $d\gamma^{**}/d\Gamma = 0$. From this, we get that a rise in m_f decreases u^{**} but increases g^{**}. Therefore, the long-run equilibrium is the wage-led demand regime and the profit-led growth regime. Recall that in the medium-run equilibrium of the MB-type investment function, we obtain either the wage-led growth regime or the profit-led growth regime depending on the conditions. In contrast, we obtain only profit-led growth in the long-run equilibrium when the expected rate of growth is not adjusted.

Next, we consider the case where the expected rate of growth is adjusted. In this case, we obtain $d\gamma^{**}/d\Gamma < 0$. However, the sign of equation (5.47) is undetermined: the sign depends on the size of δ of the investment function (5.4). If δ is smaller than the absolute value of $d\gamma^{**}/d\Gamma$, the long-run equilibrium is the wage-led growth regime. If, however, δ is larger than the absolute value of $d\gamma^{**}/d\Gamma$, then the long-run equilibrium is the profit-led growth regime. Note that when δ is small (large), the medium-run equilibrium tends to be the wage-led (profit-led) growth regime. This suggests that when the medium-run equilibrium is the wage-led (profit-led) growth regime, the long-run equilibrium is also the wage-led (profit-led) growth regime.[29]

We now focus on the effect of a rise in the capitalists' savings rate on the capacity utilization rate and the capital accumulation rate in the long-run equilibrium. Differentiating u^{**} and g^{**} with respect to s, we obtain the following equations:

$$\frac{du^{**}}{ds} = \frac{s(1-\delta)(\Gamma-n)\frac{d\gamma^{**}}{ds} - [\gamma + \delta(\Gamma-n)][\gamma + (\Gamma-n)]}{[s\gamma + s(\Gamma-n)]^2} < 0, \qquad (5.48)$$

$$\frac{dg^{**}}{ds} = \frac{1}{1-\delta}\frac{d\gamma^{**}}{ds} \leq 0. \qquad (5.49)$$

First, when γ is not adjusted, a rise in the savings rate lowers the capacity utilization rate. However, the capital accumulation rate in the long-run equilibrium is independent of s when $d\gamma^{**}/ds = 0$, and consequently, the paradox of thrift does not hold. Second, when γ is adjusted and accordingly, $d\gamma^{**}/ds < 0$, a rise in the savings rate increases both the capacity utilization rate and the rate of capital accumulation. Therefore, the paradox of thrift holds. In the Kalecki-type investment function case, we obtain the paradox of thrift irrespective of whether or not the expected rate of

---

29) We can show that such a relationship actually holds using numerical examples. For this, see Appendix 5.E.

growth is adjusted. However, in the MB-type investment function case, we obtain the paradox of thrift only when the expected rate of growth is adjusted.

We consider the long-run relationship between the employment rate and bargaining power. From the structure of the model, the effect of a rise in m_f on the employment rate is identical to the effect of a rise in θ on the employment rate. As a result, when the long-run equilibrium is the wage-led (profit-led) growth regime, a rise in the bargaining power of the firms decreases (increases) the employment rate. This result is the same as that obtained in the medium-run equilibrium.

5.3.3 Summary

Finally, we summarize the results obtained in the medium-run and long-run equilibria.

Table 5.5: Classification of regimes in the medium-run and long-run equilibria

	Kalecki (medium-run)	MB (medium-run)	Kalecki (long-run) γ: fixed; adjusted	MB (long-run) γ: fixed; adjusted
Wage-led demand	○	○	○, ○	○, ○
Wage-led growth	○	○	×, ○	×, ○
Profit-led growth	×	○	×, ×	○, ○

In Table 5.5, the symbol "○" indicates that the corresponding regime is obtained whereas the symbol "×" indicates that the corresponding regime is not obtained. For example, in the medium-run equilibrium with the Kalecki-type investment function, both the wage-led demand and the wage-led growth regimes are obtained whereas the profit-led growth regime is not obtained. In the columns headed with "long-run," the left cell corresponds to the case where the expected rate of growth is fixed while the right cell corresponds to the case where the expected rate of growth is adjusted. For example, in the long-run equilibrium with the MB-type investment function, the wage-led growth regime is not obtained when γ is fixed, while the wage-led growth regime is obtained when γ is adjusted.

5.4 Conclusions

This chapter presents a long-run Kaleckian model, and investigates which regime is obtained in the long-run equilibrium. For this purpose, we use the Kalecki-type investment function and the MB-type investment function. Moreover, we discuss the equilibrium employment rate that is not considered in detail in the existing Kaleckian models. The results are summarized as follows.

To endogenously determine the employment rate, we introduce the specification that the growth rate of labor productivity is an increasing function of the employment rate. This specification is reasonable in that labor productivity growth becomes pro-cyclical and in addition, the natural rate of growth becomes endogenous. Moreover, this specification has the effect of stabilizing the medium-run equilibrium. For in-stance, a rise in the employment rate increases the labor productivity growth, which increases the profit share. This increase of the profit share in turn decreases capacity utilization (because the medium-run is the wage-led demand regime), which, under our assumption, decreases the employment rate in the end. This negative feedback effect stabilizes the medium-run equilibrium.

When the expected growth rate is not adjusted, the long-run equilibrium with the Kalecki-type investment function is neither a wage-led growth regime nor a profit-led growth regime, while the long-run equilibrium with the MB investment function is a profit-led growth regime.

When the expected rate of growth is adjusted, the long-run equilibrium with the Kalecki-type investment function is a wage-led growth regime; in contrast, the long-run equilibrium with the MB-type investment function is a wage-led growth regime if the medium-run equilibrium is a wage-led growth regime, but is a profit-led growth regime if the medium-run equilibrium is a profit-led growth regime. Therefore, we find that the important characteristics of the Kaleckian model are also observed in the long run.

The relationship between the employment rate and the bargaining power of the firms is as follows. In the medium-run equilibrium, a rise in the bargaining power of the firms decreases the employment rate if the equilibrium is a wage-led growth regime, but increases the employment rate if the equilibrium is a profit-led growth regime. In the long-run equilibrium with the Kalecki-type investment function, the employment rate is free from the bargaining power of the firms if the expected growth rate is not adjusted.

From these observations, we find that adjusting the expected growth rate is deci-sive in determining whether or not the characteristics of the medium-run equilibrium are reflected in the characteristics of the long-run equilibrium. Naturally, adjustment of the normal capacity utilization rate also affects the results. Therefore, in the future, we intend to focus on empirical tests for the validity of these long-run adjustments. In addition, since the type of investment function affects the results, empirical tests for the investment function will also be looked into.

Appendix 5.A: Medium-run equilibrium profit share: Kalecki-type investment function

Let m_1 and m_2 be the roots of the quadratic equation (5.14). Calculating the discrim-inant of the equation, we find it to be positive. Hence, m_1 and m_2 are the two real distinct roots. Let $m_1 < m_2$. We have

$$m_1 + m_2 = \frac{\Theta}{s - \delta} > 0, \tag{5.50}$$

$$m_1 m_2 = \frac{\varepsilon(\Gamma - n)}{s - \delta} > 0. \tag{5.51}$$

That is, both m_1 and m_2 are positive. The condition for the medium-run equilibrium value of the capacity utilization rate to be positive is given by $(s - \delta)m - \varepsilon > 0$. From this, we obtain $m > \varepsilon/(s - \delta)$, which is a constraint on m^*. Let $f(m)$ be the left-hand side of equation (5.14). Substituting $m = \varepsilon/(s - \delta)$ in $f(m)$, we obtain

$$f(\varepsilon/(s - \delta)) = -\frac{\varepsilon s(\gamma - \varepsilon u_n)}{s - \delta} < 0. \tag{5.52}$$

This means that m_1 is smaller than $\varepsilon/(s - \delta)$ and that m_2 is larger than $\varepsilon/(s - \delta)$. Therefore, m_2 is the medium-run equilibrium value.

Appendix 5.B: Medium-run equilibrium profit share: MB-type investment function

Let m_1 and m_2 be the roots of the quadratic equation (5.21). Calculating the discriminant of the equation, we find it to be positive. Hence, m_1 and m_2 are the two real distinct roots. Let $m_1 < m_2$. We have

$$m_1 + m_2 = \frac{\Theta}{s(1 - \delta)} > 0, \tag{5.53}$$

$$m_1 m_2 = \frac{\varepsilon(\Gamma - n)}{s(1 - \delta)} > 0. \tag{5.54}$$

That is, both m_1 and m_2 are positive. The condition for the medium-run equilibrium value of the capacity utilization rate to be positive is given by $sm - \varepsilon > 0$. From this, we obtain $m > \varepsilon/s$, which is a constraint on m^*. Let $f(m)$ be the left-hand side of equation (5.21). Substituting $m = \varepsilon/s$ in $f(m)$, we obtain

$$f(\varepsilon/s) = -\frac{\varepsilon^2}{s} - (\gamma - \varepsilon u_n) - (1 - \varepsilon)(\Gamma - n) < 0. \tag{5.55}$$

This means that m_1 is smaller than ε/s and that m_2 is larger than ε/s. Therefore, m_2 is the medium-run equilibrium value.

Apendix 5.C: Local stability of the medium-run equilibrium: Kalecki-type investment function

To investigate the local stability of the medium-run equilibrium, we linearize the system of differential equations (5.11), (5.12), and (5.13) around the equilibrium.

$$\begin{pmatrix} \dot{u} \\ \dot{m} \\ \dot{e} \end{pmatrix} = \begin{pmatrix} J_{11} & J_{12} & 0 \\ 0 & J_{22} & J_{23} \\ J_{31} & J_{32} & J_{33} \end{pmatrix} \begin{pmatrix} u - u^* \\ m - m^* \\ e - e^* \end{pmatrix}. \tag{5.56}$$

The elements of the Jacobian matrix $\mathbf{J}$ are given by

$$J_{11} \equiv \frac{\partial \dot{u}}{\partial u} = -\alpha[(s - \delta)m - \varepsilon] < 0, \tag{5.57}$$

$$J_{12} \equiv \frac{\partial \dot{u}}{\partial m} = -\alpha(s - \delta)u < 0, \tag{5.58}$$

$$J_{22} \equiv \frac{\partial \dot{m}}{\partial m} = -(1 - m) < 0, \tag{5.59}$$

$$J_{23} \equiv \frac{\partial \dot{m}}{\partial e} = (1 - m)g_a'(e) > 0, \tag{5.60}$$

$$J_{31} \equiv \frac{\partial \dot{e}}{\partial u} = -\frac{\alpha e[(s - \delta)m - \varepsilon]}{u} + e(\delta m + \varepsilon), \tag{5.61}$$

$$J_{32} \equiv \frac{\partial \dot{e}}{\partial m} = -e[\alpha(s - \delta) - \delta u], \tag{5.62}$$

$$J_{33} \equiv \frac{\partial \dot{e}}{\partial e} = -eg_a'(e) < 0. \tag{5.63}$$

All elements are evaluated at the equilibrium value; we omit "$*$" to avoid troublesome notations.

The characteristic equation of $\mathbf{J}$ is given by

$$q^3 + a_1 q^2 + a_2 q + a_3 = 0, \tag{5.64}$$

where q denotes a characteristic root. Each coefficient of equation (5.64) is given by

$$a_1 = -\text{tr}\,\mathbf{J} = -(J_{11} + J_{22} + J_{33}), \tag{5.65}$$

$$a_2 = \begin{vmatrix} J_{22} & J_{23} \\ J_{32} & J_{33} \end{vmatrix} + \begin{vmatrix} J_{11} & 0 \\ J_{31} & J_{33} \end{vmatrix} + \begin{vmatrix} J_{11} & J_{12} \\ 0 & J_{22} \end{vmatrix} = J_{22}J_{33} - J_{23}J_{32} + J_{11}(J_{33} + J_{22}), \tag{5.66}$$

$$a_3 = -\det\mathbf{J} = -J_{11}(J_{22}J_{33} - J_{23}J_{32}) - J_{31}J_{12}J_{23}, \tag{5.67}$$

where $-a_1 = \text{tr}\,\mathbf{J}$ denotes the trace of $\mathbf{J}$; a_2, the sum of the principal minors' determinants; and $-a_3 = \det\mathbf{J}$, the determinant of $\mathbf{J}$.

The necessary and sufficient conditions for the local stability are $a_1 > 0$, $a_2 > 0$,

$a_3 > 0$, and $a_1 a_2 - a_3 > 0$. Accordingly, we need to examine these inequalities.

$$a_1 = \underbrace{[(s - \delta)m - \varepsilon]}_{\equiv A > 0} \alpha + \underbrace{(1 - m) + eg_a'(e)}_{\equiv B > 0} = \underset{+}{A}\alpha + \underset{+}{B} > 0, \tag{5.68}$$

$$a_2 = \underbrace{\{[(s - \delta)m - \varepsilon][(1 - m) + eg_a'(e)] + (s - \delta)(1 - m)eg_a'(e)\}}_{\equiv C > 0} \alpha + \underbrace{(1 - \delta u)(1 - m)eg_a'(e)}_{\equiv D > 0}$$

$$= \underset{+}{C}\alpha + \underset{+}{D} > 0, \tag{5.69}$$

$$a_3 = \underbrace{(1 - m)eg_a'(e)\{[(s - \delta)m - \varepsilon] + \varepsilon su\}}_{\equiv E > 0} \alpha = \underset{+}{E}\alpha > 0, \tag{5.70}$$

$$a_1 a_2 - a_3 = \underbrace{AC}_{+} \alpha^2 + (AD + BC - E)\alpha + \underbrace{BD}_{+}. \tag{5.71}$$

Here, we have

$$AD + BC - E = \underbrace{[(s - \delta)m - \varepsilon][(1 - m) + eg_a'(e)]^2}_{+}$$

$$+ \underbrace{(s - \delta)(1 - m)eg_a'(e)}_{+}[eg_a'(e) + \underbrace{1 - m - \delta um - \varepsilon u}_{\equiv \Lambda}]. \tag{5.72}$$

Λ will be positive if δ and ε are not extremely large. When $\Lambda > 0$, we obtain $AD + BC - E > 0$, which leads to $a_1 a_2 - a_3 > 0$. Therefore, if $\Lambda > 0$, the necessary and sufficient conditions for the local stability are satisfied. Note that $\Lambda > 0$ is a sufficient condition for $a_1 a_2 - a_3 > 0$.

Appendix 5.D: Local stability of the medium-run equilibrium: MB-type investment function

The elements of the Jacobian matrix **J** that consists of equations (5.18), (5.19), and (5.20) are given by

$$J_{11} \equiv \frac{\partial \dot{u}}{\partial u} = -\alpha(sm - \varepsilon) < 0, \tag{5.73}$$

$$J_{12} \equiv \frac{\partial \dot{u}}{\partial m} = -\alpha(su - \delta), \tag{5.74}$$

$$J_{22} \equiv \frac{\partial \dot{m}}{\partial m} = -(1 - m) < 0, \tag{5.75}$$

$$J_{23} \equiv \frac{\partial \dot{m}}{\partial e} = (1 - m)g_a'(e) > 0, \tag{5.76}$$

$$J_{31} \equiv \frac{\partial \dot{e}}{\partial u} = -\frac{\alpha e(sm - \varepsilon)}{u} + \varepsilon e, \tag{5.77}$$

$$J_{32} \equiv \frac{\partial \dot{e}}{\partial m} = -\frac{e[\alpha(su - \delta) - \delta u]}{u}, \tag{5.78}$$

$$J_{33} \equiv \frac{\partial \dot{e}}{\partial e} = -eg_a'(e) < 0. \tag{5.79}$$

All elements are evaluated at the equilibrium value.

The coefficients of the characteristic equation are given by

$$a_1 = \underbrace{(sm - \varepsilon)}_{\equiv A > 0}\alpha + \underbrace{(1 - m) + eg_a'(e)}_{\equiv B > 0} = A\alpha + B > 0, \tag{5.80}$$

$$a_2 = \left\{ \underbrace{\frac{(1 - m)eg_a'(e)(su - \delta)}{u} + (sm - \varepsilon)[(1 - m) + eg_a'(e)]}_{\equiv C > 0} \right\}\alpha + \underbrace{(1 - \delta)(1 - m)eg_a'(e)}_{\equiv D > 0}$$

$$= C\alpha + D > 0, \tag{5.81}$$

$$a_3 = \underbrace{(1 - m)eg_a'(e)[(1 - \delta)(sm - \varepsilon) + \varepsilon(su - \delta)]}_{\equiv E > 0}\alpha = E\alpha > 0, \tag{5.82}$$

$$a_1 a_2 - a_3 = \underbrace{AC}_{+}\alpha^2 + (AD + BC - E)\alpha + \underbrace{BD}_{+}. \tag{5.83}$$

Here, we have

$$AD + BC - E = \underbrace{(sm - \varepsilon)[(1 - m) + eg_a'(e)]^2}_{+}$$

$$+ \underbrace{(1 - m)eg_a'(e)(su - \delta)}_{+}\left[\frac{eg_a'(e) + \overbrace{1 - m - \varepsilon u}^{\equiv \Lambda}}{u} \right]. \tag{5.84}$$

Λ is positive if ε is not extremely large. When $\Lambda > 0$, we obtain $AD + BC - E > 0$, which leads to $a_1 a_2 - a_3 > 0$. Therefore, if $\Lambda > 0$, the necessary and sufficient conditions for the local stability are satisfied. Note that $\Lambda > 0$ is a sufficient condition for $a_1 a_2 - a_3 > 0$.

Appendix 5.E: Numerical examples in the long run: MB-type investment function

Table 5.6 shows the parameters used for the numerical examples. The initial values are set to $u_n(0) = 0.5$ and $\gamma(0) = 0.15$ (common to all cases).[30] In these examples, only the sizes of the coefficients ε and δ are different. The coefficient ε is larger (smaller)

---

30) Since the long-run equilibrium has a path-dependent property, different initial conditions produce different long-run equilibrium values.

than the coefficient δ in the wage-led (profit-led) growth regime example.

Table 5.6: Parameters used in the numerical examples

	θ	m_f	m_w	s	n	ε	δ	λ	ψ	α	ϕ	η
MB wage-led growth	0.3	0.3	0.2	0.75	0.05	0.08	0.05	0.15	1	1	1	1
MB profit-led growth	0.3	0.3	0.2	0.75	0.05	0.04	0.09	0.15	1	1	1	1

Table 5.7 shows the results when the medium-run equilibrium is a wage-led growth regime. We increase the target profit share of the firms m_f from 0.3 to 0.4. From this, we find that a rise in m_f lowers both the capacity utilization rate and the capital accumulation rate in the long-run equilibrium. In other words, in this numerical example, the long-run equilibrium is a wage-led demand regime and a wage-led growth regime. Therefore, the long-run equilibrium regime is the same as the medium-run equilibrium regime.

Table 5.7: Example where the long-run equilibrium is a wage-led growth regime (the medium-run equilibrium is a wage-led growth regime)

	u	g	m	e	u_n	γ	g_a
Benchmark	0.670	0.182	0.362	0.878	0.670	0.164	0.132
m_f: $0.3 \rightarrow 0.4$	0.650↓	0.180↓	0.370↑	0.870↓	0.650↓	0.162↓	0.130↓

Table 5.8 shows the results when the medium-run equilibrium is a profit-led growth regime. From this, we find that a rise in m_f decreases the capacity utilization rate and the capital accumulation rate in the long-run equilibrium. In other words, in this numerical example, the long-run equilibrium is both a wage-led demand regime and a profit-led growth regime. Therefore, the long-run equilibrium regime is the same as the medium-run equilibrium regime.

Table 5.8: Example where the long-run equilibrium is a profit-led growth regime (the medium-run equilibrium is a profit-led growth regime)

	u	g	m	e	u_n	γ	g_a
Benchmark	0.686	0.191	0.371	0.939	0.686	0.157	0.141
m_f: $0.3 \rightarrow 0.4$	0.636↓	0.192↑	0.402↑	0.944↑	0.636↓	0.155↓	0.142↑

Part 3: Extended Short-run Kaleckian Models

The Macroeconomic Effects of the Wage Gap between Regular and Non-Regular Employment and of Minimum Wages

6.1　Introduction

Although the debate over the so-called regular and non-regular employment has been running for several decades in Japan, this issue has become an increasingly urgent problem.[1] The situation has been aggravated both by an increase of non-regular employment due to a prolonged economic depression and by the prevalence of discriminatory treatment based on the employment pattern, that is, regular and non-regular employment.[2] The intensification of this undesirable situation motivates us to address the following questions: how does the expansion of the wage gap between regular and non-regular employees influence a macroeconomy, and what are the consequences of a significant increase in the number of non-regular employees? To investigate these questions, we build a model in which regular and non-regular workers coexist. Further, we consider the minimum wage policy; one of the policies adopted by a government to alleviate the situation. Through analyzing how the introduction of the minimum wage policy affects the economy, we clarify the relevance of minimum wages as stabilizing mechanisms.

Flaschel and Greiner (2009) have justified a minimum wage policy based on human rights.[3] Flaschel and Greiner's model is an application of Goodwin's (1967) growth cycle model, which assumes a two-class economy, consisting of working and capitalist classes. They show the existence of an endogenous and perpetual business cycle with respect to the employment rate and wage share. They also show that the

---

1) For instance, according to the labor force survey of February 2012 by the Ministry of Internal Affairs and Communications (http://www.stat.go.jp/data/roudou/longtime/03roudou.htm), the average ratio of non-regular employees to all employees (excluding executives of companies or corporations) from October 2011 to December 2011 is 35.7 %, the highest rate ever registered. For the younger generation (ages 15 to 34), the rate is 33.1%.

2) Japan has not ratified the International Labor Organization (ILO) convention 111, which prohibits discrimination with respect to employment and occupation, in particular, discrimination between regular and non-regular employees.

3) For a theoretical contribution to research on human rights, see Sen (2004).

introduction of the minimum wage within certain limits below the steady state wage share can increase the stability of an economy. In their model, the minimum wage corresponds to the minimum wage share exogenously determined by the government because labor productivity is constant. Based on Flaschel and Greiner (2009), a line of research has been developed. Flaschel and Greiner (2011) and Flaschel et al. (2012) introduce into the Goodwin model heterogeneous labor; that is, skilled and unskilled workers. The labor market is segmented. On the one hand, there is a market for skilled workers only. On the other hand, there is a market for unskilled workers and skilled workers who do not find a job in the first market. It is assumed that skilled workers do not lose their jobs because they can always find a job in the second labor market even if they do not find a job in the first one. Thus, the excess labor supply in the first labor market implies that some of the unskilled workers lose their jobs under the assumption that the labor supply is abundant. It is also assumed that only the skilled workers in the first labor market participate in the wage bargain. That is, the wages of the workers in the second labor market depend on the bargain struck by the skilled workers. Thus, the skilled workers have a large influence on the unskilled workers in the second labor market with respect to their wage determination and employment. In this framework, endogenous business cycles can occur as per Flaschel and Greiner (2009), and the introduction of the minimum wage into the second labor market can alleviate fluctuations of the economy.

The model developed in the present chapter can be seen as being in line with the above contributions. We consider a two-class economy, as did Flaschel and Greiner (2009). In addition, two types of heterogeneous labor (i.e., regular and non-regular employment) are introduced within the working class. Thus, our model is a two-class economy comprising three units, a model similar to that of Flaschel and Greiner (2011). Our model, which incorporates regular and non-regular employment is motivated by the need to focus on the dual labor markets in Japan. Ishikawa and Dejima (1994) statistically examined the dual labor market in Japan by applying a switching regression analysis to micro data for Japanese workers from Basic Surveys on Wage Structure in 1980 and 1990.[4] One of their main findings is that the labor market is characterized by two different wage equations rather than one. Their finding supported the existence of the dual labor market in Japan in this period.

We analyze the effect of the wage gap between regular and non-regular employment on the stability of the steady state equilibrium by using a Kaleckian model. We also analyze how business cycles are affected by the introduction of the minimum wage. Generally, the minimum wage system has three major roles: improving the living conditions of low-paid workers, ensuring fair competition, and promoting a stable management-labor relationship. In particular in Japan, it is often said that as the number of non-regular workers increases, the minimum wage system plays an important role as a social safety net for non-regular workers. However, few studies analyze

---

4) Their study is based on the method developed by Dickens and Lang (1985), which showed the existence of the dual labor market in the US by using a switching regression analysis.

whether the introduction of the minimum wage provides stabilizing mechanisms in Japan.

The Kaleckian model is a type of Keynesian dynamic model based on the principle of effective demand. Its basic framework was developed by Rowthorn (1981). In his model, two kinds of labor, that is, direct labor and indirect labor are considered. These two kinds of labor are also emphasized by Kalecki. Direct labor refers to labor that varies with changes in output, while indirect labor refers to fixed labor that is independent of changes in output. In this sense, we can interpret direct (indirect) labor as non-regular (regular) labor. Although Rowthorn (1981) emphasized two types of labor, surprisingly, almost all Kaleckian models have neglected the consideration of different types of labor.[5] In particular, only a few contributions analyze the effect of direct and indirect labor on the stability of the steady state equilibrium. Raghavendra (2006), one of the exceptions, extends Rowthorn's model and presents a model in which an endogenous business cycle occurs with respect to the two variables (the capacity utilization rate and profit share). Specifically, although the income distribution (the wage and profit shares) is exogenously given in Rowthorn's model, it is endogenously determined in Raghavendra's. In place of Rowthorn's investment function, which is an increasing function of the capacity utilization and the profit rate, Raghavendra introduces an investment function presented by Marglin and Bhaduri (1990), which is an increasing function of the capacity utilization and the profit share. Moreover, he adopts a non-linear investment function.

In Raghavendra's model, a limit cycle occurs under certain conditions due to the interaction between the nonlinearity of the investment function and the increasing returns to scale caused by the existence of fixed labor. The occurrence of an endogenous and perpetual business cycle is proved by the Poincaré-Bendixson theorem. This suggests an alternation of the profit-led demand and wage-led demand regimes, where the profit-led demand (wage-led demand) regime means that an increase in the profit share increases (decreases) the capacity utilization rate.[6] In this chapter, fixed and variable labor in the Raghavendra model are interpreted as regular and non-regular employment, respectively. Furthermore, we extend the model in order to analyze the stability of the steady state equilibrium and the effect of introducing minimum wages on a business cycle.

There are two differences between our model and that of Raghavendra. First, our assumptions concerning wages differ. While Raghavendra (2006) assumes equal pay for fixed labor and variable labor, we assume that regular workers earn a higher wage than do non-regular workers. Second, our formulations regarding the income distribution dynamics differ. In his model, the income distribution dynamics (the profit share) are derived from the dynamic markup pricing rule of firms and the wage curve.[7] In contrast, we adopt the conflicting-claims theory of inflation to obtain the income

---

5) For the literature considering the two types of labor in a Kaleckian model, see Lavoie (1992, 2009).

6) See Blecker (2002) for further discussion concerning various regimes in the Kaleckian model.

7) The wage curve in Raghavendra (2006) means that wage level is an increasing function of the capacity utilization rate.

distribution dynamics.[8] In particular, we introduce the reserve army effect that the target profit share of labor unions is a decreasing function of the capacity utilization rate.

We analyze the dynamics of the capacity utilization rate and the profit share by using the extended model. In the case where the steady state equilibrium is unstable in a profit-led demand regime, under certain conditions, an endogenous and perpetual business cycle occurs by the Hopf bifurcation theorem. Generally, the longer a downturn of a business cycle is, the worse the quality of life of a non-regular worker becomes. One of the policies that a government should adopt to alleviate such an undesirable situation is a minimum wage policy, which sets a lower limit to the wage share, and thus, an upper limit to the profit share.

Next, we explain the minimum wage policy. We introduce the minimum wage by setting an upper limit to the profit share. Such formalization can be regarded as the minimum wage in our model because the determination of the maximum profit share is equivalent to that of the non-regular employment minimum wage. The rationale is as follows. First, by definition, the maximum profit share is equal to the minimum wage share. Second, given labor productivity, the determination of the minimum wage share is equivalent to that of the minimum average wage of the whole economy. Third, in our model, the average wage of the whole economy is proportional to the non-regular employment wage.[9] Thus, from these three facts, the equivalence between the determinations of the maximum profit share and the non-regular employment minimum wage holds.

In our analysis, we focus on the case where the steady state equilibrium is locally unstable. The government does not accurately know the equilibrium profit share. Thus, the minimum wage determined by the government does not necessarily coincide with it. In this case, the following results are obtained by our analysis.

Under a profit-led demand regime, if the government sets a minimum wage that is lower than the steady state real wage, the size of fluctuation decreases. If a minimum wage is set at the same level as the steady state real wage, the economy converges to the steady state almost without fluctuations. If the government sets a minimum wage that is higher than the steady state real wage, the economy converges to a point that is different from the steady state. In this case, although fluctuations can be diminished, both the profit share and the capacity utilization rate that are obtained in the long run become smaller than those obtained before the introduction of the minimum wage policy.

Under a wage-led demand regime, the steady state is a saddle point. If the government simultaneously introduces a minimum wage and a maximum wage, depending on whether the initial value is located above or below the stable arm, the economy reaches different steady states. On the one hand, if the economy starts from an initial

---

8) Flaschel and Greiner (2009) present an extended version of the Goodwin model in which the income distribution dynamics are given by how the dynamic markup pricing rule and the wage rate of change depends on both capacity utilization and inflation rate.

9) See equations (6.7) and (6.8) below.

value above the stable arm, it converges to a point where the capacity utilization rate is smaller than its equilibrium value whereas the profit share is larger than its equilibrium value. On the other hand, if the economy starts from an initial value below the stable arm, it converges to a point where the capacity utilization rate is larger than its equilibrium value whereas the profit share is smaller than its equilibrium value.

The rest of the chapter is organized as follows. Section 2 describes our model. Section 3 analyzes the properties of the steady state equilibrium and its stability. Section 4, given that the steady state equilibrium is locally unstable, analyzes how the introduction of the minimum wage policy affects the economy. Section 5 concludes.

6.2   The model

We consider an economy with two heterogeneous groups of workers (regular and non-regular employment) and capitalists. Workers' income consists of wages only, and they spend all their income on consumption. Capitalists obtain their income from profits only, which is saved at a constant rate s. Then, the saving function is given by

$$g_s = sr, \quad 0 < s < 1, \tag{6.1}$$

where $g_s = S/K$ is the ratio of real savings S to the capital stock K, and r is the profit rate.

Following Marglin and Bhaduri (1990), we assume that the firms' investment function is an increasing function of the capacity utilization rate u and the profit share m.[10]

$$g_d = g_d(u, m), \quad g_{du} > 0, \ g_{dm} > 0, \tag{6.2}$$

where $g_d = I/K$ denotes the ratio of the real investment I to capital stock, g_{du} denotes the partial derivative of the investment function with respect to capacity utilization, and g_{dm} denotes the partial derivative of the investment function with respect to the profit share. For simplicity, we do not consider capital depreciation.

Let us assume that the ratio of the potential output Y^F to the capital stock is technically fixed, that is, always constant. Then, the capacity utilization rate can be represented as $u = Y/K$, where Y denotes the actual output. Note that the relation $r = mu$ holds among the profit rate, the profit share, and the capacity utilization rate. In the following analysis, without loss of generality, we assume that the ratio of the potential output to the capital stock is equal to unity.

We assume that the regular employment L_r is related to the potential output, while

---

10) In the typical Kaleckian model, the investment function is formalized as an increasing function of the profit rate and the capacity utilization rate. On the contrary, Marglin and Bhaduri (1990) assert that one of the investment function variables should be the profit share rather than the profit rate.

the non-regular employment L_{nr} is related to the actual output.

$$L_r = \alpha Y^F, \quad \alpha > 0, \tag{6.3}$$

$$L_{nr} = \beta Y, \quad \beta > 0, \tag{6.4}$$

where α and β are positive constants. Regular employment is considered to be a fixed factor, i.e., regular employees are not frequently fired or hired even if output fluctuates. Regular employment changes when scale of plants changes, and scale of plants changes when the potential output changes. Hence, we can consider that regular employment changes when the potential output changes. In contrast, non-regular employment is considered to be a variable factor, i.e., non-regular workers are fired or hired as output fluctuates. Thus, we can consider that non-regular employment changes when the actual output changes. In this chapter, for simplicity, we assume that regular employment and non-regular employment are proportional to the potential output and the actual output, respectively.[11]

The ratio of regular employment to non-regular employment leads to $L_r/L_{nr} = \alpha/(\beta u)$. This means that an increase in the capacity utilization rate leads to a decrease in this ratio. In other words, a relatively large number of non-regular workers are employed with a rise in the capacity utilization rate. Once the capacity utilization rate is determined at the steady state equilibrium, the ratio of regular employment to non-regular employment is also determined.

We assume a quantity adjustment that the capacity utilization rate increases (decreases) in accordance with an excess demand (supply) in the goods market.

$$\dot{u} = \phi(g_d - g_s), \quad \phi > 0, \tag{6.5}$$

where the parameter ϕ denotes the speed of adjustment of the goods market.

We define the level of the average labor productivity of the economy as $a = Y/L$, where L denotes the aggregate employment, that is, $L = L_r + L_{nr}$. From this, we obtain the following:

$$a = \frac{Y}{\alpha Y^F + \beta Y} = \frac{u}{\alpha + \beta u}. \tag{6.6}$$

This implies that the average labor productivity is an increasing function of the capacity utilization rate, that is, increasing returns to scale prevail. Since u is constant at the steady state equilibrium, the corresponding average labor productivity is also constant. Thus, there is no perpetual technical progress in our model.[12]

The nominal wage of regular employment w_r is supposed to be higher than that of

---

11) An empirical study by Uni (2009) shows that in Japan, the employment elasticity of output, that is, how much employment changes when the actual output changes, is small for regular employment and large for non-regular employment. This study supports our specification.

12) We can introduce perpetual technical progress by using the theory of induced technical change. See Appendix 6.A.

non-regular employment w_{nr} at a certain rate γ.[13]

$$w_r = \gamma w_{nr}, \quad \gamma > 1. \tag{6.7}$$

From these, the average wage of the economy yields

$$w = \frac{L_r}{L} w_r + \frac{L_{nr}}{L} w_{nr} = \frac{\alpha}{\alpha + \beta u} w_r + \frac{\beta u}{\alpha + \beta u} w_{nr} = \left[\frac{\gamma \alpha + \beta u}{\gamma(\alpha + \beta u)} \right] w_r. \tag{6.8}$$

The average wage is given by the weighted average of regular and non-regular employment wages. Each weight corresponds to the corresponding employment share. While the weight of regular employment is a decreasing function of the capacity utilization rate, the weight of non-regular employment is an increasing function of the capacity utilization rate. The component in the square bracket is a decreasing function of the capacity utilization rate.

Next, we formalize the equation of the price of goods p and the equation of the regular employment wage by using the theory of conflicting-claims inflation.[14] First, firms set their price so as to narrow the gap between firms' target profit share m_f and the actual profit share, and accordingly, the price changes. Second, labor unions negotiate so as to narrow the gap between the labor unions' target profit share m_w and the actual profit share, and accordingly, the nominal regular employment wage changes. The two assumptions can be written as follows:

$$\frac{\dot{p}}{p} = \theta(m_f - m), \quad 0 < \theta < 1, \ 0 < m_f < 1, \tag{6.9}$$

$$\frac{\dot{w}_r}{w_r} = (1 - \theta)(m - m_w), \quad 0 < m_w < 1, \tag{6.10}$$

where θ is a positive parameter. We interpret θ and $1 - \theta$ as the bargaining power of firms and that of labor unions, respectively. Further, by taking the reserve army effect into consideration, we assume that m_w is a decreasing function of the capacity utilization rate.

$$m_w = m_w(u), \quad m'_w < 0. \tag{6.11}$$

As the capacity utilization rate (a proxy variable of the employment rate) increases, workers' demands in wage bargaining are likely to increase, which leads workers to set a higher target wage share, and accordingly, set a lower target profit share.

Since the profit share is given by $m = 1 - (wL/pY)$ by definition, by taking the

---

13) A similar formalization is adopted by Lavoie (2009).
14) The theory of conflicting-claims inflation is presented by Rowthorn (1977). For previous studies on Kaleckian models with this theory, see, for example, Dutt (1987) and Cassetti (2003).

derivative of m with respect to time, we obtain

$$\frac{\dot{m}}{1-m} = \frac{\dot{p}}{p} - \frac{\dot{w}}{w} + \frac{\dot{a}}{a}. \tag{6.12}$$

From equations (6.8) and (6.10), the rate of change of the average wage in the whole economy is given by

$$\frac{\dot{w}}{w} = -\frac{(\gamma - 1)\alpha\beta}{(\gamma\alpha + \beta u)(\alpha + \beta u)} \cdot \dot{u} + (1 - \theta)[m - m_w(u)]. \tag{6.13}$$

From equation (6.6), the rate of change of labor productivity is given by

$$\frac{\dot{a}}{a} = \frac{\alpha}{(\alpha + \beta u)u} \cdot \dot{u}. \tag{6.14}$$

By substituting equations (6.1) and (6.2) into equation (6.5), as well as equations (6.9), (6.12), and (6.13) into equation (6.11), we can obtain the following dynamic equations with respect to the capacity utilization rate and the profit share.

$$\dot{u} = \phi[g_d(u, m) - smu], \quad \phi > 0, \tag{6.15}$$

$$\dot{m} = -(1 - m)[m - \theta m_f - (1 - \theta)m_w(u) - f(u)\dot{u}], \quad f(u) = \frac{\alpha\gamma}{(\gamma\alpha + \beta u)u}, \ f'(u) < 0. \tag{6.16}$$

Firms set m_f as large as possible. Conversely, labor unions set m_w as small as possible. Hence, we can assume that $m_f > m_w(u)$.

6.3 Characteristics of the steady state equilibrium and its stability

6.3.1 Characteristics of the steady state equilibrium

The steady state equilibrium is an equilibrium such that $\dot{u} = \dot{m} = 0$. From this, we have the simultaneous equations with respect to u^* and m^*.

$$g_d(u^*, m^*) = sm^*u^*, \tag{6.17}$$

$$m^* = \theta m_f + (1 - \theta)m_w(u^*). \tag{6.18}$$

There is also a steady state for $m^* = 1$, where the wage share is zero. We exclude the steady state in the following analysis because every worker is always employed without payment. In the following analysis, we assume that there is a unique pair of $u^* \in (0, 1)$ and $m^* \in (0, 1)$ that simultaneously satisfies equations (6.17) and (6.18).

The capacity utilization rate and the profit share at the steady state equilibrium depend on the bargaining power, the target profit share of firms, and the target profit share of labor unions. However, the steady state equilibrium does not depend on the four parameters ϕ, γ, α, and β. This property is used in the analysis of the next section.

6.3.2 The stability of the steady state equilibrium

To investigate the stability of the steady state equilibrium, we analyze the Jacobian matrix of the system of the differential equations. Let the Jacobian matrix be **J**. The matrix **J** is given as follows:

$$\mathbf{J} = \begin{pmatrix} J_{11} & J_{12} \\ J_{21} & J_{22} \end{pmatrix} = \begin{pmatrix} \frac{\partial \dot{u}}{\partial u} & \frac{\partial \dot{u}}{\partial m} \\ \frac{\partial \dot{m}}{\partial u} & \frac{\partial \dot{m}}{\partial m} \end{pmatrix}, \tag{6.19}$$

where

$$J_{11} = \phi[g_{du}(u^*, m^*) - sm^*], \tag{6.20}$$

$$J_{12} = \phi[g_{dm}(u^*, m^*) - su^*], \tag{6.21}$$

$$J_{21} = (1 - m^*)[(1 - \theta)m'_w(u^*) + f(u^*)J_{11}], \tag{6.22}$$

$$J_{22} = -(1 - m^*)[1 - f(u^*)J_{12}]. \tag{6.23}$$

Each component of **J** is evaluated at the steady state equilibrium.

Let us assume the following condition:

Assumption 6.1. $sm^* > g_{du}(u^*, m^*)$.

This means that the response of savings to the capacity utilization rate is larger than that of investments. This assumption makes the quantity adjustment of the goods market stable. Assumption 6.1 is sometimes called the Keynesian stability condition (Marglin and Bhaduri, 1990), which is often imposed in Kaleckian models. With Assumption 6.1, we can obtain $J_{11} < 0$.

Let us classify the regime according to the effect of a profit share increase on the capacity utilization.

Definition 6.1. *If the relation $g_{dm}(u^*, m^*) < su^*$ holds, the steady state equilibrium is called a wage-led demand regime. If, however, the relation $g_{dm}(u^*, m^*) > su^*$ holds, the steady state equilibrium is called a profit-led demand regime.*[15]

If the investment response to the profit share is less than the saving response, then the steady state equilibrium exhibits a wage-led demand regime. If, however, the investment response to the profit share is more than the saving response, then the steady state equilibrium exhibits a profit-led demand regime. Depending on which

---

15) A profit-led demand regime is generally defined as a regime such that an increase in the exogenously given profit share leads to a rise in the capacity utilization rate at the steady state equilibrium. However, we cannot apply this definition to our model because the profit share at the steady state equilibrium is an endogenous variable. Here, we follow the definition of Raghavendra (2006).

regime is realized in the steady state equilibrium, a wage-led demand regime or a profit-led demand regime, we have $J_{12} < 0$ or $J_{12} > 0$. From Assumption 6.1 and Definition 6.1, the sign structure of the Jacobian matrix $\mathbf{J}$ is given as follows:

$$\mathbf{J} = \begin{pmatrix} - & \pm \\ - & ? \end{pmatrix}. \tag{6.24}$$

The steady state equilibrium is locally stable if and only if the determinant of the Jacobian matrix $\mathbf{J}$ is positive and the trace is negative. Let us confirm this fact in our model.

First, calculating the determinant, we obtain

$$\det \mathbf{J} = -\underset{-}{(1 - m^*)}[\underset{-}{J_{11}} + \underset{+/-}{(1 - \theta)m'_w(u^*)J_{12}}]. \tag{6.25}$$

If the steady state equilibrium exhibits a profit-led demand regime, that is, $J_{12} > 0$, then $\det \mathbf{J} > 0$ always holds. On the contrary, if the steady state equilibrium exhibits a wage-led demand regime, that is, $J_{12} < 0$, then $\det \mathbf{J} < 0$ holds if the absolute value of $m'_w(u)$ is sufficiently large whereas $\det \mathbf{J} > 0$ holds if the absolute value of $m'_w(u)$ is sufficiently small. Further, when $\det \mathbf{J} < 0$, the discriminant of the characteristic equation is always positive. Hence, we obtain two distinct real roots.

Second, calculating the trace, we obtain

$$\operatorname{tr} \mathbf{J} = \underset{-}{J_{11}} - (1 - m^*) + \underset{+/-}{(1 - m^*)f(u^*)J_{12}}. \tag{6.26}$$

By assumption, $J_{11} < 0$. However, since J_{12} can be positive or negative, $\operatorname{tr} \mathbf{J}$ is not always negative. If the steady state equilibrium exhibits a wage-led demand regime, that is, $J_{12} < 0$, then $\operatorname{tr} \mathbf{J} < 0$ always holds. On the contrary, if the steady state equilibrium exhibits a profit-led demand regime, that is, $J_{12} > 0$, then $\operatorname{tr} \mathbf{J} > 0$ can hold.

From the above analysis, we obtain the following propositions.

Proposition 6.1. *Suppose that the steady state equilibrium exhibits a wage-led demand regime. If the reserve army effect is small, then the steady state equilibrium is locally stable. In contrast, if the reserve army effect is large, then the steady state equilibrium is locally unstable.*

Remember that the reserve army effect is given by $m'_w(u) < 0$.

Let us explain Proposition 6.1 intuitively. This proposition means that in a wage-led demand regime, the higher reserve army effect has unstable effects on the economy. Consider the case where the capacity utilization rate deviates from the steady state capacity utilization rate due to the occurrence of an exogenous shock. Suppose that the capacity utilization rate is less than the steady state equilibrium, for instance. In this case, there are two opposing effects. First, the capacity utilization rate increases due to $J_{11} < 0$, which is called the direct stable effect. Second, the fall in the capacity utilization rate leads to an increase in the profit share due to $J_{21} < 0$. As a consequence, due to $J_{12} < 0$, the capacity utilization rate decreases, which is called the indirect unstable effect. Thus, in a wage-led demand regime, whereas the direct effect is stable, the indirect effect is unstable. If the reserve army effect is large, the profit share fairly increases due to a strong effect of $J_{21} < 0$. As a result, the capacity utilization rate largely decreases via an effect of $J_{12} < 0$. That is, the indirect unstable effect is intense. In the unstable case, the steady state equilibrium is a saddle point.[16)]

Proposition 6.2. *Suppose that the steady state equilibrium exhibits a profit-led demand regime. Then, the steady state equilibrium can be locally unstable.*

This proposition means that, in a profit-led demand regime, the higher response of the capacity utilization rate to a change in the profit share can destabilize the economy. First, in a profit-led demand regime, if the capacity utilization rate is less than the steady state value, then it increases due to $J_{11} < 0$. This is the direct effect. Second, if the capacity utilization rate is less than the steady state value, then the profit share increases due to $J_{21} < 0$, which increases the capacity utilization rate due to $J_{12} > 0$. This is the indirect effect. In a profit-led demand regime, both the direct and indirect effects seem stable. However, if the indirect effect is too large, that is, if the response of the capacity utilization rate to the profit share is sufficiently large, the capacity utilization rate fairly increases due to the strong effect of $J_{12} > 0$. In this case, the capacity utilization rate increases too much and deviates from the steady state, and consequently, the steady state equilibrium is unstable.

Now, we show that endogenous and perpetual business cycles occur. By rearranging tr $\mathbf{J}$, we obtain

$$\text{tr}\,\mathbf{J} = \phi A - (1 - m^*), \quad A \equiv [g_{du}(u^*, m^*) - sm^*] + (1 - m^*)f(u^*)(g_{dm}(u^*, m^*) - su^*]. \tag{6.27}$$

The term A does not depend on the parameter ϕ, which represents the adjustment speed of the goods market. Neither the capacity utilization rate nor the profit share at the steady state equilibrium depends on ϕ. Thus, we can choose ϕ as a bifurcation parameter.

Proposition 6.3. *Suppose that the steady state exhibits a profit-led demand regime and that the term A is positive. Then, a limit cycle occurs when the speed of adjustment of the goods market lies within some range.*

Proof. Set $\phi_0 = (1 - m^*)/A > 0$. Taking a positive value ϕ arbitrarily, we have tr $\mathbf{J} = 0$ for $\phi = \phi_0$, tr $\mathbf{J} < 0$ for $\phi < \phi_0$, and tr $\mathbf{J} > 0$ for $\phi > \phi_0$. Thus, $\phi = \phi_0$ is a Hopf bifurcation point. That is, there is a continuous family of non-stationary, periodic solutions of the system around $\phi = \phi_0$.   ∎

---

16) We consider both the capacity utilization rate and the profit share as state variables rather than jump variables. Unlike models with dynamic optimization, our model has no mechanism to set initial values on the saddle path.

This proposition means that, as the adjustment speed of the goods market increases, there appears a point at which the stable steady state equilibrium switches to the unstable one. As Raghavendra (2006) has shown, we also obtain a similar result: given a phase in which both the profit share and the capacity utilization rate simultaneously either increase or decrease, and a phase in which one increases while the other decreases, the former phase alternates with the latter. This implies an apparent alternation of the profit-led demand and wage-led demand regimes.

Next, we consider the parameter γ, which represents the wage gap between regular and non-regular employment. Note that γ does not affect the equilibrium. Therefore, γ appears only in the part $f(u^*)$ of $\operatorname{tr} \mathbf{J}$. Furthermore, we find that

$$\frac{\partial f(u; \gamma)}{\partial \gamma} = \frac{\alpha \beta}{u(\gamma \alpha + \beta u)^2} > 0. \tag{6.28}$$

This means that in a case in which the steady state equilibrium exhibits a profit-led demand regime, a rise in γ amplifies the instability of the steady state equilibrium.

Proposition 6.4. *Suppose that the steady state equilibrium exhibits a profit-led demand regime. Then, an expansion of the gap between regular and non-regular employment makes the steady state equilibrium unstable.*

Furthermore, we obtain the following proposition.

Proposition 6.5. *Suppose that the steady state equilibrium is unstable in a profit-led demand regime. Then, a limit cycle occurs within a certain range of the wage gap between regular and non-regular employment.*

Proof. Set

$$\gamma_0 = \frac{\beta}{\alpha} \cdot \frac{(u^*)^2[(1 - m^*) - J_{11}]}{\{[J_{11} - (1 - m^*)]u^* + (1 - m^*)J_{12}\}} > 0.$$

Taking a positive value γ arbitrarily, we have $\operatorname{tr} \mathbf{J} = 0$ for $\gamma = \gamma_0$, $\operatorname{tr} \mathbf{J} < 0$ for $\gamma < \gamma_0$, and $\operatorname{tr} \mathbf{J} > 0$ for $\gamma > \gamma_0$. Thus, $\gamma = \gamma_0$ is a Hopf bifurcation point. That is, there is a continuous family of non-stationary, periodic solutions of the system around $\gamma = \gamma_0$. ∎

As the wage gap expands, there appears a point at which the stable steady state equilibrium switches to the unstable one. Thus, an increase in the wage gap makes the economy more unstable. To stabilize the economy, it is desirable to shrink the wage gap between regular and non-regular employment.

Note that the steady state capacity utilization rate does not depend on the parameters α and β. Given the steady state capacity utilization rate, we consider the effect of a rise in β/α on the stability of the steady state equilibrium. Then, a rise in β/α means that a relatively large number of non-regular employees are employed compared to the number of regular employees. The ratio β/α appears only in the part $f(u^*)$ of tr $\mathbf{J}$. From equation (6.16), we find that

$$\frac{\partial f(u;\beta/\alpha)}{\partial(\beta/\alpha)} = -\frac{u^2}{u[\gamma + (\beta/\alpha)u]^2} < 0. \tag{6.29}$$

This means that in a case in which the steady state equilibrium exhibits a profit-led demand regime, the higher the ratio β/α is, the smaller tr $\mathbf{J}$ is. From this, we obtain the following proposition.

Proposition 6.6. *Suppose that the steady state equilibrium exhibits a profit-led demand regime. Then, a rise in the relatively large number of non-regular employees compared with the number of regular employees makes the steady state equilibrium stable.*

This proposition shows that an increase in the relatively large number of non-regular employees will have the effect of making the economy stable. Thus, if the government tries to decrease the relatively large number of non-regular employees, the economy becomes unstable. However, we cannot conclude that a government should adopt an employment policy to increase non-regular employment in order to stabilize the economy. Rather, from propositions 6.4 and 6.6, we emphasize a policy mix between wage and employment policies; even though the economy becomes unstable due to a decrease in non-regular employees, a government makes an effort to stabilize the economy by conducting a policy to shrink the wage gap between regular and non-regular employment.

6.4   Introduction of minimum wages

As one of the policies adopted by the government, a minimum wage policy is considered next. The minimum wage is introduced by setting an upper limit to the profit share. We consider such formalization justifiable because the determination of the maximum profit share is equivalent to that of the minimum wage of non-regular employment.[17] The equivalence is obtained from the following three facts. First, by definition, the introduction of the maximum profit share ($m_{\max}$) is equal to that of the minimum wage share ($1 - m_{\max}$). Second, given the labor productivity ($a = Y/L$), the determination of the minimum wage share is equivalent to that of the minimum average wage of the whole economy, that is, $1 - m_{\max} = w/(pa)$. Third, by substituting equation (6.7) into equation (6.8), the average wage of the whole economy is proportional to the wage of non-regular employment, that is, $w = \left(\frac{\gamma\alpha+\beta u}{\alpha+\beta u}\right)w_{nr}$, where $\left(\frac{\gamma\alpha+\beta u}{\alpha+\beta u}\right) > 1$ for all $u \in (0,1)$. Note that the minimum average wage of the economy

---

17) However, if policymakers set the upper limit to the profit share, firms might choose to relocate to another country to seek higher profits.

$w_{\min}$ corresponding to $m_{\max}$ lies between w_{nr} and w_r from equation (6.8) and the third fact, that is, $w_r > w > w_{\min} > w_{nr}$.[18]

Here, as per Flaschel and Greiner (2009, 2011) and Flaschel et al. (2012), we analyze how the introduction of the minimum wage affects the dynamics of the profit share and the capacity utilization rate.

In this section, to facilitate our analysis, numerical simulations are used. For this purpose, we need to specify the investment function and the target profit share of labor unions. Here, we assume the following functional forms:[19]

$$g_d = \psi u^\delta m^\varepsilon, \quad \psi > 0,\ 0 < \delta < 1,\ \varepsilon > 0, \tag{6.30}$$

$$m_w = \sigma_0 - \sigma_1 u, \quad 0 < \sigma_0 < 1,\ \sigma_1 > 0. \tag{6.31}$$

If Okun's law, that is, a positive correlation between the employment rate and the capacity utilization rate, holds, we can regard the capacity utilization rate as a proxy variable of the employment rate. Such a method is adopted by Tavani et al. (2011).[20]

6.4.1   The case of a profit-led demand regime

In this subsection, we assume that the steady state equilibrium exhibits a profit-led demand regime and that a limit cycle occurs. Moreover, we conduct a numerical simulation that is roughly consistent with business cycles in the Japanese economy.

Figure 6.1 plots data for the capacity utilization rate and the profit share between the period 1980–2007. These data are smoothed by means of the Hodrick-Prescott filter. From Figure 6.1, we see that the capacity utilization and the profit share show a clockwise movement along an upward-sloping orbit, which implies that the profit share is pro-cyclical to capacity utilization, that is, the wage share is counter-cyclical to capacity utilization. Moreover, the capacity utilization fluctuates between 75% and 100% and the profit share between 15% and 30%.

---

18) Concretely, the value in the square brackets in equation (6.8) is smaller than unity for any $u \in (0, 1)$. This means that the relation $w < w_r$ holds. Again, the value $\left(\frac{\gamma\alpha+\beta u}{\alpha+\beta u}\right)$ of the third fact is greater than unity for any $u \in (0, 1)$, which means that the relation $w > w_{nr}$ holds.

19) In the case where the investment function is specified as in equation (6.30), there is also a steady state for $m^* = 0$. We will also exclude it because in this case, the profit rate leads to zero and hence, capital stock will not be accumulated.

20) For Kaleckian models that strictly consider the endogenous determination of the employment rate, see Sasaki (2010, 2011, 2012, 2013).

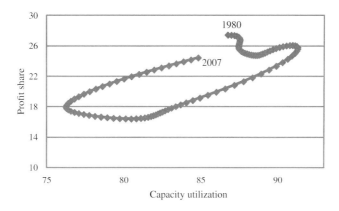

Figure 6.1: Capacity utilization and profit share in Japan (1980–2007)

From Figure 6.1,[21] we find that the Japanese economy exhibits a profit-led demand regime. In fact, by using VAR models, Azetsu et al. (2010) and Nishi (2010) empirically show that the Japanese economy exhibits a profit-led demand regime. Using a method similar to Flaschel et al. (2007) and Barbosa-Filho and Taylor (2006), Sonoda (2013) estimates the demand and distribution regimes in Japan between the period 1977–2007. He concludes that labor productivity is pro-cyclical to capacity utilization, real wage is counter-cyclical, and in total, the wage share is counter-cyclical.[22] Consequently, the profit share becomes pro-cyclical to the capacity utilization rate.

Next, we set the parameters to produce a cyclical pattern as in Figure 6.1.

Wage gap: According to the Basic Survey on Wage Structure by the Ministry of Health, Labour and Welfare, the ratio of wages for ordinary workers to wages for part-time workers is calculated as $100/60 = 1.61$. Therefore, we set $\gamma = 1.6$.

Labor input coefficients of regular and non-regular workers: According to data by the Ministry of Internal Affairs and Communications, the ratio of regular workers to non-regular workers is calculated as $L_r/L_{nr} = 7/3 = 2.33$. Note that in our theoretical model, the ratio is given by $L_r/L_{nr} = \alpha/(\beta u)$. If the equilibrium capacity utilization rate is 0.7, we have $L_r/L_{nr} = 2.77$ if we set $\alpha = 2$ and $\beta = 1$. The percentage of non-regular workers has recently increased. It was less than 30% between the period 1980–2007. Therefore, the value 2.77 seems reasonable.

Saving rate: Naastepad and Storm (2007) calculate that the propensity to save from profits in Japan between the period 1960–2000 is approximately 0.5, and hence, we set $s = 0.5$.

21) Sources: Indices of Industrial Production (Ministry of Economy, Trade and Industry) for the capacity utilization rate and Financial Statements Statistics of Corporations by Industry (Ministry of Finance) for the profit share.
22) Yoshikawa (1994) also points out that the wage share in Japan is counter-cyclical to the capacity utilization rate.

Parameters of investment function: Naastepad and Storm (2007) also estimate the investment function of the Japanese economy. However, their specification of the investment function differs from ours, and accordingly, we cannot employ their results as they are. Nevertheless, their results indicate that the elasticity of investment with respect to the profit share is much larger than that with respect to the output (a proxy variable of the capacity utilization rate). Hence, we use a much larger value for ε than for δ. With our specification of the investment function, $\varepsilon > 1$ corresponds to a profit-led demand regime, and hence, we set $\varepsilon = 2$ to satisfy this restriction.

For other parameters than those mentioned above, we cannot obtain reliable estimates. Accordingly, we set the parameters so that the equilibrium values of the capacity utilization rate and the profit share would roughly approximate the Japanese data.

Summarizing the above discussion, we set the parameters as follows:

$$\psi = 1.3, \ \delta = 0.2, \ \varepsilon = 2, \ \phi = 5, \ s = 0.5, \ \theta = 0.4,$$
$$m_f = 0.7, \ \sigma_0 = 0.1, \ \sigma_1 = 0.1, \ \alpha = 2, \ \beta = 1, \ \gamma = 1.6, \ m_{\max} = 0.35.$$

Calculating the steady state with the above parameters, we obtain $u^* = 0.72$ and $m^* = 0.30$.

Given the arbitrary initial value, a limit cycle occurs (see Figure 6.2).[23] The limit cycle is stable. That is, if the initial value is set far from the steady state, it converges to the limit cycle. Even if the initial value is set in the neighborhood of the steady state, it converges to the limit cycle, which is shown in Figure 6.2.

---

23) As a robustness check, we examine the range of a parameter that produces limit cycles. First, we consider the adjustment speed of the goods market ϕ. As long as the other parameters are constant, limit cycles can occur with the range of $\phi \in [4.2, 8.6]$. Second, we consider the elasticity of investment with respect to the profit share. As long as the other parameters are constant, limit cycles can occur with the range of $\varepsilon \in [1.92, 4.99]$. With a value of $\varepsilon > 5$, interior solutions are not obtained.

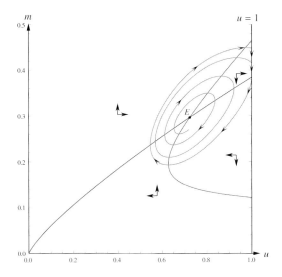

Figure 6.2: The occurrence of a limit cycle

Here, we introduce $m_{\max}$. Depending on how the government sets $m_{\max}$, we obtain different results.

First, we consider a case in which the exogenously given $m_{\max}$ is more than the maximum value (i.e., the top) of the limit cycle without introducing minimum wages (for instance, $m_{\max} = 0.5$). From the phase diagram, we can see that the initial value in this case converges to the limit cycle faster than does the initial value in the case without $m_{\max}$ as long as the initial value is located outside of the limit cycle and its transition to the limit cycle reaches $m_{\max}$ before it converges to the limit cycle.

Second, we consider a case in which $m_{\max}$ is set between the maximum value of the limit cycle and the steady state equilibrium. Then, from the analysis of the phase diagram, we find that the size of the limit cycle becomes smaller. This means that the size of fluctuation decreases. In other words, by introducing a minimum wage, the size of business cycles can be reduced. Figure 6.3 shows the limit cycles in the case of $m_{\max} = 0.35$. Figure 6.4 shows the limit cycles of these two cases before and after introducing a minimum wage. Clearly, we can see that the size of business cycles diminishes.[24]

---

24) When the steady state equilibrium exhibits a profit-led demand regime and is stable, the economy converges to equilibrium with oscillations. In this case, if the minimum wage policy is effective in that the pair of u and m reaches the maximum profit share line along its transitional process, then the size of business cycles diminishes compared to a case where the minimum wage policy is ineffective. Therefore, even where limit cycles do not occur, as long as the minimum wage policy is effective, the policy can alleviate business cycles.

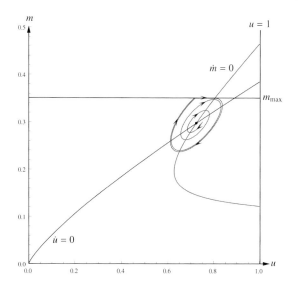

Figure 6.3: Introduction of a minimum wage

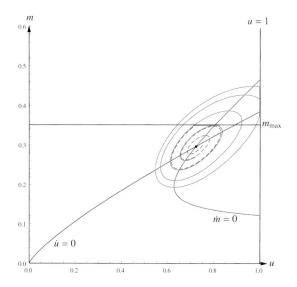

Figure 6.4: Comparisons of the two cycles

Third, we consider m_{max} exactly the same as the steady state profit share. Then, from the phase diagram, the economy converges to the steady state almost without fluctuations. That is, if the government knows the steady state equilibrium in advance, by setting the minimum wage at the same level of the steady state, it can lead the economy to converge to the steady state.

Fourth, we consider a case in which m_{max} is set less than the steady state equilibrium. If the government does not actually know the equilibrium, it is significant to consider such a case. Then, from the phase diagram, the economy converges to a point on line $\dot{u} = 0$ almost without fluctuations. For example, as shown in Figure 6.5, the economy converges to point P. That is, although fluctuations can be diminished, both the profit share and the capacity utilization rate obtained in the long run become smaller than those obtained before the introduction of the minimum wage policy. Figure 6.5 shows the case of $m_{max} = 0.25$.

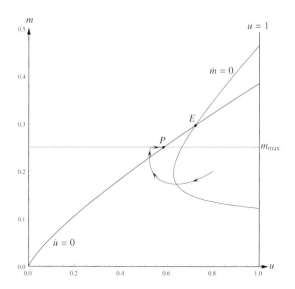

Figure 6.5: Introduction of a minimum wage that is larger than the equilibrium

Let us compare the real wage of point E and that of point P. The real wage of regular employment and that of non-regular employment are given by using the capacity utilization rate and the profit share as follows:[25]

$$\frac{w_r}{p} = \frac{\gamma u}{\gamma\alpha + \beta u}(1 - m),\tag{6.32}$$

$$\frac{w_{nr}}{p} = \frac{u}{\gamma\alpha + \beta u}(1 - m).\tag{6.33}$$

From this, the real wage is an increasing function of the capacity utilization rate and a decreasing function of the profit share. By rearranging the formulae, we obtain the iso-real wage curves in the (u, m)-space.

$$m = 1 - \frac{1}{\gamma}\frac{w_r}{p}\left(\frac{\alpha\gamma}{u} + \beta\right),\tag{6.34}$$

$$m = 1 - \frac{w_{nr}}{p}\left(\frac{\alpha\gamma}{u} + \beta\right).\tag{6.35}$$

Each curve becomes a rectangular hyperbola. In the first quadrant of the (u, m)-space, the lower and the more to the right these curves are located, the higher are the associated real wages.

Whether point E or P gives a higher real wage depends on two things: the shape of the iso-real wage curve and the relative positions between points E and P. Iso-real wage curves and points E and P are shown in Figure 6.6. The real wage associated with the dotted iso-real wage curve is higher than that associated with the solid one. In the left figure, point E gives a higher real wage compared to point P. The employment rate (capacity utilization rate) in E is also high compared to its counterpart because u in E is higher than u in P. On the contrary, in the right figure, a higher real wage is given in point P compared to point E. However, the employment rate in P is low compared to that in E because u in P is smaller than u in E.

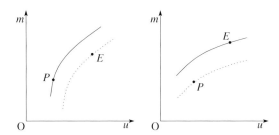

Figure 6.6: Iso-real wage curves and the two equilibria

---

25) Taking the derivatives of equations (6.32) and (6.33) with respect to γ, we obtain $\frac{\partial(w_r/p)}{\partial\gamma} > 0$ and $\frac{\partial(w_{nr}/p)}{\partial\gamma} < 0$, respectively. This means that an expansion of the wage gap between regular and non-regular employment leads to an increase in the real wage of regular employees and a decrease in the real wage of non-regular employees.

6.4.2   The case of a wage-led demand regime

We consider a case in which the steady state equilibrium exhibits a wage-led demand regime.

First, we consider a case in which the reserve army effect is small and consequently the steady state equilibrium is stable. Figure 6.7 shows the phase diagram in a wage-led demand regime case.

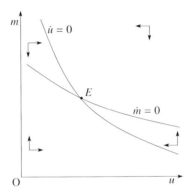

Figure 6.7: Phase diagram in a case where the stable steady state equilibrium exhibits a wage-led demand regime

Next, we consider a case in which the reserve army effect is large and consequently, the steady state equilibrium is unstable. Steady state E is the saddle point in Figure 6.8. Thus, if the economy starts from the initial value above the stable arm, for instance, point A_0, it converges to a point where the capacity utilization rate is zero and the profit share is unity. If the economy starts from the initial value below the stable arm, for instance, point B_0, it converges to a point where the capacity utilization rate is unity and the profit share is zero.

Here, we introduce $m_{\max}$ and $m_{\min}$. If the government does not actually know the steady state equilibrium, the minimum wage given by the government does not necessarily coincide with the steady state profit share. The interval $[m_{\min}, m_{\max}]$ represents the feasible combinations of the profit share determined by the government as the minimum wage policy. Then, as shown in Figure 6.8, starting from point A_0, the economy converges to point A, while when starting from point B_0, it converges to point B. If we compare point A with point B, point B is superior to point A because the real wage associated with B is higher than that associated with A. Further, the employment rate in B is also high compared to that in A because u in B is higher than u in A.

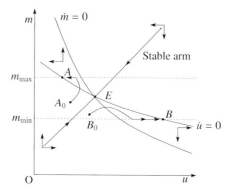

Figure 6.8: Phase diagram in a case where the unstable steady state equilibrium exhibits a wage-led demand regime

6.5   Concluding remarks

In this chapter, we have developed a Kaleckian model in which two types of labor (regular and non-regular employment) are incorporated. We have analyzed how the expansion of the wage gap between regular and non-regular employment affects the economy.

First, if the steady state equilibrium exhibits a wage-led demand regime, an increase in the wage gap does not affect the stability of equilibrium. In this case, the size of the reserve army effect affects the stability of the equilibrium. If the reserve army effect is strong, the steady state equilibrium is unstable. However, even if the steady state equilibrium is unstable, the introduction of a minimum and/or maximum wage prevents the capacity utilization and profit share from diverging. In this case, it is possible that depending on conditions, we obtain a real wage and an employment rate that are higher than the steady state equilibrium values.

Second, if the steady state equilibrium exhibits a profit-led demand regime, an increase in the wage gap destabilizes the equilibrium. It is possible that depending on conditions, an increase in the wage gap produces endogenous and perpetual business cycles. In addition, an increase in non-regular employment relative to regular employment stabilizes the steady state equilibrium. However, we must note that the government should not literally increase non-regular employment. On the contrary, the government should adopt a policy mix that decreases both the non-regular employment and the wage gap. The introduction of a minimum wage is desirable in that it mitigates fluctuations of business cycles. However, the introduction of an inappropriate minimum wage policy that sets a minimum wage higher than the steady state equilibrium value consequently leads to a real wage and an employment rate lower than the steady state values.

Finally, we must note that our model is a short- to medium-run model, not a long-run model, in a strict sence. As stated in the text, if we assume Okun's law, the capacity utilization rate has a one-to-one relationship with the employment rate. However, these two variables are strictly different. In this chapter, for convenience, we identify the capacity utilization rate with the employment rate, but we cannot in a strict sense. To build a long-run model that distinguishes between the capacity utilization rate and the employment rate and investigate the effects on employment in detail will be left for future research.

Appendix 6.A: Introducing induced technical change

As the text shows, the average labor productivity changes with changes in the capacity utilization rate along the transitional dynamics toward the steady state equilibrium, but after the economy reaches equilibrium, there is no perpetual technical progress in our model because the capacity utilization rate remains constant. However, we can introduce perpetual technical progress into the model by using the idea of induced technical change, which we turn to in this Appendix.

Suppose, for simplicity, that the labor input coefficients α and β are decreasing at the same constant rate $\lambda > 0$. Then, we can write α and β as follows:

$$\alpha = \alpha_0 e^{-\lambda t}, \tag{6.36}$$

$$\beta = \beta_0 e^{-\lambda t}, \tag{6.37}$$

where α_0 and β_0 are positive constants. In this case, the rate of change in the average labor productivity is given by

$$\frac{\dot{a}}{a} = \frac{\alpha}{(\alpha + \beta u)u} \cdot \dot{u} + \lambda. \tag{6.38}$$

That is, λ is added to equation (6.14).

Here, we introduce induced technical change and assume that λ is an increasing function of the wage share, that is, a decreasing function of the profit share.

$$\lambda = \lambda(m), \quad \lambda' < 0. \tag{6.39}$$

This idea is also adopted by Tavani *et al.* (2011) and similar to the ideas of Taylor (2004, ch. 7) and Foley and Michl (1999, ch. 14).

With equation (6.39), the element of the Jacobian matrix J_{22} is modified to

$$J_{22} = -(1 - m^*)[1 - f(u^*)J_{12} - \lambda'(m^*)]. \tag{6.40}$$

From this, we can see that $\lambda'(m^*) < 0$ is likely to make J_{22} negative, which makes the dynamic system more stable. Indeed, the trace and the determinant of $\mathbf{J}$ are rewritten as follows:

$$\text{tr}\,\mathbf{J} = \underset{-}{J_{11}} - (1-m^*) + (1-m^*)\underset{+/-}{f(u^*)J_{12}} + (1-m^*)\underset{-}{\lambda'(m^*)}, \qquad (6.41)$$

$$\det\mathbf{J} = -(1-m^*)[\underset{-}{J_{11}} + (1-\theta)\underset{-}{m'_w(u^*)}\underset{+/-}{J_{12}} - \underset{-}{\lambda'(m^*)}\underset{-}{J_{11}}]. \qquad (6.42)$$

Accordingly, the term $\lambda'(m^*) < 0$ is likely to make the $\text{tr}\,\mathbf{J}$ negative and $\det\mathbf{J}$ positive.

Therefore, introducing induced technical change makes the dynamic system more stable. However, qualitative results do not change considerably as long as the extent of induced technical change is small enough.

Chapter 7

International Competition and Distributive Conflict in an Open Economy Kaleckian Model

7.1 Introduction

Thus far, a number of Kaleckian models have been developed, and the relation between income distribution and aggregate demand has been investigated.[1] From those models, we derived a familiar result: that there are two types of demand regime, wage-led and profit-led, according to the parameter constellation of investment and saving functions.[2] A wage-led demand regime indicates an economy in which a rise in the profit share decreases aggregate demand and a profit-led demand regime indicates an economy in which a rise in the profit share increases aggregate demand.

Most of the Kaleckian models that investigate the relation between income distribution and aggregate demand assume a closed economy and abstract from international trade. The real economy is nevertheless an open economy, and accordingly there are complications in applying analytical results based on the assumption of a closed economy to the real world. It is necessary to construct an open economy model and derive effective implications for the real economy.

Some of the Kaleckian models have, in fact, taken into account an open economy case.[3] Blecker (1989) is a pioneering work that introduces international price competition into the Kaleckian model. By adding net export into demand components, Blecker shows that an increase in the wage share can lower international price competitiveness and has a negative impact on investment, which implies that a wage-led

---

1) As for the empirical studies on the relation between income distribution and aggregate demand based on the Kaleckian framework, see Stockhammer and Onaran (2004), Barbosa-Filho and Taylor (2006), Naastepad and Storm (2007), Hein and Vogel (2008), Stockhammer, Onaran, and Ederer (2009), and Stockhammer, Hein, and Grafl (2011).

2) For a theoretical explanation of the demand regime, see Blecker (2002).

3) Cordero (2002) constructs an open economy Kaleckian model that integrates the theory of conflicting-claims inflation. This model assumes, however, that price is determined in the international goods market and formalizes only workers' bargaining process. La Marca (2010), using an open economy version of the stock-flow consistent model, considers the dynamics of the capacity utilization rate, profit share, and trade balance. Von Arnim (2011) constructs an open economy Kaleckian model and considers the effect of the wage policy on growth and distribution by using Monte Carlo simulation.

demand regime is hard to obtain. Another novel idea of Blecker (1989) is the assumption that firms restrain their prices in terms of international price competition, whereas traditional Kaleckian models assume that firms determine their price as they like. This modification implies that international competition strictly affects income distribution in the domestic country.

Blecker (1989) nevertheless assumes that the measure of international price competition (i.e., the ratio of domestic unit labor cost to import prices) is exogenously given and hence does not explicitly consider the process in which international competition influences income distribution. We therefore need to endogenize income distribution to improve the open economy model.

A representative way to endogenize the process of income distribution in a Kaleckian model is to use the theory of conflicting-claims inflation developed by Rowthorn (1977).[4] This theory assumes that both firms and workers have their own target values of each distributive share and then negotiate over the price and the nominal wage in response to the gap between the actual share and their own targets.

The Cassetti (2002) model is one that takes into account the open economy case using the theory of conflicting-claims inflation. He considers a situation in which inflation of domestic products due to class conflict changes the real exchange rate, and this change affects the growth rate of the economy through exports and imports. His model is important in that it simultaneously introduces international price competition and the determination of income distribution.

Cassetti's (2002) model nevertheless leaves room for further investigation. When extending a Kaleckian model with conflict-inflation to an open economy model, he uses equations that determine the wage and price dynamics in a closed economy without any modifications. In other words, he assumes that in the face of international price competition in the international goods market, firms and workers never consider foreign competition, which is unrealistic. To investigate income distribution in an open economy, we must consider the effect of international price competition on the conflict between firms and workers.

Missaglia (2007) is a study that considers this aspect. Missaglia assumes that the price equation of firms depends on the real exchange rate; when the terms of trade deteriorate, firms restrain their prices. Missaglia's (2007) approach is still unsatisfactory because he does not consider the effect of international price competition on the wage bargaining of workers. The same problem holds for Blecker (1998), which is an extension of Blecker (1989).

With the ongoing globalization of the real world, just as firms have to consider international competition in setting their prices, workers also have to consider international competition in formulating their wage demands. Increasing wages recklessly in an open economy causes a decrease in the price competitiveness of the domestic industry and a decline in market share on the international market, which in turn

---

4) For closed economy Kaleckian models with the theory of conflicting-claims inflation, see Cassetti (2003) and Dutt (1987).

causes a fall in domestic labor demand and leads to a loss of employment. In addition, if international capital flow is allowed, firms facing losses due to international price competition transfer their production base to foreign countries to seek cheaper labor. Accordingly, the pressure on domestic workers will intensify. It is therefore reasonable to suppose that workers who engage in wage bargaining pay attention to the relative price of domestic and foreign products.[5]

When both firms and workers consider international price competition, the effect of price pressure on income distribution has two channels. Whether the wage share or the profit share increases when international competition intensifies depends on how much firms and workers share the burden arising from price restraint.

Accordingly, the Blecker (2011) model assumes that international price competition affects both firms and workers. In this model, the target profit share of firms depends on the real exchange rate, and moreover, the rate of change in the nominal wage that is determined by wage bargaining depends on the real exchange rate. In his approach, however, the target profit share of workers is assumed to be constant. It is because the price of imports is indexed to the nominal wage that changes in the real exchange rate affect the nominal wage, not because the international price competition affects the target of workers. As stated above, however, it is possible that under severe international competition, labor unions revise the target downward. It is therefore necessary to build a conflict model that considers this possibility.

In addition, the Blecker (2011) model separates the determination of output (capacity utilization) from the determination of income distribution and the real exchange rate. In other words, the goods market has nothing to do with the profit share and the real exchange rate that are determined in the labor market; there is a feedback from the labor market to the goods market, but not from the goods market to the labor market.

In the present chapter, we therefore present a Kaleckian model in which international price competition affects both firms' decisions and workers' decisions. In addition, there is bilateral feedback from the labor market to the goods market and from the goods market to the labor market.[6] Using this model, we investigate the stability of the steady state equilibrium and the effect of international price competition

---

5) For a model that assumes the effect of international price competition on the wage bargaining of workers, see Blecker (1996). He also introduces a real world example that supports this assumption: the labor union of Xerox Corporation accepts a sharp wage cut to prevent work from moving abroad in the face of international price competition.

6) At the steady state equilibrium of our model, the rate of inflation is constant. Accordingly, the equilibrium capacity utilization rate can be called the "Non-Accelerating Inflation Rate of *Utilization*." As long as we identify the capacity utilization rate with the employment rate, we can regard $1 - u^*$ as the "Non-Accelerating Inflation Rate of Unemployment (NAIRU)," where u^* denotes the equilibrium value of the capacity utilization rate. The equilibrium capacity utilization rate depends on both the bargaining power of workers and that of firms. For example, an increase in the bargaining power of workers either positively or negatively affects the NAIRU. This result is similar to the results obtained in Storm and Naastepad (2007) and Naastepad and Storm (2010), and stands in marked contrast to the mainstream NAIRU-view, which implies that deregulation of labor market and resultant reduction in the bargaining power of workers is necessary for lowering the rate of unemployment. However, strictly speaking, the capacity utilization rate and the employment rate are different variables, and hence, we need to build a model in which the employment rate is an endogenous variable if we want to find the NAIRU.

on the equilibrium values. From our analysis, we obtain the following new results.

First, with regard to the stability of the equilibrium, as long as the effect of the real exchange rate on trade balance is sufficiently small, the equilibrium is likely to be stable irrespective of which demand regime is realized in the equilibrium. By contrast, if the real exchange rate effect is large, then the equilibrium is likely to be unstable, and depending on conditions, cyclical fluctuations can occur.

Second, with regard to the comparative static analysis, even if the domestic economy is characterized by a profit-led demand regime, unlike in a closed economy, a rise in the bargaining power of firms can depress the capacity utilization rate. Moreover, even if the domestic economy is characterized by a wage-led demand regime, unlike in a closed economy, a rise in the bargaining power of workers can depress the capacity utilization rate.

The remainder of the chapter is organized as follows. Section 2 presents our model. Section 3 investigates the dynamics of the model. Section 4 conducts comparative static analysis. Section 5 is the conclusion.

7.2   Model

Consider a small open economy in which workers and capitalists coexist. Workers consume all their wages and capitalists save a fraction s of their profits. Workers and capitalists consume both domestic and foreign goods. The goods market is imperfectly competitive, and hence, firms set prices according to a mark-up pricing rule. Moreover, firms have an investment function independent of savings. The capital stock and investment consist only of domestic goods.

7.2.1   Dynamics of capacity utilization

Suppose that firms operate with a fixed coefficient production function. The ratio of potential output Y^F to the capital stock K is assumed to be constant. We can then write the capacity utilization rate as $u = Y/K$, where Y denotes actual output.[7] From this, we have $r = mu$, where r and m denote the profit rate and profit share, respectively.

Following Marglin and Bhaduri (1990), we assume that the firms' investment function is increasing in both the capacity utilization rate and profit share:

$$\frac{I}{K} = g_d(u, m), \quad g_{du} > 0, \ g_{dm} > 0, \tag{7.1}$$

where g_{du} denotes the partial derivative with respect to the capacity utilization rate and g_{dm} the partial derivative with respect to the profit share.

Let us specify consumption demand. Total domestic consumption demand consists of demand for domestic goods and foreign goods. First, we assume that total

---

7) The capacity utilization rate is defined as Y/Y^F. Since we have $Y/Y^F = (Y/K)/(K/Y^F)$, we can use Y/K as the capacity utilization rate as long as K/Y^F is technologically fixed and constant.

nominal consumption of domestic goods is a fraction α of total nominal consumption expenditure.

$$p(C_w^D + C_c^D) = \alpha[wE + (1 - s)rpK], \tag{7.2}$$

where p denotes the price of domestic goods, C_w^D workers' real consumption of domestic goods, C_c^D capitalists' real consumption of domestic goods, w the nominal wage, and E employment. Next, we assume that total nominal consumption of foreign goods (i.e., total nominal imports) is a fraction $1-\alpha$ of total nominal consumption expenditure.

$$ep^f(C_w^M + C_c^M) = (1 - \alpha)[wE + (1 - s)rpK], \tag{7.3}$$

where e denotes the nominal exchange rate in terms of home currency, p^f the price of foreign goods that is exogenously given, C_w^M workers' real consumption of foreign goods, and C_c^M capitalists' real consumption of foreign goods.

Following Cassetti (2002), we assume that the expenditure coefficient for domestic goods is a function of the real exchange rate $\varepsilon = ep^f/p$.

$$\alpha = \alpha(\varepsilon), \quad 0 < \alpha(\varepsilon) < 1. \tag{7.4}$$

How the expenditure coefficient changes when the real exchange rate changes depends on the elasticity of substitution ρ between domestic goods and foreign goods. If ρ is less than unity, then α is a decreasing function of ε. However, if ρ is more than unity, then α is an increasing function of ε.

We specify demand for exports. Nominal exports equal real exports multiplied by the price of domestic goods. We assume that real exports are increasing in both the real exchange rate and foreign real incomes Y^f.

$$p \cdot EX = p \cdot EX(\varepsilon, Y^f) = p \cdot ex(\varepsilon) \cdot K \cdot Y^f, \quad ex' > 0, \tag{7.5}$$

where $ex(\varepsilon)$ denotes real exports per capital stock. For simplicity, we assume that real exports are linear in foreign real incomes.[8]

The goods market clearing condition leads to

$$\begin{aligned}
pY &= pC + pI + pEX - ep^f M \\
&= (pC^D + ep^f C^M) + pI + pEX - ep^f M \\
&= pC^D + pI + pEX, \tag{7.6}
\end{aligned}$$

8) In our specification, the income elasticity of export demand is unity. In contrast, in balance-of-payments-constrained growth models, originally founded by Thirlwall (1979), the sizes of the income elasticities of export and import demands are important in determining the rate of economic growth. However, as discussed below, we assume that foreign incomes Y^f is constant. Therefore, the size of the income elasticity of export demand does not affect our results.

where C denotes total consumption made up of the consumption of domestic goods $C^D = C_w^D + C_c^D$ and that of foreign goods $C^M = C_w^M + C_c^M$, and M denotes imports. Note that $C^M = M$. Dividing both sides of equation (7.6) by pK and substituting equations (7.2), (7.3), (7.4), and (7.5) in the resultant expression, we obtain

$$g_d(u, m) = [1 - \alpha(\varepsilon)]u + \alpha(\varepsilon)sum - ex(\varepsilon)Y^f. \tag{7.7}$$

Equation (7.7) is a condition that holds in the equilibrium of the goods market. However, the equilibrium of the goods market is not instantaneously attained. If we denote the right-hand side of equation (7.7) as g_s, the excess demand of the goods market is given by $g_d - g_s$. Here, for simplicity, we assume that Y^f is constant and unity.

We assume that in the goods market, quantity adjustment prevails.

$$\dot{u} = \phi(g_d - g_s), \quad \phi > 0, \tag{7.8}$$

where ϕ denotes the speed of adjustment of the goods market. Equation (7.8) shows that excess demand leads to a rise in the capacity utilization rate, while excess supply leads to a decline in the capacity utilization rate. Substituting equation (7.1) and the right-hand side of equation (7.7) in equation (7.8), we obtain the dynamics of the capacity utilization rate.

$$\dot{u} = \phi\{g_d(u, m) - [1 - \alpha(\varepsilon)]u - \alpha(\varepsilon)sum + ex(\varepsilon)\}. \tag{7.9}$$

7.2.2   Dynamics of the profit share

Differentiating the definition of the profit share $m = 1 - [w/(pa)]$ with respect to time, we obtain

$$\frac{\dot{m}}{1 - m} = \hat{p} - \hat{w} + \hat{a}, \tag{7.10}$$

where $\hat{x} = \dot{x}/x$ denotes the rate of change in a variable x and a the level of labor productivity. In this subsection, we specify each term on the right-hand side of equation (7.10).

We specify changes in the domestic price and the nominal wage by using Rowthorn's (1977) conflicting-claims theory of inflation. First, suppose that firms set their price to close the gap between their target profit share m_f and the actual profit share. Second, suppose that the growth rate of the nominal wage that workers manage to negotiate depends on the gap between their target profit share m_w and the actual profit share.

$$\hat{p} = \theta_f(m_f - m), \tag{7.11}$$

$$m_f = m_f(\varepsilon; \mu), \ m_{f\varepsilon} > 0, \ m_{f\mu} > 0, \ 0 < m_f < 1, \ \mu > 0, \ \theta_f > 0,$$

$$\hat{w} = \theta_w(m - m_w), \tag{7.12}$$

$$m_w = m_w(\varepsilon, u; \omega), \ m_{w\varepsilon} < 0, \ m_{wu} < 0, \ m_{w\omega} < 0, \ 0 < m_w < 1, \ \omega > 0, \ \theta_w > 0,$$

where μ and ω are shift parameters, and denote the bargaining power of firms and of workers, respectively. The parameters θ_f and θ_w are the adjustment speed of the price and of the nominal wage, respectively.

In our model, the two target profit shares are determined endogenously.

First, we assume that the target profit share of firms is an increasing function of the real exchange rate ($m_{f\varepsilon} > 0$). This means that domestic firms set their price by considering international price competition with foreign firms. When the price competitiveness of domestic firms lowers, domestic firms cut their target profit share and hence their prices to defend their market share in the international goods market.

Second, we assume that the target profit share of workers is decreasing in both the real exchange rate and the capacity utilization rate ($m_{w\varepsilon} < 0$ and $m_{wu} < 0$). An increase in the price of the domestic goods has a negative effect on employment and workers thus set their target profit share considering the price decrease. When the real exchange rate decreases and price competitiveness worsens, workers therefore compromise to raise the target profit share. We can identify an increase in the capacity utilization rate with an increase in the employment rate. When the employment rate increases, workers' attitude in bargaining becomes stronger, leading them to seek a higher target wage share, that is, a lower target profit share. This is known as the "reserve army effect."

Third, we assume that the target profit share of firms is increasing in the bargaining power of firms ($m_{f\mu} > 0$) and that the target profit share of workers is decreasing in the bargaining power of workers ($m_{w\omega} < 0$).

The growth rate of labor productivity is determined endogenously. Here, we assume that labor productivity growth is an increasing function of the capacity utilization rate.

$$\hat{a} = g_a(u), \quad g_a' > 0. \tag{7.13}$$

This specification is similar to the "reserve-army creation effect" described in Sasaki (2011, 2012), where the growth rate of labor productivity is an increasing function of the employment rate. If the employment rate is positively related with the capacity utilization rate,[9] That is, if Okun's law holds, we can use capacity utilization in place of the employment rate (Tavani, Flaschel, and Taylor, 2011). As the employment rate (capacity utilization) increases and the labor market tightens, the bargaining power of workers increases, which exerts an upward pressure on wages, leading capitalists to adopt labor-saving technical changes. In other words, capitalists intentionally create unemployment (Bhaduri, 2006; Dutt, 2006; Flaschel and Skott, 2006; Sasaki, 2010, 2011).

---

9) In the short-run, it is reasonable to think that the capacity utilization rate and the employment rate move in the same direction. However, in the long-run, these two variables are different, and so, we should consider the dynamics of the two variables separately. If we separate the dynamics of the two variables, as the closed economy models of Sasaki (2010, 2013) show, the number of differential equations increases, and so, analysis gets more complicated. Therefore, in the present chapter, we do not separate the dynamics of the rate of utilization from those of the employment rate. Separate analysis will be left for future research.

Substituting equations (7.11), (7.12), and (7.13) in equation (7.10), we obtain the dynamics of the profit share.

$$\frac{\dot{m}}{1-m} = \theta_f[m_f(\varepsilon;\mu) - m] - \theta_w[m - m_w(\varepsilon, u; \omega)] + g_a(u). \qquad (7.14)$$

7.2.3   Dynamics of the real exchange rate

We specify the dynamics of the real exchange rate. The rate of change in the real exchange is given as

$$\hat{\varepsilon} = \hat{e} + \hat{p}^f - \hat{p}, \qquad (7.15)$$

where the rate of change in the price of foreign goods, $\hat{p}^f$ is constant and exogenously given. Following Blecker and Seguino (2002) and Blecker (2011), we introduce a crawling peg system in regard to the nominal exchange rate:

$$\hat{e} = \lambda(\bar{\varepsilon} - \varepsilon), \quad \bar{\varepsilon} > 0, \ \lambda > 0, \qquad (7.16)$$

where λ denotes the speed of adjustment. The currency authority has a target level of the real exchange rate $\bar{\varepsilon}$ and adjusts the nominal exchange rate according to the gap between the target and the actual levels.[10] We introduce this crawling peg mechanism to investigate how the exchange rate policy of monetary authority affects the steady state equilibrium. The target level of the real exchange rate affects the equilibrium value of ε as well as the adjustment path of ε.

Substituting equations (7.11) and (7.16) in equation (7.15), we obtain the following equation of the dynamics of the real exchange rate:

$$\hat{\varepsilon} = \lambda(\bar{\varepsilon} - \varepsilon) + \hat{p}^f - \theta_f[m_f(\varepsilon;\mu) - m]. \qquad (7.17)$$

7.3   Dynamics of the model

From the above analysis, the dynamics of the capacity utilization rate, profit share, and real exchange rate are given as

$$\dot{u} = \phi\{g_d(u, m) - [1 - \alpha(\varepsilon)]u - \alpha(\varepsilon)sum + ex(\varepsilon)\}, \qquad (7.18)$$

$$\dot{m} = (1 - m)\{\theta_f[m_f(\varepsilon;\mu) - m] - \theta_w[m - m_w(\varepsilon, u; \omega)] + g_a(u)\}, \qquad (7.19)$$

$$\dot{\varepsilon} = \varepsilon\{\lambda(\bar{\varepsilon} - \varepsilon) + \hat{p}^f - \theta_f[m_f(\varepsilon;\mu) - m]\}. \qquad (7.20)$$

The steady state is a situation where $\dot{u} = \dot{m} = \dot{\varepsilon} = 0$. We let the steady state values be denoted as u^*, m^*, and ε^*. In the following analysis, we assume that there

---

10) According to Blecker (2011), we assume that the central bank automatically sterilizes any reserve inflows and outflows that are necessary to manage the nominal exchange rate. Accordingly, the money supply and interest rate, which are not explicitly shown in our model, are both unaffected.

are steady state values such that $0 < u^* < 1$, $0 < m^* < 1$, and $\varepsilon^* > 0$. As the numerical simulations in Appendix 7.B show, such a steady state actually exists, but this result depends on functional specifications.

The elements of the Jacobian matrix $\mathbf{J}$ that corresponds to the system of the differential equations are given by

$$J_{11} \equiv \frac{\partial \dot{u}}{\partial u} = \phi\{g_{du} - [1 - \alpha(\varepsilon)] - \alpha(\varepsilon)sm\}, \tag{7.21}$$

$$J_{12} \equiv \frac{\partial \dot{u}}{\partial m} = \phi[g_{dm} - \alpha(\varepsilon)su], \tag{7.22}$$

$$J_{13} \equiv \frac{\partial \dot{u}}{\partial \varepsilon} = \phi\{\alpha'(\varepsilon)u(1 - sm) + ex'(\varepsilon)\}, \tag{7.23}$$

$$J_{21} \equiv \frac{\partial \dot{m}}{\partial u} = (1 - m)[\theta_w m_{wu} + g_a'(u)] = (1 - m)\Omega, \quad \Omega \equiv \theta_w m_{wu} + g_a'(u), \tag{7.24}$$

$$J_{22} \equiv \frac{\partial \dot{m}}{\partial m} = -(\theta_f + \theta_w)(1 - m) < 0, \tag{7.25}$$

$$J_{23} \equiv \frac{\partial \dot{m}}{m\varepsilon} = (1 - m)(\theta_f m_{f\varepsilon} + \theta_w m_{w\varepsilon}), \tag{7.26}$$

$$J_{31} \equiv \frac{\partial \dot{\varepsilon}}{\partial u} = 0, \tag{7.27}$$

$$J_{32} \equiv \frac{\partial \dot{\varepsilon}}{\partial m} = \theta_f \varepsilon > 0, \tag{7.28}$$

$$J_{33} \equiv \frac{\partial \dot{\varepsilon}}{\partial \varepsilon} = -\varepsilon(\lambda + \theta_f m_{f\varepsilon}) < 0. \tag{7.29}$$

All the elements are evaluated at the steady state values. In what follows, we explain elements whose signs are ambiguous.

To conduct the analysis further, we introduce the following assumption.

Assumption 7.1. *The condition* $g_{du} - [1 - \alpha(\varepsilon)] - \alpha(\varepsilon)sm < 0$ *holds.*

This condition is an open economy version of the Keynesian stability condition in which we assume that the quantity adjustment in the goods market is stable. We then have $J_{11} < 0$.

Next, we introduce the following definition.

Definition 7.1. *We define* $g_{dm} - \alpha(\varepsilon)su < 0$ *as the domestically wage-led demand regime and* $g_{dm} - \alpha(\varepsilon)su > 0$ *as the domestically profit-led demand regime.*

The element J_{12} shows the direct effect of an increase in the profit share on the capacity utilization rate. If the sign is positive, a rise in the profit share increases domestic demand directly, which we call a *domestically* profit-led demand case.[11] If the sign is negative, a rise in the profit share decreases domestic demand directly, which

---

11) We can rewrite equation (7.22) as follows: $J_{12} = \phi[g_{dm} - \alpha u + \alpha(1 - s)u]$. The first term on the right-hand side shows a positive effect of a rise in the profit share on investment. The second term shows a negative impact of an increase in the profit share on consumption for domestic goods from wage income,

we call a *domestically* wage-led demand case. Note here that the partial relationship between the profit share and the capacity utilization rate, which is represented by J_{12}, differs from the overall relationship between them. In regard to the overall relation between the profit share and the capacity utilization rate, we add the following definition.

Definition 7.2. *We call the situation where for any of the parameter changes that affect income distribution, the profit share and the capacity utilization rate move in the opposite direction in the steady state equilibrium an overall wage-led demand regime. We call the situation where for any of the parameter changes that affect income distribution, the profit share and the capacity utilization rate move in the same direction in the steady state equilibrium an overall profit-led demand regime.*

In section 7.4, we will show cases where a domestically wage-led demand (profit-led demand) regime can be compatible with an overall profit-led demand (wage-led demand) regime.

The element J_{13} shows the effect of an increase in the real exchange rate on the trade balance (normalized by capital stock) $TB = ex(\varepsilon) - [1 - \alpha(\varepsilon)](1 - sm)u$. If ρ is more than unity, we have $\alpha'(\varepsilon) > 0$, which leads to $J_{13} > 0$. This corresponds to $\partial TB/\partial\varepsilon > 0$, which means that the Marshall-Lerner condition (ML condition, hereafter) is satisfied. If ρ is less than unity, we have $\alpha'(\varepsilon) < 0$, which leads to $J_{13} < 0$, depending on the size of $ex'(\varepsilon) > 0$. In this case, the ML condition is not satisfied.

The element J_{21} shows the effect of an increase in the capacity utilization rate on the profit share. If the reserve army effect exceeds the reserve army creation effect, we have $\Omega < 0$, leading to $J_{21} < 0$. This corresponds to the case where the profit share is counter-cyclical to the capacity utilization rate. On the contrary, if the reserve army creation effect exceeds the reserve army effect, we have $\Omega > 0$, leading to $J_{21} > 0$. This corresponds to the case where the profit share is pro-cyclical to the capacity utilization rate.

The element J_{23} shows the effect of an increase in the real exchange rate on the profit share. If firms are more responsive than workers, that is, if the absolute value of $m_{f\varepsilon}$ is greater than that of $m_{w\varepsilon}$, then $J_{23} > 0$. In contrast, if workers are more responsive than firms, that is, if the absolute value of $m_{w\varepsilon}$ is greater than that of $m_{f\varepsilon}$, then $J_{23} < 0$. If firms are responsive, firms bear the burden arising from international price competition more than workers, but if workers are more responsive, workers bear the burden arising from international price competition more than firms.

By deriving the characteristic equation that corresponds to the Jacobian matrix **J** and examining the corresponding characteristic roots, we can investigate the local stability of the steady state equilibrium.[12] For clarification of analysis, we use the

---

and the third term shows a positive effect of a rise in the profit share on consumption for domestic goods from profit income. Thus, the term "domestically profit-led demand" denotes the case where a rise in the profit share increases domestic demand, and the term "domestically wage-led demand" denotes the case where a rise in the profit share decreases domestic demand.

12) For details of the stability analysis, see Appendix 7.A.

following two assumption:

Assumption 7.2. *Both $g_{dm} - \alpha(\varepsilon)su < 0$ and $\Omega > 0$ hold.*

Assumption 7.3. *Both $g_{dm} - \alpha(\varepsilon)su > 0$ and $\Omega < 0$ hold.*

Assumption 7.2 corresponds to the case where the economy is in a domestically wage-led demand regime and the reserve army creation effect exceeds the reserve army effect. Then, we have both $J_{12} < 0$ and $J_{21} > 0$. Assumption 7.3 corresponds to the case where the economy is in a domestically profit-led demand regime and the reserve army effect exceeds the reserve army creation effect. We then have $J_{12} > 0$ and $J_{21} < 0$.

Using these assumptions, we obtain the following proposition:

Proposition 7.1. *Suppose that the effect of the real exchange rate on the trade balance is small, that is, the absolute value of $\partial TB/\partial \varepsilon$ is small. Then, irrespective of whether or not the ML condition is satisfied, the combination of either a domestically wage-led demand regime and $\Omega > 0$ or a domestically profit-led demand regime and $\Omega < 0$ makes the steady state equilibrium stable.*

Proof. See Appendix 7.A.1.   ■

As Appendix 7.C shows, in a closed economy, the combination of a domestically wage-led demand regime and $\Omega > 0$ (i.e., the reserve army creation effect exceeds the reserve army effect), or a domestically profit-led demand regime and $\Omega < 0$ (the reserve army effect exceeds the reserve army creation effect) is a stability condition. In the open economy, if the effect of the real exchange rate on the trade balance is small, these combinations are also stability conditions.

We also obtain two further propositions:

Proposition 7.2. *Suppose that the effect of the real exchange rate on the trade balance is large, that is, the absolute value of $\partial TB/\partial \varepsilon$ is large. Then, on the one hand, if the ML condition is satisfied, the combination of a domestically wage-led demand regime and $\Omega > 0$ makes the steady state equilibrium unstable. On the other hand, if the ML condition is not satisfied, under the combination of a domestically wage-led demand regime and $\Omega > 0$, limit cycles occur when the speed of adjustment of the goods market lies within some range.*

Proof. See Appendix 7.A.2.   ■

Proposition 7.3. *Suppose that the effect of the real exchange rate on the trade balance is large, that is, the absolute value of $\partial TB/\partial \varepsilon$ is large. Then, on the one hand, if the ML condition is satisfied, under the combination of a domestically profit-led demand regime and $\Omega < 0$, limit cycles occur when the speed of adjustment of the goods market lies within some range. On the other hand, if the ML condition is not satisfied, the combination of a domestically profit-led demand regime and $\Omega < 0$ makes the steady state equilibrium unstable.*

Proof. Proof. See Appendix 7.A.3.   ■

We now explain why limit cycles occur when the speed of adjustment of the goods market is medium. First, when ϕ is sufficiently close to zero, the capacity utilization rate is not adjusted and the analysis of the dynamic system therefore amounts to the analysis of the subsystem that consists of the profit share and the real exchange rate. After some calculations, we find that the dynamics of the subsystem are stable. Second, when ϕ is sufficiently large, the capacity utilization rate is adjusted immediately and the effect of the capacity utilization rate on the dynamic system therefore does not last. In this case, too, the analysis of the dynamic system amounts to the analysis of the subsystem that consists of the profit share and the real exchange rate. When ϕ takes an intermediate value, the capacity utilization rate changes with lags. The capacity utilization rate therefore has a lasting effect on the dynamic system and, accordingly, cyclical fluctuations occur.

Propositions 7.1, 7.2, and 7.3 are summarized in Figure 7.1.

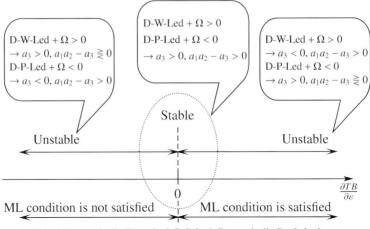

Figure 7.1: Diagram of stability analysis

7.4 Comparative static analysis

This section examines the effect of changes in the saving rate of capitalists, the bargaining powers of firms and workers, and the target value of the real exchange rate on the steady state values of the rate of capital utilization, profit share, and the real exchange rate.[13] Here, we only consider the stable steady state: Assumption 7.1 holds, either Assumption 7.2 ($J_{12} < 0$ and $J_{21} > 0$) or Assumption 7.3 ($J_{12} > 0$ and $J_{21} < 0$) holds, the trade balance does not respond much to the real exchange rate (i.e., the absolute value of $\partial TB/\partial \varepsilon$ is sufficiently small), and $\det \mathbf{J} < 0$ holds. In addition, we suppose here that the ML condition is always satisfied, that is, $J_{13} > 0$ holds.[14]

7.4.1   Saving rate of capitalists

We represent the effect of a change in the saving rate of capitalists on the capacity utilization rate as follows:

$$\frac{du^*}{ds} = \frac{\alpha \varepsilon (1 - m)mu[\lambda + \theta_f \theta_w (m_{f\varepsilon} - m_{w\varepsilon})]}{\det \mathbf{J}} < 0. \tag{7.30}$$

Equation (7.30) thus means that the paradox of thrift holds even in an open economy version of the Kaleckian model: an increase in the saving rate of capitalists reduces the capacity utilization rate.

The effects of a change in the saving rate of capitalists on the profit share and the real exchange rate are given by

$$\frac{dm^*}{ds} = \frac{-\alpha mu J_{21} J_{33}}{\det \mathbf{J}}, \tag{7.31}$$

$$\frac{d\varepsilon^*}{ds} = \frac{\alpha mu J_{21} J_{32}}{\det \mathbf{J}}. \tag{7.32}$$

As described above, an increase in the saving rate of capitalists decreases the capacity utilization rate. When the reserve army creation effect exceeds the reserve army effect ($J_{21} > 0$), a decline in the capacity utilization rate reduces labor productivity growth and thus the profit share ($dm^*/ds < 0$). Furthermore, a fall in the profit share decreases the real exchange rate ($d\varepsilon^*/ds < 0$) because a loss of profitability urges capitalists to raise the price of domestic goods.

If, however, the reserve army effect is stronger than the reserve army creation effect ($J_{21} < 0$), a rise in the saving rate of capitalists leads to a rise in the profit share ($dm^*/ds > 0$). This is because a fall in the capacity utilization rate decelerates nominal wage growth. An increase in profitability, moreover, leaves room for lowering the price of domestic goods. Consequently, an increase in the saving rate of capitalists raises the real exchange rate ($d\varepsilon^*/ds > 0$).

---

13) The current analysis abstracts from the effect of the price of foreign goods on the steady state values. This is because, for the home country, a rise in the target value of the real exchange rate is equivalent to a rise in the price of foreign goods in the sense that they both produce the same results.

14) The results of the comparative static analysis in the cases where the ML condition does not hold is more complicated than those in the cases where the condition holds. We therefore do not investigate the former case.

7.4.2   Bargaining powers of firms and workers

The next task is to investigate the effects of the bargaining power of firms and workers on the steady state values of the key endogenous variables. Because it is difficult to derive purely analytical results from our model, we here confine ourselves to pointing out that the propositions obtained in a closed version of a Kaleckian model may not be applied to an open economy case.

We represent an effect of an increase in the firms' bargaining power on the capacity utilization rate as follows:

$$\frac{du^*}{d\mu} = \frac{-\theta_f m_{f\mu} J_{13} J_{32} + \theta_f m_{f\mu} J_{12} J_{33} - \theta_f m_{f\mu} J_{13} J_{22} + \theta_f m_{f\mu} J_{12} J_{23}}{\det \mathbf{J}}. \tag{7.33}$$

As Appendix 7.C shows, in a closed economy, a rise in the bargaining power of firms has a strictly positive impact on the capacity utilization rate under a domestically profit-led demand regime. In an open economy, however, this may not occur.

Assume that the capacity utilization rate is domestically profit-led ($J_{12} > 0$). The first and second terms on the right-hand side of equation (7.33) are thus positive, whereas the third and fourth terms are negative if $J_{23} > 0$. If the latter effects are larger than the former effects, a rise in the bargaining power of firms reduces the capacity utilization rate even under a domestically profit-led demand regime. The story behind such a situation is explained as follows. An increase in the firms' bargaining power puts upward pressure on the price of domestic goods, which in turn leads to a decline in the real exchange rate. A direct effect of a decrease in the real exchange rate is that it worsens the trade balance and the capacity utilization rate (the third term); its indirect effect is that it reduces the profit share and thus shrinks domestic demand under a domestically profit-led demand regime if firms bear the burden arising from international price competition more than workers (the fourth term).

The effect of an increase in the workers' bargaining power on the capacity utilization rate is given as

$$\frac{du^*}{d\omega} = \frac{-\theta_w m_{w\omega} J_{13} J_{32} + \theta_w m_{w\omega} J_{12} J_{33}}{\det \mathbf{J}}. \tag{7.34}$$

A well-known implication of equation (7.34) is that it is hard to allow workers to strengthen their bargaining power in an open economy.[15] The first (negative) term on the right-hand side of equation (7.34) implies that an increase in the workers' bargaining power reduces firms' profitability and forces firms to push up the price of domestic goods; a rise in the price of domestic goods, in turn, decreases the capacity utilization rate by deteriorating terms of trade. This gives a reason to justify weakening the bargaining power of workers that confront international price competition, irrespective of which demand regime is realized.

---

15) This point is stressed by Blecker (2011) and Cassetti (2012). They show that cutting down a mark-up rate of domestic goods as well as decreasing nominal wages causes higher growth under a domestically wage-led demand case in an open economy.

Next, we represent the impact of a change in the firms' bargaining power on the profit share as follows:

$$\frac{dm^*}{d\mu} = \frac{-\theta_f m_{f\mu} J_{11} J_{33} + \theta_f m_{f\mu} J_{13} J_{21} - \theta_f m_{f\mu} J_{11} J_{23}}{\det \mathbf{J}}. \tag{7.35}$$

It is likely that an increase in the bargaining power of firms raises the profit share, but the result is not so simple in an open economy framework. For instance, if θ_w is sufficiently small, we have $J_{21} > 0$ and $J_{23} > 0$, both the second and third terms on the right-hand side of equation (7.35) show a negative sign, which implies that there is a possibility of increasing bargaining power of firms reducing the profit share. Strengthening its bargaining power raises the price of domestic goods and decreases the real exchange rate. A decline in the real exchange rate, in turn, leads to decreases in the capacity utilization rate. If the adjustment speed of the nominal wage is sufficiently slow, then the reserve army creation effect becomes larger than the reserve army effect, and the profit share decreases (the second term). Also, if the adjustment speed of the nominal wage is sufficiently slow, then firms bear the burden arising from international price competition more than workers, and the profit share decreases (the third term).

In contrast, the effect of a change in the workers' bargaining power on the profit share is very simple.

$$\frac{dm^*}{d\omega} = \frac{-\theta_w m_{w\omega} J_{11} J_{33}}{\det \mathbf{J}} < 0. \tag{7.36}$$

Irrespective of the sign of J_{23}, the right-hand side of equation (7.36) is necessarily negative. In other words, irrespective of whether or not firms are more responsive than workers, strengthening workers' bargaining power decreases the profit share. This is because an increase in workers' bargaining power ω decreases their target profit share m_w, which has a negative impact on the profit share.

We represent the effect of a change in the firms' bargaining power on the real exchange rate as follows:

$$\frac{d\varepsilon^*}{d\mu} = \frac{\theta_f m_{f\mu}(J_{11} J_{22} - J_{12} J_{21}) + \theta_f m_{f\mu} J_{11} J_{32}}{\det \mathbf{J}}. \tag{7.37}$$

Under either Assumption 7.2 or Assumption 7.3, the sign of the first term on the right-hand side of equation (7.37) is negative, whereas the sign of the second term is positive. The result is therefore ambiguous.

The effect of a change in the workers' bargaining power on the real exchange rate is given as

$$\frac{d\varepsilon^*}{d\omega} = \frac{\theta_w m_{w\omega} J_{11} J_{32}}{\det \mathbf{J}} < 0. \tag{7.38}$$

Equation (7.38) shows that an increase in the workers' bargaining power reduces firms' profitability and firms increase the price of domestic goods, which in turn decreases the real exchange rate.

7.4.3   Target value of the real exchange rate

Governments often seek to raise the real exchange rate (devalue the currency) with the intention of improving the trade balance and stimulating output and employment. To begin with, we consider the effect of an increase in the target value of the exchange rate on its own steady state value:

$$\frac{d\varepsilon^*}{d\bar{\varepsilon}} = \frac{-\lambda(J_{11}J_{22} - J_{12}J_{21})}{\det \mathbf{J}} > 0. \tag{7.39}$$

Because $d\varepsilon^*/d\bar{\varepsilon} > 0$ is obtained from $J_{11}J_{22} - J_{12}J_{21} > 0$, raising the target value of the real exchange rate increases its steady-state value. As mentioned above, if the ML condition is satisfied, we have $J_{13} > 0$, and hence, $\partial TB/\partial \varepsilon > 0$. Therefore, when governments devalue their home currencies, the trade balance is necessarily improved because of a rise in the real exchange rate.

However, even if the trade balance is improved, the capacity utilization rate does not necessarily increase. Next, we investigate whether the attempt to depreciate the exchange rate (i.e., raising the target value of the real exchange rate) succeeds in stimulating output.

$$\frac{du^*}{d\bar{\varepsilon}} = \frac{\lambda J_{13}J_{22} - \lambda J_{12}J_{23}}{\det \mathbf{J}}. \tag{7.40}$$

The sign of the first term on the right-hand side of equation (7.40) is positive, which implies that a rise in the real exchange rate improves the trade balance, whereas the sign of the second term is ambiguous. The depreciation policy therefore may not work. The story behind the failure of that policy is explained as follows.

Suppose that the economy exhibits a domestically profit-led demand regime ($J_{12} > 0$) and workers are more responsive to changes in the real exchange rate than firms ($J_{23} < 0$). Under these assumptions, the sign of the second term on the right-hand side of equation (7.40) is negative. A rise in the real exchange rate caused by the depreciation policy stimulates foreign demand as long as the ML condition is satisfied (the first term). At the same time, the depreciation policy triggers workers to demand a higher nominal wage, which causes a decline in the profit share and stagnation of domestic demand. The total effect is therefore ambiguous. To succeed in the depreciation policy under a domestically profit-led demand regime, it is necessary for firms to bear the burden arising from international price competition.

Next, we assume that a domestically wage-led demand regime is realized ($J_{12} < 0$) and firms are more responsive to changes in the real exchange rate than workers ($J_{23} > 0$). In this case, currency depreciation may not work because the sign of the second term is negative. A rise in the real exchange rate increases the profit share by increasing the price of domestic goods, which in turn causes a decline in domestic demand. Under a domestically wage-led demand regime, the nominal wage must therefore rise higher than the price of domestic goods to stimulate aggregate demand by means of the depreciation policy.

Finally, we represent the effect of a change in the real exchange rate on the profit share as follows:

$$\frac{dm^*}{d\bar{\varepsilon}} = \frac{-\lambda J_{13}J_{21} + \lambda J_{11}J_{23}}{\det \mathbf{J}}. \tag{7.41}$$

If, on the one hand, the reserve army creation effect is stronger than the reserve army effect, the depreciation policy raises the capacity utilization rate by improving the trade balance, and increases the profit share (i.e., the sign of the first term on the right-hand side of equation (7.41) is positive). On the other hand, if the reserve army effect is stronger than the reserve army creation effect, the policy decreases the profit share (i.e., the sign of the first term is negative).

In addition, when firms are more responsive to changes in the real exchange rate than workers, the depreciation policy raises the price of domestic goods and increases the profit share (i.e., the sign of the second term is positive). When workers are more responsive, however, this policy reduces the profit share through higher nominal wage growth (i.e., the sign of the second term is positive).

7.4.4   Summary

Table 7.1 shows the results of comparative static analysis in cases where a domestically wage-led demand regime is realized and the reserve army creation effect is larger than the reserve army effect, while Table 7.2. shows the results of cases in which a domestically profit-led demand regime is realized and the reserve army effect is larger than the reserve army creation effect.

Let us review the key points obtained from our analysis.

First, the paradox of thrift holds even in the open economy Kaleckian model.

Second, to succeed in a depreciation policy for stimulating aggregate demand, it is necessary for the government to consider both the demand regime in the domestic economy and whether workers or firms bears more of the burden of international price competition.

Third, the domestic relation between the profit share and the capacity utilization rate differs from the overall relation between them. For instance, as Table 7.2 shows, a rise in the bargaining power of firms may increase the profit share and decrease the capacity utilization rate under a domestically profit-led demand regime, which implies that a domestically profit-led demand regime can be compatible with an overall wage-led demand regime. Thus, a domestic demand regime is not sufficient to tell us whose bargaining power should be raised to increase aggregate demand. Moreover, the overall regime is merely a consequence of comparative static analysis with regard to the parameter changes that affect income distribution. Therefore, we should concentrate on the effects of the bargaining powers of firms and workers on the capacity utilization rate rather than the domestic and /or overall demand regime. In what follows, we compare our results with regard to the bargaining power with those of Blecker (2011) and Cassetti (2012).[16]

In Blecker (2011), a decrease in the target profit share of workers decreases the steady state value of the profit share but has an ambiguous effect on the steady state value of the capacity utilization rate under a domestically wage-led demand regime. Furthermore, under this regime, a decrease in the degree of the market share of the firm (i.e., a decline in the price of domestic goods) decreases the profit share but increases the capacity utilization rate in the steady state equilibrium. Thus, Blecker (2011) obtains $du^*/dm_w > 0$ or < 0 and $du^*/dm_f < 0$.

Cassetti (2012) also assumes a domestically wage-led growth regime. In this situation, a domestically wage-led demand regime holds if the Keynesian stability condition is satisfied. A decrease in the target value of the profit share of workers decreases the steady state value of the rate of capital accumulation, and an increase in the target profit share of firms has negative impact on the steady-state value of the capital accumulation rate (i.e., $dg^*/dm_w > 0$ and $dg^*/dm_f < 0$).

In our model, a decrease in the bargaining power of workers is represented by an increase in m_w while an increase in the bargaining power of firms is represented by a rise in m_f. If we assume a domestically wage-led demand regime, we have $du^*/dm_w > 0$ or < 0 and $du^*/dm_f > 0$ or < 0. This is because the effect of a change in the bargaining power on the capacity utilization rate depends on which domestic demand regime is realized and which agents, firms or workers, bear more of the burden arising from international price competition. Depending on the combination of these two factors, there are various scenarios that might unfold under international competition.

Table 7.1: Results for comparative static analysis under a domestically wage-led demand regime and $\Omega > 0$

	u^*	m^*	ε^*
s	−	−	−
μ	+ or −	+ or −	+ or −
ω	+ or −	−	−
$\bar{\varepsilon}$	+ or −	+ or −	+

---

16) In the following discussion, we change the notations of Blecker (2011) and Cassetti (2012) into ours. Cassetti (2012) considers raw material imports, whereas we do not because our aim is to investigate the effect of international competition on wage bargaining (especially on the target profit shares of workers and firms) and not to investigate the effect of internationalization through raw material imports.

Table 7.2: Results for comparative static analysis under a domestically profit-led demand regime and $\Omega < 0$

	u^*	m^*	ε^*
s	$-$	$+$	$+$
μ	$+$ or $-$	$+$ or $-$	$+$ or $-$
ω	$-$	$-$	$-$
$\bar{\varepsilon}$	$+$ or $-$	$+$ or $-$	$+$

7.5 Conclusions

This chapter has presented an open economy Kaleckian model, considering the process in which international price competition affects wage bargaining between firms and workers and the effect of such bargaining on the stability of the equilibrium and the steady-state values of the endogenous variables. In particular, the analysis shows that some of the propositions obtained from a closed economy Kaleckian model do not hold in an open economy model, and even some previous results from open economy Kaleckian models are overturned or shown to be special cases. Our results can be summarized as follows.

Stability analysis. (1) The stability conditions in a closed economy case (i.e., the combination of either a domestically wage-led demand regime and a larger reserve army creation effect or a domestically profit-led demand regime and a larger reserve army effect) are accepted in an open economy case where a change in the real exchange rate has a small impact on the trade balance. (2) By contrast, if a change in the real exchange rate has a larger impact on the trade balance, the steady state becomes unstable. (3) Moreover, if the ML condition is satisfied under the combination of a domestically profit-led demand regime and a larger reserve army effect, limit cycles occur as long as the speed of adjustment of the goods market lies within some range.

Comparative static analysis. (4) The paradox of thrift is true even in an open economy setting. (5) Strengthening the firms' bargaining power may depress an economy that exhibits a domestically profit-led demand regime, but may not reduce the capacity utilization rate under a domestically wage-led demand regime. We therefore conclude that not only the domestic demand regimes but also which agents, firms or workers, bear the burden arising from international price competition determines the effect of the bargaining power on the aggregate demand. (6) Furthermore, the success of a depreciation policy for stimulating output and employment depends on how to spread the burden of international price competition between firms and workers as well as the demand regime.

Appendix 7.A: Stability analysis and proofs of propositions

The characteristic equation that corresponds to the Jacobian matrix $\mathbf{J}$ is given as

$$q^3 + a_1 q^2 + a_2 q + a_3 = 0, \tag{7.42}$$

where q denotes a characteristic root. The coefficients of equation (7.42) are given by

$$a_1 = -\text{tr}\,\mathbf{J} = -(J_{11} + J_{22} + J_{33}) > 0, \tag{7.43}$$

$$a_2 = (J_{22}J_{33} - J_{23}J_{32}) + (J_{11}J_{33}) + (J_{11}J_{22} - J_{12}J_{21}), \tag{7.44}$$

$$a_3 = -\det\mathbf{J} = -J_{11}(J_{22}J_{33} - J_{23}J_{32}) + J_{21}(J_{12}J_{33} - J_{13}J_{32}), \tag{7.45}$$

where $\text{tr}\,\mathbf{J}$ denotes the trace of $\mathbf{J}$ and $\det\mathbf{J}$ the determinant of $\mathbf{J}$.

The necessary and sufficient conditions for the local stability of the steady state equilibrium are given by $a_1 > 0$, $a_2 > 0$, $a_3 > 0$, and $a_1 a_2 - a_3 > 0$. We investigate whether or not these conditions are satisfied. In our model, the coefficients of the characteristic equation are linear functions of ϕ, the speed of adjustment of u, and hence, $a_1 a_2 - a_3$ is a quadratic function of ϕ, where[17]

$$a_1 = \Delta_1 \phi + \Delta_2, \tag{7.46}$$

$$a_2 = \Delta_3 \phi + \Delta_4, \tag{7.47}$$

$$a_3 = \Delta_5 \phi, \tag{7.48}$$

$$a_1 a_2 - a_3 = f(\phi) \equiv (\Delta_1 \Delta_3)\phi^2 + (\Delta_1 \Delta_4 + \Delta_2 \Delta_3 - \Delta_5)\phi + \Delta_2 \Delta_4. \tag{7.49}$$

In the following analysis, we explain the coefficients Δ_1, Δ_2, Δ_3, Δ_4, and Δ_5.

To begin with, the signs of Δ_1, Δ_2, and Δ_4 are immediately obtained as

$$\Delta_1 = [1 - \alpha(\varepsilon)] + \alpha(\varepsilon)sm - g_{du} > 0, \tag{7.50}$$

$$\Delta_2 = (\theta_f + \theta_w)(1 - m) + \varepsilon(\lambda + \theta_f m_{f\varepsilon}) > 0, \tag{7.51}$$

$$\Delta_4 = \varepsilon(1 - m)[(\theta_f + \theta_w)\lambda + \theta_f \theta_w(m_{f\varepsilon} - m_{w\varepsilon})] > 0. \tag{7.52}$$

$\Delta_1 > 0$ is obtained from Assumption 7.1, and $\Delta_4 > 0$ is obtained from both $m_{f\varepsilon} > 0$ and $m_{w\varepsilon} < 0$.

Next, the coefficient Δ_3 can be expressed as

$$\Delta_3 = \{[1 - \alpha(\varepsilon)] + \alpha(\varepsilon)sm - g_{du}\}[(\theta_f + \theta_w)(1 - m) + \varepsilon(\lambda + \theta_f m_{f\varepsilon})]$$
$$- (1 - m)[g_{dm} - \alpha(\varepsilon)su]\Omega. \tag{7.53}$$

From this, if Assumption 7.2 holds, that is, $g_{dm} - \alpha(\varepsilon)su < 0$ and $\Omega > 0$ hold, we have

---

17) We use the fact that the speed of adjustment of the goods market ϕ affects the dynamic process of the model but not the steady state values.

$\Delta_3 > 0$, and if Assumption 7.3 holds, that is, $g_{dm} - \alpha(\varepsilon)su > 0$ and $\Omega < 0$ hold, we also have $\Delta_3 > 0$.

The coefficient Δ_5 can be expressed as

$$\Delta_5 = \varepsilon(1 - m)\{[1 - g_{du} - \alpha(\varepsilon)(1 - sm)][(\theta_f + \theta_w)\lambda + \theta_f\theta_w(m_{f\varepsilon} - m_{w\varepsilon})] \\ - \Omega\{[g_{dm} - \alpha(\varepsilon)su](\lambda + \theta_f m_{f\varepsilon}) + \theta_f[\alpha'(\varepsilon)u(1 - sm) + ex'(\varepsilon)]\}\}. \quad (7.54)$$

The first line of the right-hand side of equation (7.54) is always positive. Let us focus on the second line.

First, when Assumption 7.2 holds and the ML condition is satisfied, the sign of the second line depends on the absolute size of the following term:

$$-\theta_f\Omega[\alpha'(\varepsilon)u(1 - sm) + ex'(\varepsilon)]. \quad (7.55)$$

If expression (7.55) is small, we have $\Delta_5 > 0$, leading to $a_3 > 0$. This effect is small when $\alpha'(\varepsilon) > 0$ is small and $ex'(\varepsilon) > 0$ is small, that is, when the expenditure coefficient for domestic goods is not so responsive to the real exchange rate and when export demand is not so responsive to the real exchange rate. In other words, when the trade balance is not so responsive to the real exchange rate, then $\partial TB/\partial\varepsilon > 0$ is small. By contrast, if Assumption 7.2 holds and the ML condition is not satisfied, $\Delta_5 > 0$ necessarily holds.

Second, when Assumption 7.3 holds and the ML condition is satisfied, $\Delta_5 > 0$ necessarily holds. By contrast, when Assumption 7.3 holds and the ML condition is not satisfied, we have $\Delta_5 > 0$ as long as the absolute value of $\partial TB/\partial\varepsilon < 0$ is small, which is to say, close to zero.

Finally, we investigate the sign of $\Delta_1\Delta_4 + \Delta_2\Delta_3 - \Delta_5$. On the one hand, if the sign is positive, we always have $a_1a_2 - a_3 > 0$. On the other hand, if the sign is negative and its absolute value is large, we have $a_1a_2 - a_3 < 0$.

$$\Delta_1\Delta_4 + \Delta_2\Delta_3 - \Delta_5 \\ = [(\theta_f + \theta_w)(1 - m) + \varepsilon(\lambda + \theta_f m_{f\varepsilon})]^2(1 - \alpha + \alpha sm - g_{du}) \\ - (1 - m)\Omega\{(\theta_f + \theta_w)(1 - m)(g_{dm} - \alpha su) - \theta_f\varepsilon[\alpha'(\varepsilon)u(1 - sm) + ex'(\varepsilon)]\}. \quad (7.56)$$

The first line of the right-hand side of equation (7.56) is always positive. Let us focus on the second line.

When Assumption 7.2 holds and the ML condition is satisfied, the second line of equation (7.56) is always positive and hence, we have $\Delta_1\Delta_4 + \Delta_2\Delta_3 - \Delta_5 > 0$, leading to $a_1a_2 - a_3 > 0$. By contrast, when Assumption 7.2 holds and the ML condition is not satisfied, we have $\Delta_1\Delta_4 + \Delta_2\Delta_3 - \Delta_5 > 0$ as long as the absolute value of $\partial TB/\partial\varepsilon < 0$ is small, which is to say, close to zero.

When Assumption 7.3 holds and the ML condition is satisfied, we have $\Delta_1\Delta_4 + \Delta_2\Delta_3 - \Delta_5 > 0$ if $\partial TB/\partial\varepsilon > 0$ is small because the second line is positive. By contrast, when Assumption 7.3 holds and the ML condition is not satisfied, $\Delta_1\Delta_4 + \Delta_2\Delta_3 - \Delta_5 > 0$

necessarily holds.

7.A.1 Proof of proposition 7.1

Irrespective of the sign of $\partial TB/\partial\varepsilon$, if the absolute value of $\partial TB/\partial\varepsilon$ is small, we have $\Delta_5 > 0$ and $\Delta_1\Delta_4 + \Delta_2\Delta_3 - \Delta_5 > 0$. From this, we have $a_1 > 0$, $a_2 > 0$, $a_3 > 0$, and $a_1a_2 - a_3 > 0$. All the necessary and sufficient conditions are therefore satisfied.

7.A.2 Proof of proposition 7.2

First part: If $\partial TB/\partial\varepsilon > 0$ is large, we have $\Delta_5 < 0$ and $\Delta_1\Delta_4 + \Delta_2\Delta_3 - \Delta_5 > 0$. Then, we have $a_1 > 0$, $a_2 > 0$, $a_3 < 0$, and $a_1a_2 - a_3 > 0$, which means that one condition is not satisfied. The steady state equilibrium is therefore unstable.

Second part: If the absolute value of $\partial TB/\partial\varepsilon < 0$ is large, we have $\Delta_5 > 0$ and $\Delta_1\Delta_4 + \Delta_2\Delta_3 - \Delta_5 < 0$. If the absolute value of $\Delta_1\Delta_4 + \Delta_2\Delta_3 - \Delta_5 < 0$ is large, it is possible that the sign of $f(\phi)$ alternates. The quadratic function $f(\phi)$ is convex downwards and its intercept is positive. If the discriminant of $f(\phi) = 0$ is positive, the equation $f(\phi) = 0$ has two positive real roots: for $\phi \in (0, \phi_1)$, we have $a_1 > 0$, $a_2 > 0$, $a_3 > 0$, and $a_1a_2 - a_3 > 0$; for $\phi \in (\phi_1, \phi_2)$, we have $a_1 > 0$, a_2, $a_3 > 0$, and $a_1a_2 - a_3 < 0$; and for $\phi > \phi_2$, we have $a_1 > 0$, $a_2 > 0$, $a_3 > 0$, and $a_1a_2 - a_3 > 0$. The Hopf bifurcation thus occurs at $\phi = \phi_1$ and $\phi = \phi_2$. Indeed, at $\phi = \phi_1$ and $\phi = \phi_2$, we have $a_1 > 0$, $a_2 > 0$, $a_3 > 0$, $a_1a_2 - a_3 = 0$, and $\partial(a_1a_2 - a_3)/\partial\phi|_{\phi=\phi_1 \text{ or } \phi_2} \neq 0$, which mean that all the conditions for the Hopf bifurcation are satisfied. There is therefore a continuous family of non-constant, periodic solutions of the system around $\phi = \phi_1$ and $\phi = \phi_2$.

7.A.3 Proof of proposition 7.3

First part: If $\partial TB/\partial\varepsilon > 0$ is large, we have $\Delta_5 > 0$ and $\Delta_1\Delta_4 + \Delta_2\Delta_3 - \Delta_5 < 0$. When the absolute value of $\Delta_1\Delta_4 + \Delta_2\Delta_3 - \Delta_5 < 0$ is large, it is possible that the sign of $f(\phi)$ alternates. The quadratic function $f(\phi)$ is convex downwards and its intercept is positive. If the discriminant of $f(\phi) = 0$ is positive, the equation $f(\phi) = 0$ has two positive real roots: for $\phi \in (0, \phi_1)$, we have $a_1 > 0$, $a_2 > 0$, $a_3 > 0$, and $a_1a_2 - a_3 > 0$; for $\phi \in (\phi_1, \phi_2)$, we have $a_1 > 0$, $a_2 > 0$, $a_3 > 0$, and $a_1a_2 - a_3 < 0$; and for $\phi > \phi_2$, we have $a_1 > 0$, $a_2 > 0$, $a_3 > 0$, and $a_1a_2 - a_3 > 0$. The Hopf bifurcation thus occurs at $\phi = \phi_1$ and $\phi = \phi_2$. Indeed, at $\phi = \phi_1$ and $\phi = \phi_2$, we have $a_1 > 0$, $a_2 > 0$, $a_3 > 0$, $a_1a_2 - a_3 = 0$, and $\partial(a_1a_2 - a_3)/\partial\phi|_{\phi=\phi_1 \text{ or } \phi_2} \neq 0$, which means that all the conditions for the Hopf bifurcation are satisfied. There is therefore a continuous family of non-constant, periodic solutions of the system around $\phi = \phi_1$ and $\phi = \phi_2$.

Second part: If the absolute value of $\partial TB/\partial\varepsilon < 0$ is large, we have $\Delta_5 < 0$ and $\Delta_1\Delta_4 + \Delta_2\Delta_3 - \Delta_5 > 0$. We then have $a_1 > 0$, $a_2 > 0$, $a_3 < 0$, and $a_1a_2 - a_3 > 0$, which means that one condition is not satisfied. The steady state equilibrium is therefore unstable.

Appendix 7.B: Numerical simulations

Using numerical simulations, we show that the Hopf bifurcation actually occurs. For this purpose, we have to specify functional forms.

$$\text{Investment function: } g_d = \gamma_0 u^{\gamma_1} m^{\gamma_2}, \quad \gamma_0 > 0, \ 0 < \gamma_1 < 1, \ \gamma_2 > 0. \tag{7.57}$$

Here, following Blecker (2002) and Sasaki (2010), we use the Cobb-Douglas investment function. Roughly speaking, the parametric restriction $0 < \gamma_2 < 1$ corresponds to a domestically wage-led demand regime while $\gamma_2 > 1$ corresponds to a domestically profit-led demand regime.

$$\text{Firms' target profit share: } m_f = \alpha_0 + \alpha_1 \varepsilon, \quad 0 < \alpha_0 < 1, \ \alpha_1 > 0, \tag{7.58}$$

$$\text{Workers' target profit share: } m_w = \beta_0 - \beta_1 u - \beta_2 \varepsilon, \quad 0 < \beta_0 < 1, \ \beta_1 > 0, \ \beta_2 > 0, \tag{7.59}$$

$$\text{Labor productivity growth: } g_a = \eta u, \quad \eta > 0, \tag{7.60}$$

$$\text{Expenditure coefficient: } \alpha(\varepsilon) = B_0 \varepsilon^{\rho-1}, \quad B_0 > 0, \ 0 < \rho < +\infty, \tag{7.61}$$

$$\text{Export demand function: } ex(\varepsilon) = A_0 \varepsilon^{\psi}, \quad A_0 > 0, \ 0 < \psi < +\infty. \tag{7.62}$$

In what follows, we present a numerical example that corresponds to the case where $\Omega < 0$, the economy is in a domestically profit-led demand regime, and $\partial TB/\partial\varepsilon > 0$ is large. First, we set the parameters as follows: $s = 0.7$; $\gamma_0 = 0.2$; $\gamma_1 = 0.2$; $\gamma_2 = 1.7$; $\alpha_0 = 0.3$; $\alpha_1 = 0.01$; $\beta_0 = 0.3$; $\beta_1 = 0.2$; $\beta_2 = 0.01$; $A_0 = 0.4$; $\psi = 1500$; $\theta_f = 0.3$; $\theta_w = 0.7$; $\eta = 0.01$; $\lambda = 1$; $\bar{\varepsilon} = 1$; $p^f = 0.01$; $B_0 = 0.3$; $\rho = 150$.

In this numerical example, the open economy version of the Keynesian stability condition holds, workers are more responsive than firms, the two endogenously determined target profit shares are more than zero and less than unity, the inequality $m_f > m_w$ holds, and the endogenously determined expenditure share is $0 < \alpha(\varepsilon^*) < 1$.

We set initial conditions to $u(0) = 0.15$, $m(0) = 0.25$, and $\varepsilon(0) = 0.98$. As Figure 7.2 shows, there are two Hopf bifurcation points.

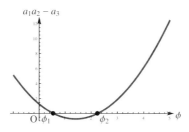

Figure 7.2: Existence of two Hopf bifurcation points

Using $\phi = 1$ as the speed of adjustment of the goods market, we obtain the following figures with regard to the time series of the endogenous variables (Figures 7.3–7.6).

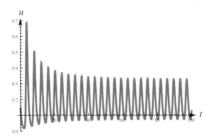

Figure 7.3: Dynamics of capacity utilization

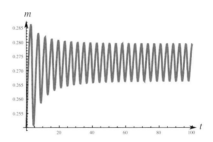

Figure 7.4: Dynamics of the profit share

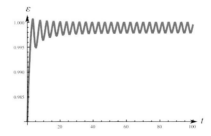

Figure 7.5: Dynamics of the real exchange rate

Trade balance

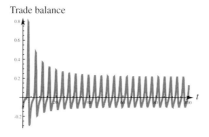

Figure 7.6: Dynamics of the trade balance

Appendix 7.C: Closed economy model

We briefly explain the closed economy model, which is a model that removes import and export demand as well as the effect of the real exchange rate from the open economy model. In this case, the dynamics of the capacity utilization rate and the profit share are as follows:

$$\dot{u} = \phi[g_d(u, m) - sum], \tag{7.63}$$

$$\dot{m} = (1 - m)\{\theta_f[m_f(\mu) - m] - \theta_w[m - m_w(u; \omega)] + g_a(u)\}. \tag{7.64}$$

The steady state equilibrium is given by $\dot{u} = \dot{m} = 0$.

The elements of the Jacobian matrix are given by

$$J_{11} = \phi(g_{du} - sm), \tag{7.65}$$

$$J_{12} = \phi(g_{dm} - su), \tag{7.66}$$

$$J_{21} = (1 - m)[\theta_w m_w'(u; \omega) + g_a'(u)] = (1 - m)\Omega, \tag{7.67}$$

$$J_{22} = -(\theta_f + \theta_w)(1 - m) < 0. \tag{7.68}$$

All the elements are evaluated at the steady state equilibrium values.

Similar to the open economy model, we use the following three assumptions. Assumption 7.1': $g_{du} - sm < 0$; Assumption 7.2': $g_{dm} - su < 0$ and $\Omega > 0$; Assumption 7.3': $g_{dm} - su > 0$ and $\Omega < 0$.

From Assumption 7.1', we have tr $\mathbf{J} < 0$. The determinant is given by

$$\det \mathbf{J} = \phi(1 - m)[(\theta_f + \theta_w)(sm - g_{du}) - (g_{dm} - su)\Omega]. \tag{7.69}$$

Under Assumption 7.2', we have det $\mathbf{J} > 0$. In addition, under Assumption 7.3', we have det $\mathbf{J} > 0$. If Assumptions 7.1' and 7.2' hold simultaneously or if Assumptions 7.1' and 7.3' hold simultaneously, we have both tr $\mathbf{J} < 0$ and det $\mathbf{J} > 0$, which thus satisfies the necessary and sufficient conditions for the local stability of the equilibrium.

We investigate the effects of exogenous increases in μ (i.e., the bargaining power of firms) and ω (i.e., the bargaining power of workers) on the equilibrium capacity utilization rate. Totally differentiating the equilibrium conditions, we obtain

$$\frac{du^*}{d\mu} = \frac{\phi(1-m)\theta_f m_{f\mu}(g_{dm} - su)}{\det \mathbf{J}}, \tag{7.70}$$

$$\frac{du^*}{d\omega} = \frac{\phi(1-m)\theta_w m_{w\omega}(g_{dm} - su)}{\det \mathbf{J}}. \tag{7.71}$$

We have $\det \mathbf{J}$ from the stability condition. Then, if $g_{dm} - su > 0$, we have $du^*/d\mu > 0$ and $du^*/d\omega < 0$, and if $g_{dm} - su < 0$, we have $du^*/d\mu < 0$ and $du^*/d\omega > 0$. Consequently, if the economy is in a profit-led demand regime, an increase in the bargaining power of firms and an increase in the bargaining power of workers increases and decreases the capacity utilization rate, respectively. Whereas if the economy is in a wage-led demand regime, an increase in the bargaining power of firms and an increase in the bargaining power of workers decreases and increases the capacity utilization rate, respectively.

References

Aghion, P., Howitt, P., 1992. A model of growth through creative destruction. Econometrica 60 (2), 323–351.

Agliardi, E., 1988. Microeconomic foundations of macroeconomics in the post-Keynesian approach. Metroeconomica 39 (3), 275–297.

Amadeo, E., 1986. Notes on capacity utilisation, distribution and accumulation. Contributions to Political Economy 5 (1), 83–94.

Arnim, R., 2011. Wage policy in an open-economy Kalecki-Kaldor model: a simulation study. Metroeconomica, 62 (2), 235–264.

Arrow, K. J., 1962. The economic implications of learning by doing. Review of Economic Studies 29 (3), 155–173.

Asada, T., Semmler, W., 1995. Growth and finance: an intertemporal model. Journal of Macroeconomics 17 (4), 623–649.

Auerbach, P., Skott, P., 1988. Concentration, competition and distribution: a critique of theories of monopoly capital. International Review of Applied Economics 2 (1), 42–61.

Azetsu, K., Koba, T., Nakatani, T., 2010. Empirical analysis of a Kaleckian-type model of growth and distribution. Political Economy Quarterly 47 (1), 56–65 (in Japanese).

Barbosa-Filho, N. H., Taylor, L., 2006. Distributive and demand cycles in the US economy: A structuralist Goodwin model. Metroeconomica 57 (3), 389–411.

Benhabib, J., Nishimura, K., 1979. The Hopf-bifurcation and the existence and stability of closed orbits in multisector models of optimal economic growth. Journal of Economic Theory 21 (3), 421–444.

Bernanke, B. S., Gürkaynak, R. S., 2001. Is growth exogenous? Taking Mankiw, Romer, and Weil seriously. In Bernanke, B. S., Rogoff, K. (Eds.). NBER Macroeconomics Annual 2001. Cambridge MA: MIT Press.

Bhaduri, A. 2006. Endogenous economic growth: a new approach. Cambridge Journal of Economics 30 (1), 69–83.

Bhaduri, A., 2008. On the dynamics of profit-led and wage-led growth. Cambridge Journal of Economics 32, 147–160.

Bhaduri, A., Marglin, S., 1990. Unemployment and the real wage: the economic basis for contesting political ideologies. Cambridge Journal of Economics 14 (4), 375–393.

Blecker, R. A., 1989. International competition, income distribution and economic growth. Cambridge Journal of Economics 13, 395–412.

Blecker, R. A., 1996. The new economic integration: structuralist models of north-south trade and investment liberalization. Structural Change and Economic Dynamics 7 (3), 321–345.

Blecker, R.A., 1998. International competition, relative wages, and the balance-of-payments constraint. Journal of Post Keynesian Economics 20 (4), 495–526.

Blecker, R. A., 2002. Distribution, demand and growth in neo-Kaleckian macro-models. In Setterfield, M. (Ed.). The Economics of Demand-Led Growth, Challenging the Supply-Side Vision of the Long Run. Cheltenham: Edward Elgar , pp. 129–152.

Blecker, R. A. 2011. Open economy models of distribution and growth. In Hein, E., Stockhammer, E. (Eds.). A Modern Guide to Keynesian Macroeconomics and Economic Policies. Cheltenham: Edward Elgar, pp. 215–239.

Blecker, R.A., Seguino, S. 2002. Macroeconomic effects of reducing gender wage inequality in an export-oriented, semi-industrialized economy. Review of Development Economics 6 (1), 103–119.

Cassetti, M., 2002. Conflict, inflation, distribution and terms of trade in the Kaleckian model. In Setterfield M. (Ed). The Economics of Demand-Led Growth, Challenging the Supply-Side Vision of the Long Run. Cheltenham: Edward Elgar, pp. 189–211.

Cassetti, M., 2003. Bargaining power, effective demand and technical progress: a Kaleckian model of growth. Cambridge Journal of Economics 27 (3), 449–464.

Cassetti, M., 2006. A note on the long-run behaviour of Kaleckian models. Review of Political Economy 18 (4), 497–508.

Cassetti, M., 2012. Macroeconomic outcomes of changing social bargains: the feasibility of a wage-led demand open economy reconsidered. Metroeconomica 63 (1), 64–91.

Charles, S., 2008a. Teaching Minsky's financial instability hypothesis: a manageable suggestion. Journal of Post Keynesian Economics 31 (1), 125–138.

Charles, S., 2008b. Corporate debt, variable retention rate and the appearance of financial fragility. Cambridge Journal of Economics 32 (5), 781–795.

Charles, S., 2008c. A post-Keynesian model of accumulation with a Minskyan financial structure. Review of Political Economy 20 (3), 319–331.

Chiarella, C., Flaschel, P., 1998. Dynamics of natural rates of growth and employment. Macroeconomic Dynamics 2 (3), 345–368.

183

Choi, H., 1995. Goodwin's growth cycle and the efficiency wage hypothesis. Journal of Economic Behavior & Organization 27, 223–235.

Cordero, J. A. 2002. A model of growth and conflict inflation for a small open economy. Metroeconomica 53 (3), 261–289.

Cordero, J. A., 2008. Economic growth under alternative monetary regimes: inflation targeting vs. real exchange rate targeting. International Review of Applied Economics 22 (2), 45–160.

Del Monte, A., 1975. Grado di monopolio e sviluppo economico. Rivista Internazionale di Scienze Sociali 83 (3), 231–263.

Dickens, W. T., Lang, K., 1985. A test of dual labor market theory. American Economic Review 75 (4), 792–805.

Dockner, E. J., Feichtinger, G., 1991. On the optimality of limit cycles in dynamic economic systems. Journal of Economics 53 (1), 31–50.

Duménil, G., Lévy, D., 1999. Being Keynesian in the short term and classical in the long term: the traverse to classical long-term equilibrium. The Manchester School 67 (6), 684–716.

Dutt, A. K., 1992. Conflict inflation, distribution, cyclical accumulation and crises. European Journal of Political Economy 8 (4), 579–597.

Dutt, A. K., 1997. Equilibrium, path dependence and hysteresis in post-Keynesian models. In Arestis, P., Palma, G. and Sawyer, M. (Eds.). Markets, Unemployment and Economic Policy: Essays in Honour of Geoff Harcourt, Vol. 2. London: Routledge.

Dutt, A. K., 1987. Alternative closures again: a comment on growth, distribution and inflation. Cambridge Journal of Economics 11 (1), 75–82.

Dutt, A. K., 1992. Conflict inflation, distribution, cyclical accumulation and crises. European Journal of Political Economy 8 (4), 579–597.

Dutt, A. K., 1997. Equilibrium, path dependence and hysteresis in post-Keynesian models. In Arestis, P., Palma, G., Sawyer, M. (Eds.). Markets, Unemployment and Economic Policy: Essays in Honour of Geoff Harcourt, Vol. 2. London: Routledge.

Dutt, A. K., 2006. Aggregate demand, aggregate supply and economic growth. International Review of Applied Economics 20, 319–336.

Dutt, A. K., Amadeo, E. J., 1993. A post-Keynesian theory of growth, interest and money. Baranzini, M., Harcourt, G. C. (Eds.). The Dynamics of The Wealth of Nations: Growth, Distribution and Structural Change. New York: St. Martin's Press.

Evans, G. W., Honkapohja, S., Romer, P., 1998. Growth cycles. American Economic Review 88 (3), 495–515.

Flaschel, P., Greiner, A., 2009. Employment cycles and minimum wages: a macro view. Structural Change and Economic Dynamics 20 (4), 279–287.

Flaschel, P., Greiner, A., 2011. Dual labor markets and the impact of minimum wages on atypical employment. Metroeconomica, 62 (3), 512–531.

Flaschel, P., Greiner, A., Logeay, C., Proano, C., 2012. Employment cycles, low income work and the dynamic impact of wage regulations. A macro perspective. Journal of Evolutionary Economics 22 (2), 235–250.

Flaschel, P., Kauermann, G., Semmler, W., 2007. Testing wage and price Phillips curves for the United States. Metroeconomica 58 (4), 550–581.

Flaschel, P., Skott, P., 2006. Steindlian models of growth and stagnation. Metroeconomica 57 (3), 303–338.

Foley, D. K., 2003. Endogenous technical change with externalities in a classical growth model. Journal of Economic Behavior & Organization 52, 167–189.

Foley, D. K., Michl, T. R., 1999. Growth and Distribution. Cambridge MA: Harvard University Press.

Francois, P., Lloyd-Ellis, H., 2003. Animal spirits through creative destruction. American Economic Review 93 (3), 530–550.

Furukawa, Y., 2007. Endogenous growth cycles. Journal of Economics 91 (1), 69–96.

Gandolfo, G., 1996. Economic Dynamics, 3rd edition. Berlin: Springer-Verlag.

Giavazzi, F., Wyplosz, C., 1985. The zero root problem: a note on the dynamic determination of the stationary equilibrium in linear models. Review of Economic Studies 52 (2), 353–357.

Goodwin, R., 1967. A growth cycle. In Feinstein, C. H. (Ed.). Socialism, Capitalism and Economic Growth, Essays Presented to Maurice Dobb. Cambridge: Cambridge University Press.

Grossman, G. M., Helpman, E., 1991. Quality ladders in the theory of growth. Review of Economic Studies 58 (1), 43–61.

Harvie, D., 2000. Testing Goodwin: growth cycles in ten OECD. Cambridge Journal of Economics 24 (3), 349–376.

Hein, E., 2006. Interest, debt and capital accumulation: a Kaleckian approach. International Review of Applied Economics 20 (3), 337–352.

Hein, E., 2007. Interest rate, debt, distribution and capital accumulation in a post Kaleckian model. Metroeconomica 56 (2), 310–339.

Hein, E., Lavoie, M., van Treeck, T., 2010. Harrodian instability and the 'normal rate' of capacity utilization in Kaleckian models of distribution and growth–a survey. Metroeconomica 63 (1), 139–169.

Hein, E., Lavoie, M., van Treeck, T., 2011. Some instability puzzles in Kaleckian models of growth and distribution: a critical survey. Cambridge Journal of Economics 35 (3), 587–612.

Hein, E., Vogel, E., 2008. Distribution and growth reconsidered: empirical results for six OECD countries. Cambridge Journal of Economics 32 (3), 479–511.

Ishikawa, T., Dejima, T., 1994. Dual Structure in the Japanese Labor Market. In. Ishikawa, T. (Ed.). Distribution of Wealth and Income in Japan. Tokyo: University of Tokyo Press, pp. 169–209, (in Japanese).

Kaldor, N., 1966. Causes of the slow rate of economic growth in the United Kingdom. Reprinted in Kaldor, N., 1978. Further Essays on Economic Theory. London: Duckworth.

Kalecki, M., 1954. Theory of Economic Dynamics. London: George Allen and Unwin.

Kalecki, M., 1971. Selected Essays on The Dynamics of The Capitalist Economy. Cambridge, UK: Cambridge University Press.

La Marca, M., 2010. Real exchange rate, distribution and macro fluctuations in export-oriented economies. Metroeconomica 61 (1), 124–151

Lavoie, M., 1992. Foundations of Post-Keynesian Economic Analysis. Cheltenham: Edward Elgar.

Lavoie, M., 1995a. Interest rate in post-Keynesian models of growth and distribution. Metroeconomica 46 (2), 146–177.

Lavoie, M., 1995b. The Kaleckian model of growth and distribution and its neo-Ricardian and neo-Marxian critiques. Cambridge Journal of Economics 19 (6), 789–818.

Lavoie, M., 1996. Traverse, hysteresis and normal rates of capacity utilization in Kaleckian models of growth and distribution. Review of Radical and Political Economics 28 (4), 113–147.

Lavoie, M., 2002. The Kaleckian growth model with target return pricing and conflict inflation. In Setterfield, M. (Ed.). The Economics of Demand-Led Growth, Challenging the Supply-Side Vision of the Long Run. Cheltenham: Edward Elgar.

Lavoie, M., 2003. Kaleckian effective demand and Sraffian normal prices: towards a reconciliation. Review of Political Economy 15 (1), 53–74.

Lavoie, M., 2006. Introduction to Post-Keynesian Economics. New York: Palgrave Macmillan.

Lavoie, M., 2009. Cadrisme within a Post-Keynesian model of growth and distribution. Review of Political Economy 21 (3), 369–391.

Lavoie, M., 2010. Surveying short-run and long-run stability issues with the Kaleckian model of growth. In Setterfield, M. (Ed.). Handbook of Alternative Theories of Economic Growth. Cheltenham: Edward Elgar.

Lavoie, M., Rodríguez, G., Seccareccia, M., 2004. Similitudes and discrepancies in post-Keynesian and Marxist theories of investment: a theoretical and empirical investigation. International Review of Applied Economics 18 (2), 127–149.

Leijonhufvud, A., 1973. Effective demand failures. Swedish Journal of Economics 75, 27–48.

León-Ledesma, M. A., Lanzafame, M., 2010. The endogenous nature of the "natural" rate of growth. In Setterfield, M. (Ed.). Handbook of Alternative Theories of Economic Growth. Cheltenham: Edward Elgar.

León-Ledesma, M. A., Thirlwall, A. P., 2002. The endogeneity of the natural rate of growth. Cambridge Journal of Economics 26, 441–459.

Libânio, G. A., 2009. Aggregate demand and the endogeneity of the natural rate of growth: evidence from Latin American economies. Cambridge Journal of Economics 33 (5), 967–984.

Lima, G. T., 2004. Endogenous technological innovation, capital accumulation and distributional dynamics. Metroeconomica 55 (4), 386–408.

Lima, G. T., Meirelles, A. J. A., 2007. Macrodynamics of debt regimes, financial instability and growth. Cambridge Journal of Economics 31 (4), 563–580.

Marglin, S., 1984. Growth, Distribution, and Prices. Cambridge MA: Harvard University Press.

Marglin, S., Bhaduri, A., 1990. Profit Squeeze and Keynesian Theory. In Marglin, S., Schor, J. (Eds.). The Golden Age of Capitalism: Reinterpreting the Postwar Experience. Oxford: Clarendon Press, pp. 153–186.

Marquetti, A., 2004. Do rising real wages increase the rate of labor-saving technical change? Some econometric evidence. Metroeconomica 55 (4), 432–441.

Marx, K., 1976. Capital, Vol. 1. Harmondsworth: Penguin.

Michl, T., 2008. Tinbergen rules the Taylor rule. Eastern Economic Journal 34, 293–309.

Missaglia, M., 2007. Demand policies for long-run growth: being Keynesian both in the short and in the long run. Metroeconomica 58 (1), 74–94.

Mohun, S., Veneziani, R., 2008. Goodwin cycles and the US economy, 1948–2004. In Flaschel, P., Landesmann, M. (Eds.). Mathematical Economics and the Dynamics Of Capitalism. London: Routledge.

Mott, T., Slattery, E., 1994. The influence of changes in income distribution on aggregate demand in a Kaleckian model: stagnation vs. exhilaration reconsidered. In Davidson, P., Kregel, J. A. (Eds.). Employment, Growth and Finance. Cheltenham: Edward Elgar.

Naastepad, C.W.M., Storm, S., 2007. OECD demand regimes (1960–2000). Journal of Post Keynesian Economics 29 (2), 211–246.

Naastepad, C.W.M., Storm, S., 2010. Feasible egalitarianism: demand-led growth, labour and technology. In Setterfield, M. (Ed.). Handbook of Alternative Theories of Economic Growth. Cheltenham: Edward Elgar.

Nishi, H., 2010. An empirical analysis of income distribution and demand formation pattern of the Japanese economy using vector autoregressive model. Political Economy Quarterly 47 (3), 67–78 (in Japanese).

Ohno, T., 2009. Post-Keynesian effective demand and capital-labour substitution. Metroeconomica 60 (3), 525–536.

Park, M. S., 1997. Normal values and average values. Metroeconomica 48 (2), 188–199.

Pasinetti, L. L., 1974. Growth and Income Distribution. Cambridge: Cambridge University Press.

Pohjola, M. T., 1981. Stable, cyclic and chaotic growth: the dynamics of a discrete-time version of Goodwin's growth cycle model. Journal of Economics 41 (1–2), 27–38.

Raghavendra, S., 2006. Limits to investment exhilarationism. Journal of Economics 87 (3), 257–280.

Robinson, J., 1962. Essays in Theory of Economic Growth. London: Macmillan.

Romer, P. M., 1990. Endogenous technological change. Journal of Political Economy 98 (5), 71–101.

Rowthorn, R. E., 1977. Conflict, inflation and money. Cambridge Journal of Economics 1 (3), 215-239.

Rowthorn, R. E., 1981. Demand, real wages and economic growth. Thames Papers in Political Economy Autumn, 1–39.

Rowthorn, R. E., 1999. Unemployment, wage bargaining and capital-labour substitution. Cambridge Journal of Economics 23, 413–425.

Ryzhenkov, A. V., 2009. A Goodwinian model with direct and roundabout returns to scale (an application to Italy). Metroeconomica 60 (3), 343–399.

Sasaki, H., 2009. Cyclical growth in a Goodwin-Kalecki-Marx model. Tohoku Economics Research Group Discussion Papers, No. 246.

Sasaki, H., 2010. Endogenous technical change, income distribution, and unemployment with inter-class conflict. Structural Change and Economic Dynamics 21 (2), 123–134.

Sasaki, H., 2011. Conflict, growth, distribution, and employment: a long-run Kaleckian model. International Review of Applied Economics 25 (5), 539–557.

Sasaki, H., 2012. Is the long-run equilibrium wage-led or profit-led? A Kaleckian approach. Structural Change and Economic Dynamics 23 (3), 231–144.

Sasaki, H., 2013. Cyclical growth in a Goodwin-Kalecki-Marx model. Journal of Economics 108 (2), 145–171.

Sasaki, H., Matsuyama, J., Sako, K., 2013 The macroeconomic effects of the wage gap between regular and non-regular employment and of minimum wages. Structural Change and Economic Dynamics 26, 61–72,

Sasaki, H., Sonoda, R., Fujita, S., 2013 International competition and distributive class conflict in an open economy Kaleckian model. Metroeconomica 64 (4), 683–715.

Sato, Y., 1985. Marx-Goodwin growth cycles in a two-sector economy. Journal of Economics 45 (1), 21–34.

Sedgley, N., Elmslie, B., 2004. The conventional wage share vs. full employment: implications for the development of growth theory. Cambridge Journal of Economics 28, 875–888.

Sen, A., 2004. Elements of a theory of human rights. Philosophy and Public Affairs 32 (4), 315–356.

Setterfield, M., 2009. Macroeconomics without the LM curve: an alternative view. Cambridge Journal of Economics 33 (2), 273–293.

Shah, A., Desai, M., 1981. Growth cycles with induced technical change. Economic Journal 91, 1006–1010.

Skott, P., 1989. Effective demand, class struggle and cyclical growth. International Economic Review 30 (1), 231–247.

Skott, P., 2008. Theoretical and empirical shortcomings of the Kaleckian investment function. Department of Economics Working Paper 2008-11, University of Massachusetts Amherst.

Skott, P., 2010a. Theoretical and empirical shortcomings of the Kaleckian investment function. Metroeconomica 59 (3), 441–478.

Skott, P., 2010b. Growth, instability and cycles: Harrodian and Kaleckian models of accumulation and income distribution. In Setterfield, M. (Ed.). Handbook of Alternative Theories of Economic Growth. Cheltenham: Edward Elgar.

Skott, P., Zipperer, B., 2010. An empirical evaluation of three post Keynesian models. Working Paper 2010-08, University of Massachusetts Amherst.

Sonoda, R., 2013. Two types of Phillips curves and the dynamics of distribution in Japan. ch. 4 of PhD Thesis, Kyoto University, Japan (in Japanese).

Sportelli, M. C., 1995. A Kolmogoroff generalized predator-prey model of Goodwin's growth cycle. Journal of Economics 61 (1), 35–64.

Sportelli, M. C., 2000. Dynamic complexity in a Keynesian growth-cycle model involving Harrod's instability. Journal of Economics 71 (2), 167–198.

Stockhammer, E., 2004. Is there an equilibrium rate of unemployment in the long run?. Review of Political Economy 16 (1), 59–77.

Stockhammer, E., 2008. Is the NAIRU theory a Monetarist, new Keynesian, post Keynesian or a Marxist theory? Metroeconomica 59, 479–510.

Stockhammer, E., Hein, E., Grafl, L., 2011. Globalization and the effects of changes in functional income distribution on aggregate demand in Germany. International Review of Applied Economics 25 (1), 1–23.

Stockhammer, E., Onaran, Ö., 2004. Accumulation, distribution and employment: a structural VAR approach to a Kaleckian macro model. Structural Change and Economic Dynamics 15, 421–447.

Stockhammer, E., Onaran, Ö., Ederer, S., 2009. Functional income distribution and aggregate demand in the Euro area. Cambridge Journal of Economics 33 (1), 139–159.

Storm, S., Naastepad, C. W. M., 2007. It is high time to ditch the NAIRU. Journal of Post Keynesian Economics 29 (4), 531–554.

Storm, S., Naastepad, C. W. M., 2008. The NAIRU reconsidered: why labour market deregulation may raise unemployment. International Review of Applied Economics 22 (5), 527–544.

Tavani, D., Flaschel, P., Taylor, L., 2011. Estimated non-linearities and multiple equilibria in a model of distributive-demand cycles. International Review of Applied Economics 25 (5), 519–538.

Taylor, L., 2004. Reconstructing Macroeconomics: Structuralist Proposals and Critiques of the Mainstream. Cambridge MA: Harvard University Press.

Thirlwall, A. P., 1979. The balance of payments constraint as an explanation of international growth rate differences. Banca Nazionale del Lavoro Quarterly Review 32 (1), 45–53.

Uni, H., 2009. The Economics of Institution and Regulation. Kyoto: Nakanishiya Shuppan (in Japanese).

van de Klundert, T., van Schaik, T., 1990. Unemployment persistence and loss of productive capacity: a Keynesian approach. Journal of Macroeconomics 12 (3), 363–380.

van der Ploeg, F., 1987. Growth cycles, induced technical change, and perpetual conflict over the distribution of income. Journal of Macroeconomics 9 (1), 1–12.

Velupillai, K. V., 2006. A disequilibrium macrodynamic model of fluctuations. Journal of Macroeconomics 28 (1), 752–767.

Verdoorn, P. J., 1949. Fattori che regolano lo sviluppo della produttivit a del lavoro. L'Industria 1, 14–28 (Factors that determine the growth of labour productivity, translated by Thirlwall, A. P. In McCombie, J., Pugno, M., Soro, B. (Eds.).

Productivity Growth and Economic Performance: Essays on Verdoorn's Law. London: Macmillan, 2002).

Vogel, L., 2009. The endogeneity of the natural rate of growth: an empirical study for Latin American countries. International Review of Applied Economics 23 (1), 41–53.

Wälde, K., 2005. Endogenous growth cycles. International Economic Review 46 (3), 867–894.

Wolfstetter, E., 1982. Fiscal policy and the classical growth cycle. Journal of Economics 42 (4), 375–393.

Yoshida, H., 1999. Harrod's "Knife-Edge" reconsidered: an application of the Hopf bifurcation theorem and numerical simulations. Journal of Macroeconomics 21 (3), 537–562.

Yoshikawa, H., 1994. Labor share and growth-cycle in Japanese economy. In Ishikawa, T. (Ed.). Distribution of Wealth and Income in Japan, Tokyo: University of Tokyo Press (in Japanese), pp. 107–140.

You, J. I., 1994. Macroeconomic structure, endogenous technical change and growth. Cambridge Journal of Economics 18 (2), 213–233.

Zipperer, B., Skott, P., 2011. Cyclical patterns of employment, utilization, and profitability. Journal of Post Keynesian Economics 34 (1), 25–57.

Index

192